ROYAL HISTORICAL SOCIETY

STUDIES IN HISTORY

New Series

FRENCH REVOLUTIONARIES AND ENGLISH REPUBLICANS

THE CORDELIERS CLUB, 1790–1794

(1)

Nº. Iᵉʳ.

JOURNAL

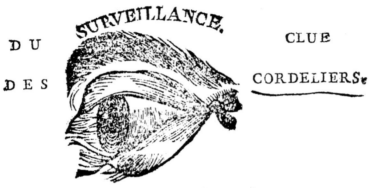

DU   SURVEILLANCE.   CLUB

DES   CORDELIERS.

SOCIÉTÉ

DES AMIS DES DROITS DE L'HOMME
ET DU CITOYEN.

Du mardi 28 juin 1791.

FRENCH REVOLUTIONARIES AND ENGLISH REPUBLICANS

THE CORDELIERS CLUB, 1790–1794

Rachel Hammersley

THE ROYAL HISTORICAL SOCIETY
THE BOYDELL PRESS

First published 2005

A Royal Historical Society publication
Published by The Boydell Press
an imprint of Boydell & Brewer Ltd
PO Box 9, Woodbridge, Suffolk IP12 3DF, UK
and of Boydell & Brewer Inc.
668 Mt Hope Avenue, Rochester, NY 14620, USA
website: www.boydellandbrewer.com

ISBN 0 86193 273 0

ISSN 0269–2244

A catalogue record for this book is available
from the British Library

Library of Congress Cataloging-in-Publication Data
Hammersley, Rachel, 1974–
    French revolutionaries and English republicans : the Cordeliers Club,
1790–1794 / Rachel Hammersley.
        p. cm. – (Royal Historical Society studies in history. New series,
ISSN 0269–2244)
    Summary: "An in-depth study of the radical Cordeliers Club and its
influence on political and constitutional thought of the time" – Provided
by publisher.
    Includes bibliographical references and index.
    ISBN 0–86193–273–0 (hardback : alk. paper)
    1. Club des Cordeliers. 2. France – History – Revolution, 1789–1799
– Societies, etc. 3. Republicanism – Great Britain – Influence.
4. Republicanism – France – History – 18th century. 5. Revolutionaries
– France – History. 6. France – Politics and government – 1789–1799.
I. Title. II. Series.
    DC183.5.H35 2005
    321.8'6'06044 – dc22   2004024110

This book is printed on acid-free paper

Printed in Great Britain by
dge, Wiltshire

Contents

List of Illustrations

The illustrations are reproduced by permission of the British Library

Publication of this volume was aided by a grant from the Scouloudi Foundation, in association with the Institute of Historical Research.

FOR MY PARENTS, WITHOUT WHOM . . .

Acknowledgements

I first became interested in English republicanism and its influence in eighteenth-century France during my MA course at the University of Sussex in 1996–7. Since then I have incurred a large number of intellectual debts and it gives me great pleasure to be able to offer my thanks and acknowledgement here to some of the people who have helped me to bring this project to fruition. It goes without saying that any errors are mine.

I am grateful to the librarians and archivists at the following institutions for their help and assistance: the University of Sussex Library, the British Library, the London Library, the Historical Manuscripts Commission, the Institute of Historical Research, Cambridge University Library, the Brotherton Library at the University of Leeds, the Archives Nationales, the Bibliothèque Nationale de France, the Bibliothèque Historique de la Ville de Paris, and the Houghton Library at Harvard University. The University of Sussex has been my intellectual home throughout the completion of this project and I wish to thank my colleagues in the Graduate Research Centre in the Humanities and in the History Department for providing me with a stimulating environment in which to work. Financial assistance has been provided by the University of Sussex and by the Leverhulme Trust, and I am immensely grateful for that support.

I am particularly grateful to my DPhil. supervisors Blair Worden and Richard Whatmore who from the beginning shared their immense knowledge and expertise with me, and in doing so helped to guide and shape this project. I also wish to express my thanks to my examiners Donald Winch and Michael Sonenscher whose insightful comments provided the inspiration for my transformation of the thesis into a book. That transformation was also aided by the responses of a number of other people who read parts or all of the work. They include Colin Brooks, Ian Bullock, Henry C. Clark, Martyn Hammersley and Maurice Hutt. I have also benefited from fruitful conversations with David Armitage, Peter Campbell, Pierre Lurbe, Olivier Lutaud, Elizabeth Tuttle and Brian Young. My ideas have been further shaped by the comments and responses to papers presented at various conferences and seminars. It would be impossible to thank each of these people individually, but I am grateful to them all the same. Trips abroad were made more pleasant and more comfortable by the hospitality and friendship of Fabrice Bensimon, Nathalie Caron, Ann Thomson and Phyllis Weliver.

Earlier fruits of this research have appeared in the following collections and journals: E. Tuttle (ed.), *Confluences XVII: républic anglais et idée de tolerance* (Paris 2000); *The History of European Ideas* xxvii (2001); and *The Journal of British Studies* (forthcoming). I am grateful to the editors and publishers for permission to reproduce some of that material here. I am also grateful to the anonymous reader for the *Journal of British Studies* for some extremely perceptive comments.

Following a chance meeting in Paris in 2002, Colin Jones's support for this project has been invaluable. His advice, and that of two anonymous readers, helped me to improve the manuscript significantly and to think more carefully about the bigger picture. I am also grateful to the Editorial Board of the Studies in History Series and to the editorial team, and in particular to Christine Linehan for her painstaking attention to detail.

My greatest debt is to my family who have been unstinting in their support from beginning to end. Without that support this book simply would not exist. In recognition of this fact I have dedicated it to my parents, but I also wish to extend my thanks to others – in particular my brother and my grandparents. Last of all I wish to thank my husband John. He continued to believe in this project when I doubted it and he has inspired me, guided me and sustained me.

Rachel Hammersley

Abbreviations

AHR	American Historical Review
AHRF	Annales historiques de la Révolution française
AN	Archives Nationales, Paris
BHVP	Bibliothèque Historique de la Ville de Paris
BL	British Library, London
BN	Bibliothèque Nationale, Paris
EHR	English Historical Review
FHS	French Historical Studies
JBS	Journal of British Studies
JMH	Journal of Modern History
P&P	Past and Present
WMQ	William and Mary Quarterly

Introduction

Regicide and republic

On 25 September 1792 the first French republic was officially proclaimed.[1] This historic announcement was followed, almost exactly four months later, by the execution of Louis Capet, formerly Louis XVI of France. Similar events to these had taken place almost one hundred and fifty years earlier across the Channel in England.[2] There, King Charles I had also been tried and executed (on 30 January 1649) although, in the English case, the abolition of the monarchy and the establishment of a republic had followed, rather than preceded, the regicide.

Despite its short life, the English republic of the 1650s left a legacy of republican writings and stimulated an enduring republican tradition. The works of John Milton, Marchamont Nedham and James Harrington – written during the 1650s – were followed by those of Algernon Sidney and Henry Neville in the 1680s. Amid the standing army controversy of the 1690s, many of these works were republished by John Toland. It was Toland who was largely responsible for establishing the notion of a seventeenth-century English republican tradition.[3] In the eighteenth century, English republican ideas survived in the works of British commonwealthmen, such as John Trenchard, Thomas Gordon, Thomas Hollis, James Burgh, Richard Price and Joseph Priestley.[4]

English republicanism has been the subject of many scholarly books and articles, and the connections between it and a broader republican tradition have been comprehensively explored.[5] By contrast, French republicanism has

---

[1] The royal office had already been abolished on 21 September; 22 September was taken as marking the first day of the republican calendar.

[2] The two cases are discussed and compared in M. Walzer (ed.), *Regicide and revolution: speeches at the trial of Louis XVI*, Cambridge 1974.

[3] On the creation of that tradition see B. Worden, 'Introduction' to E. Ludlow, *A voyce from the watch tower, V: 1660–1662*, ed. B. Worden, London 1978, 1–80; *Roundhead reputations: the English civil wars and the passions of posterity*, London 2001, 21–121; and 'Whig history and Puritan politics: the *Memoirs* of Edmund Ludlow revisited', *Historical Research* lxxv (2002), 209–37.

[4] C. A. Robbins, *The eighteenth-century commonwealthman: studies in the transmission, development and circumstance of English liberal thought from the restoration of Charles II until the war with the thirteen colonies*, Cambridge, Mass. 1959.

[5] Z. Fink, *The classical republicans: an essay in the recovery of a pattern of thought in seventeenth-century England*, Evanstan 1945; F. Raab, *The English face of Machiavelli: a changing interpretation, 1500–1700*, London 1964; J. G. A. Pocock, *The Machiavellian*

received surprisingly little attention. Moreover, when it has been discussed it has tended to be seen in a purely francophone context.[6] This might imply that the republicanism that emerged in France in the 1790s was wholly unconnected to the broader tradition – stretching from ancient Greece and Rome through to eighteenth-century Britain and North America. But this seems implausible. Rather, it would appear that the reason for the scholarly neglect of French republicanism is to be found in the particular nature of the two historiographical traditions most relevant to it: the history of republicanism and the history of the French Revolution. The way in which these two areas have been revived and developed in recent years has resulted in consideration of French republicanism, and its connection to the broader tradition, falling into the gulf between them.

The historiographical context

During the second half of the twentieth century, republicanism became an important topic of historical interest. One of the seminal texts was J. G. A. Pocock's *The Machiavellian moment*. Pocock's book is of particular significance because he drew together the fruits of much previous historical research in different areas within a single theoretical framework.[7] As with any seminal

---

moment: Florentine political thought and the Atlantic republican tradition, Princeton 1975; B. Worden, 'Classical republicanism and the Puritan revolution', in H. Lloyd-Jones, V. Pearl and B. Worden (eds), *History and imagination: essays in honour of H. R. Trevor-Roper*, London 1981, 182–200, and 'The commonwealth kidney of Algernon Sidney', *JBS* xxiv (1985), 1–40; J. Scott, *Algernon Sidney and the English republic, 1623–1677*, Cambridge 1988, and *Algernon Sidney and the restoration crisis, 1677–1683*, Cambridge 1991; A. C. Houston, *Algernon Sidney and the republican inheritance in England and America*, Princeton 1991; B. Worden, 'English republicanism', in J. Burns and M. Goldie (eds), *The Cambridge history of political thought, 1450–1750*, Cambridge 1991, 443–75; 'Marchamont Nedham and the beginnings of English republicanism, 1649–56'; 'James Harrington and *The Commonwealth of Oceana*, 1656'; 'Harrington's *Oceana*: origins and aftermath, 1651–1660'; and 'Republicanism and the restoration, 1660–1683', all in D. Wootton (ed.), *Republicanism, liberty, and commercial society, 1649–1776*, Stanford 1994, 45–193; Q. Skinner, *Liberty before liberalism*, Cambridge 1998; D. Norbrook, *Writing the English republic: poetry, rhetoric and politics, 1627–1660*, Cambridge 1999; S. D. Glover, 'The Putney debates: popular versus elitist republicanism', *P&P* clxiv (1999), 47–80.
6   See, for example, C. Nicolet, *L'Idée républicaine en France (1789–1924): essai d'histoire critique*, Paris 1982; P. Raynaud, 'Destin de l'idéologie républicaine', *Esprit* xii (1973), 17–29.
7   Pocock drew on research on renaissance Italy, seventeenth-century England and eighteenth-century Britain and North America. On renaissance Italy see H. Baron, *The crisis of the early Italian renaissance: civic humanism and republican liberty in an age of classicism and tyranny*, 2nd edn, Princeton 1966; F. Gilbert, *Machiavelli and Guicciardini: politics and history in sixteenth-century Florence*, Princeton 1965. On eighteenth-century Britain and North America see Robbins, *The eighteenth-century commonwealthman*; 'Algernon Sidney's *Discourses concerning government*: textbook of revolution', *WMQ* (1947), 267–95; and 'The

work, *The Machiavellian moment* has not gone without criticism. Pocock has been challenged on his definition of a republican or civic humanist language; his treatment of that language as homogeneous; and his argument that it was Harrington and not Locke who provided the touchstone for American republicanism.[8] However, there is another crucial issue. In his own reply to some of his critics 'The Machiavellian moment revisited', which appeared in the *Journal of Modern History* in 1981, Pocock made explicit something that had been implicit in the work itself.[9] The story he was telling, he explained, was one of the progressive movement of republican ideas *away* from Europe.

Since the publication of *The Machiavellian moment*, a number of historians have sought to challenge the Anglo-American centredness of Pocock's work. Books and articles have appeared on Dutch republicanism, and attempts have also been made to examine the writings of various European thinkers from a republican perspective.[10] However, as the two volumes of essays on European

strenuous Whig, "Thomas Hollis of Lincoln's Inn" ', *WMQ* (1950), 406–53, repr. in B. Taft (ed.), *Absolute liberty: a selection from the articles and papers of Caroline Robbins*, Connecticut 1982, 168–205; B. Bailyn, 'General introduction' to *Pamphlets of the American Revolution, 1750–1776*, ed. B. Bailyn, Cambridge, Mass. 1965, i. 3–202, and *The ideological origins of the American Revolution*, Cambridge, Mass. 1967; G. S. Wood, *The creation of the American republic, 1776–1787*, Chapel Hill 1969. For a general overview of the historiography of the American Revolution see R. E. Shalhope, 'Towards a republican synthesis: the emergence of an understanding of republicanism in American historiography', *WMQ* (1972), 49–77, and 'Republicanism and early American historiography', *WMQ* (1982), 334–56; D. T. Rodgers, 'Republicanism: the career of a concept', *Journal of American History* lxxix (1992), 11–38; A. Gibson, 'Ancients, moderns and Americans: the republicanism–liberalism debate revisited', *History of Political Thought* xxi (2000), 261–307. Pocock's book is so well known that I do not intend to dwell on it here.

8 See D. Wootton, 'Introduction: the republican tradition: from commonwealth to common sense', in Wootton, *Republicanism, liberty, and commercial society*, 13–19. On the third point see I. Kramnick, *Republicanism and bourgeois radicalism: political ideology in late eighteenth-century England and America*, Ithaca 1990, and J. O. Appleby, *Liberalism and republicanism in the historical imagination*, Cambridge, Mass. 1992.

9 J. G. A. Pocock, 'The Machiavellian moment revisited: a study in history and ideology', *JMH* liii (1981), 49–71.

10 On Dutch republicanism see E. Haitsma Mulier, *The myth of Venice and Dutch republican thought in the seventeenth century*, Assen 1980, and 'The language of seventeenth-century republicanism in the United Provinces: Dutch or European?', in A. Pagden (ed.), *The languages of political theory in early modern Europe*, Cambridge 1987, 179–95; M. Van Gelderen, *The political thought of the Dutch revolt, 1555–1590*, Cambridge 1992. Montesquieu, Rousseau and Mably have all been approached from a republican perspective: J. N. Shklar, 'Montesquieu and the new republicanism', in G. Bock, Q. Skinner and M. Viroli (eds), *Machiavelli and republicanism*, Cambridge 1990, 265–79; R. A. Leigh, 'Jean-Jacques Rousseau and the myth of antiquity in the eighteenth-century', in R. R. Bolgar (ed.), *Classical influences on western thought, AD 1650–1870*, Cambridge 1979, 155–68; M. Viroli, 'The concept of *ordre* and the language of classical republicanism in Jean-Jacques Rousseau', in Pagden, *Languages of political theory*, 159–78, and *Jean-Jacques Rousseau and the 'well-ordered society'*, Cambridge 1988; J. Hope Mason, 'Individuals in society: Rousseau's republican vision', *History of Political Thought* x (1989), 89–112; M. M. Goldsmith, 'Liberty, virtue, and the rule of law, 1689–1770', in Wootton, *Republicanism*,

republicanism published by Cambridge University Press demonstrate, it is only very recently that attention has begun to be paid to the role of republican ideas in eighteenth-century France.[11]

Like the intellectual history of the republican tradition the historiography of the French Revolution has its own seminal text, which was also written during the 1970s. François Furet's *Penser la révolution française* appeared in France in 1978 and was then translated into English in 1981 under the title *Interpreting the French Revolution*.[12] The importance of Furet's book has not been lost on historians. As Gary Kates declared, 'no other book has shaped the research agenda for French revolutionary scholarship in the 1980s and 1990s more than this one'.[13] The significance of Furet's work lies largely in the challenge that it launched against Albert Soboul and the Marxist interpretation of the Revolution, which had been dominant for most of the twentieth century.[14]

Furet's work was not itself the first attack on the orthodox position, but is better seen, like Pocock's *The Machiavellian moment*, as the culmination of a more long-term shift. By the 1970s various aspects of the Marxist explanation of the Revolution had begun to be questioned. For example, there was a growing realisation that it was very difficult clearly to differentiate and define the nobility, the bourgeoisie and the popular classes in *ancien régime* France. Running parallel to the emerging crisis in academic interpretations of the Revolution was a wider sense of disenchantment with Marxism as a political doctrine. Given the close links that had existed, since the beginning of the century, between the academic historical study of the French Revolution and Marxist politics, this disenchantment could not but have an effect on historical scholarship.[15]

---

liberty, and commercial society, 197–232; R. Wokler, 'Rousseau and his critics on the fanciful liberties we have lost', in R. Wokler (ed.), *Rousseau and liberty*, Manchester 1995, 189–212; H. Rosenblatt, *Rousseau and Geneva: from the* First discourse *to the* Social contract, *1749–1762*, Cambridge 1997; K. M. Baker, 'A script for a French Revolution: the political consciousness of the *abbé* Mably', *Eighteenth-Century Studies* xiv (1981), 235–63, repr. in K. M. Baker, *Inventing the French Revolution: essays on French political culture in the eighteenth century*, Cambridge 1990, 86–106; J. K. Wright, *A classical republican in eighteenth-century France: the political thought of Mably*, Stanford 1997.

[11] M. Van Gelderen and Q. Skinner (eds), *Republicanism: a shared European heritage*, I: *Republicanism and constitutionalism in early modern Europe*; II: *The values of republicanism in early modern Europe*, Cambridge 2002.

[12] F. Furet, *Penser la Révolution française*, Paris 1978, trans. by E. Forster as *Interpreting the French Revolution*, Cambridge 1981.

[13] G. Kates (ed.), *The French Revolution: recent debates and new controversies*, London–New York 1998, 5.

[14] For a useful summary of the historiography of the French Revolution during the twentieth century see W. Doyle, *Origins of the French Revolution*, 3rd edn, Oxford 1999, 5–41.

[15] It is worth noting, however, that Marxist interpretations of the French Revolution did not die out completely: G. C. Comninel, *Rethinking the French Revolution: Marxism and the revisionist challenge*, London–New York 1987.

It was in the midst of this crisis within the Marxist interpretation of the French Revolution that Furet found fertile ground both for his critique of the work of Marxist historians and for his own alternative interpretation.[16] In *Penser la révolution française* Furet criticised the concentration of Marxist historians on social and economic factors and instead placed an emphasis on the political and intellectual history of the Revolution. As Furet himself explained, 'The first task of the historiography of the French Revolution must be to rediscover the analysis of its political dimension.'[17] He argued that political authority is a matter of linguistic authority and his research thus concentrated on revolutionary language and rhetoric. However, when Furet considered the language of republicanism, he tended to focus on its francophone origins, and its development during the nineteenth century, rather than on its connections to the wider republican tradition.[18]

Bridging the traditions

Inspired by both Pocock and Furet, some scholars have begun to examine the language of revolutionary republicanism and to investigate its origins.[19] They have started to explore whether there was an eighteenth-century French republican tradition similar to those that developed in Britain and North America – a tradition that made possible the transition from theory to prac-

---

[16] For more detail on the empirical forerunners to Furet see Doyle, *Origins of the French Revolution*, 10–34.

[17] Furet, *Interpreting the French Revolution*, 27.

[18] See, in particular, F. Furet and M. Ozouf (eds), *Le Siècle de l'avènement républicain*, Paris 1993. The exception here is the American republic, which does receive some attention.

[19] See, in particular, K. M. Baker, 'Transformations of classical republicanism in eighteenth-century France', *JMH* lxxiii (2001), 32–53; J. K. Wright, 'The idea of a republican constitution in old regime France', in Van Gelderen and Skinner, *Republicanism*, i. 289–306; M. Sonenscher, 'Republicanism, state finances and the emergence of commercial society in eighteenth-century France – or from royal to ancient republicanism and back', in Van Gelderen and Skinner, *Republicanism*, ii. 275–92 (I am grateful to both Kent Wright and Michael Sonenscher for providing me with copies of their articles prior to publication). See also Baker, *Inventing the French Revolution*; B. Fontana (ed.), *The invention of the modern republic*, Cambridge 1994; R. Monnier, 'L'Invention de la république et la dynamique culturelle démocratique', *History of European Ideas* xx (1995), 243–52; M. Sonenscher, 'The nation's debt and the birth of the modern republic: the French fiscal deficit and the politics of the French Revolution of 1789', *History of Political Thought* xviii (1997), 64–103, 267–325; R. Monnier, ' "Démocratie representative" ou "république démocratique": de la querelle des mots (république) à la querelle des anciens et des modernes', *AHRF* (2001), iii. 1–21. Unfortunately Raymonde Monnier's important article 'Républicanism et revolution française', *FHS* xxvi (2003), 87–118, appeared too late for me to engage with it as fully as I would have liked. Of less direct relevance to this study is Andrew Jainchill's article, which deals with the persistence of classical republican ideas in France beyond Thermidor. It too appeared too late for detailed consideration here: 'The constitution of the year III and the persistence of classical republicanism', *FHS* xxvi (2003), 399–435.

tice after 1789, and influenced the outbreak of the Revolution and the establishment of a French republic three years later.

As its title suggests, Keith Baker's article 'Transformations of classical republicanism in eighteenth-century France' directly links French revolutionary republicanism to the broader tradition. Referring to Pocock, Baker seeks to distinguish 'republicanism as the belief in a specific form of government from classical republicanism as a political idiom'.[20] He traces the development of the latter in eighteenth-century France in the accounts of French history written by Henri de Boulainvilliers and the *abbé* Mably, and in the works of Rousseau and of Guillaume-Joseph Saige.[21] Baker concludes 'that classical republicanism was available as an oppositional language in France throughout the eighteenth century' and 'that the language of classical republicanism was indeed a significant feature of French political culture on the eve of the French Revolution'.[22] He then goes on to investigate how and why, in the French revolutionary context, this language provided the basis for the Terror. Highlighting the emphasis within classical republicanism on constant vigilance and surveillance of the authorities, he identifies what he describes as 'three mutations of classical republicanism'.[23] These mutations – metastasisation, moralisation and messianism – he associates with Jean Paul Marat, Maximilien Robespierre and Antoine Saint-Just, respectively. All three, he argues, involved radicalisation of the language of classical republicanism and contributed towards its 'transformation . . . into a philosophy of terror'.[24]

Two of the essays in the recent volumes on European republicanism address the question of pre-revolutionary French republicanism in more detail.[25] In 'The idea of a republican constitution in old regime France' Kent Wright sketches a history of republicanism in France during the eighteenth century, centred on the notion of the 'ancient constitution'. Having alluded to the importance of the Huguenot resistance theorists of the sixteenth century, Wright emphasises the significance of the aristocratic opposition that emerged towards the end of the reign of Louis XIV, and in particular the works of Boulainvilliers. He explains that Boulainvilliers described the French monarchy as a modern despotism that had replaced the aristocratic republic of the Frankish nobility. The Frankish nobles had formed an 'egalitarian citizenry' which elected both a small council and an executive monarch.[26] Wright goes on to show how, during the course of the eighteenth century, republican discussions of the 'ancient constitution' – in the works of

---

[20] Baker, 'Transformations of classical republicanism', 35.
[21] On Saige see Baker, *Inventing the French Revolution*, 128–52.
[22] Idem, 'Transformations of classical republicanism', 39, 42.
[23] Ibid. 43.
[24] Ibid. 53.
[25] Van Gelderen and Skinner, *Republicanism*, i, ii.
[26] Wright, 'Republican constitution', 292.

Montesquieu, Mably and Saige – moved away from the feudal and aristocratic assumptions of Boulainvilliers's account and turned French republicanism into a 'fully contemporary political programme'.[27] As Wright acknowledges, Rousseau's republicanism was unusual in that it did not deal with the question of the 'ancient constitution'. It was, none the less, integrated with that tradition in the works of Saige, and it influenced the 'modern republicanism' of Emmanuel-Joseph Sieyès.[28] On Wright's account it was Mably who provided the means by which the 'ancient constitution' could be used to overturn France's absolutist monarchy, but it was Rousseau who was the main source of inspiration for the republicanism that filled the gap left behind. Turning to the debates over the drawing up of a new constitution in the summer and autumn of 1789. Wright argues that the Declaration of the Rights of Man and of the Citizen revealed 'the crystallisation of a specifically Gallic republicanism, focused on the three planks, national sovereignty, law as the expression of the general will, and the separation of powers'.[29] Moreover he suggests that each of the positions advanced within those constitutional debates had their roots in eighteenth-century French republicanism.

A somewhat different perspective is adopted in Michael Sonenscher's article 'Republicanism, state finances and the emergence of commercial society in eighteenth-century France – or from royal to ancient republicanism and back'. Sonenscher takes as his point of departure the financial situation in eighteenth-century France and in particular the complicated interrelationship between war, trade and public credit. At face value, republican government did not seem ideally suited to these circumstances. Consequently, 'Advocating a republican form of government meant finding a way to match an absolute monarchy's capacity to preserve its freedom from external subjection while simultaneously maintaining the domestic political liberty associated with a republic.'[30] Sonenscher examines two potential solutions to this problem that were explored during the eighteenth century: the 'patriot king' solution and the 'debt-reduction' solution. The roots of the former lay in the writings of Charles Davenant and viscount Bolingbroke. It involved the creation of a balanced republican constitution with a strong patriot king at its head. Sonenscher traces the development of this idea in the works of the marquis de Montalembert, Jean-Louis Favier and, most signifi-

27 Ibid. 300.
28 On Sieyès see K. M. Baker, 'Representation', in K. M. Baker (ed.), *The French Revolution and the creation of modern political culture*, I: *The political culture of the old regime*, Oxford 1987, 469–92, and the revised version of this article in Baker, *Inventing the French Revolution*, 224–51; Sonenscher, 'The nation's debt', 267–325; and P. Pasquino, 'The constitutional republicanism of Emmanuel Sieyès', in Fontana, *Invention of the modern republic*, 107–17.
29 Wright, 'Republican constitution', 304. See also J. K. Wright, 'National sovereignty and the general will', in D. Van Kley (ed.), *The French idea of freedom: the old regime and the declaration of rights of 1789*, Stanford 1994, 199–233. On the constitutional debates of 1789 see also Baker, *Inventing the French Revolution*, 252–305.
30 Sonenscher, 'Republicanism', 277.

cantly, Mably. The main advocates of the debt-reduction solution were Jacques Pierre Brissot and Étienne Clavière. The introduction of a scheme of debt-reduction, based on the American system of continental currency, was designed to 'create a single, common interest as the basis of a patriotic commitment to the public good'.[31] The revolutionary war, Sonenscher claims, revealed the extent of the problems arising from the combination of republican government and public debt. In contrast to Baker he sees this as the key explanation for the Terror: 'The imperatives of public safety meant that the price of preserving the modern funding system was to dispense with political liberty.'[32] Sonenscher ends by sketching out Sieyès's rather different solution to the problem.

These articles suggest a distinction within French revolutionary republicanism between 'the republicanism of the moderns' and 'the republicanism of the ancients'.[33] Several recent monographs have expanded our understanding of the development of 'modern republicanism' in revolutionary France. In his *Republicanism and the French Revolution*, Richard Whatmore focuses on Jean-Baptiste Say and his associates – including Clavière and Brissot.[34] He demonstrates their opposition to the ancient republicanism of Mably and the Jacobins, and their attempt to create a form of modern republicanism, which drew both on their own Genevan experiences and on the American republican model. This version of republicanism was designed to suit the large states of the modern world and to be compatible with both commerce and civilisation. A similar story is told in James Livesey's *Making democracy in the French Revolution*, though Livesey focuses on the much neglected period of the Directory and on the ministry of François de Neufchâteau.[35] He describes the development of a new form of 'democratic republicanism' between 1795 and 1800, one adapted to commercial society and resting on the notion of a happy and industrious citizenry able to combine acting for the public good with the pursuit of their own private interests. In both accounts the need to bring about a transformation of manners is treated as both the essential foundation of modern republicanism and its stumbling block.

While our understanding of revolutionary republicanism has been enriched by the accounts of modern republicanism presented by Whatmore and Livesey, the study of ancient republicanism in revolutionary France remains in its infancy. Some research has been undertaken on the role played

---

[31] Ibid. 283.

[32] Ibid. 290.

[33] This distinction is explicitly drawn in Baker, 'Transformations of classical republicanism', 32–3.

[34] R. Whatmore, *Republicanism and the French Revolution: an intellectual history of Jean-Baptiste Say's political economy*, Oxford 2000.

[35] J. Livesey, *Making democracy in the French Revolution*, Cambridge, Mass. 2001.

by ancient texts and ideas in late eighteenth-century France.[36] In addition, the question of Rousseau's influence upon the Revolution, and particularly on the creation of revolutionary republicanism, has been explored extensively.[37] Largely overlooked, however, has been the considerable interest generated by English republicanism in eighteenth-century France.

English republicanism in eighteenth-century France

In 1756 the French statesman René Louis de Voyer de Paulmy, marquis d'Argenson, wrote in his diary: 'Meanwhile there blows from England a philosophical wind: murmurs are heard of the words "liberty", "republicanism"; already minds have been penetrated and one knows the extent to which opinion governs the world.'[38] Though writing more than thirty years before the Revolution, d'Argenson was already aware of the significance of the English ideas about republicanism and liberty that were making their way across the Channel.

The mixed and shifting French attitudes towards England during the eighteenth century have been well documented.[39] The similarities between the two nations and their proximity to one another made the drawing of comparisons a popular pastime. Ironically, both anglophilia and anglophobia tended

---

36 On the reception of ancient ideas in late eighteenth-century France see H. T. Parker, *The cult of antiquity and the French revolutionaries: a study in the development of the revolutionary spirit*, Chicago 1939; C. Mossé, *L'Antiquité dans la Révolution française*, Paris 1989; M. Raskolnikoff, *Des Anciens et des modernes*, Paris 1990, and *Histoire romaine et critique historique dans l'Europe des lumières*, Rome 1992; P. Vidal-Naquet, *Politics ancient and modern*, trans. J. Lloyd, Cambridge 1995.

37 On Rousseau's influence on the revolutionaries see D. Mornet, *Les Origines intellectuelles de la Révolution française (1715–1787)*, 5th edn, Paris 1954; J. McDonald, *Rousseau and the French Revolution, 1762–1791*, London 1965; C. Blum, *Rousseau and the republic of virtue: the language of politics in the French Revolution*, Ithaca 1986; R. Barny, *L'Éclatement révolutionnaire du Rousseauisme*, Paris 1988; J. Swenson, *On Jean-Jacques Rousseau considered as one of the first authors of the Revolution*, Stanford 2000. Furet and Baker have also emphasised Rousseau's importance in this respect: Furet, *Interpreting the French Revolution*; Baker, *Inventing the French Revolution*.

38 'Cependant il souffle d'Angleterre un vent philosophique: en entend murmurer ces mots de *liberté*, de *républicanisme*; déjà les esprits en sont pénétrés et l'on sait à quel point l'opinion gouverne le monde': R. L. de Voyer de Paulmy, marquis d'Argenson, *Mémoires*, ed. P. Jannet, Paris 1858, v. 346. On d'Argenson see N. O. Henry, 'Democratic monarchy: the political theory of the marquis d'Argenson', unpubl. PhD diss. New Haven 1968. The translations throughout are my own.

39 For a well known example of French anglophilia see Voltaire, *Letters concerning the English nation*, Oxford 1994. Secondary sources on the subject include G. Bonno, *La Constitution britannique devant l'opinion française de Montesquieu à Bonaparte*, Paris 1931; F. Acomb, *Anglophobia in France, 1763–89: an essay in the history of constitutionalism and nationalism*, Durham, NC 1950; D. Jarrett, *The begetters of revolution: England's involvement with France, 1759–1789*, London 1973; J. Grieder, *Anglomania in France, 1740–1789: fact, fiction and political discourse*, Geneva–Paris 1985.

to be driven by the same fundamental questions: how had England become so successful? And how could the French emulate that success and overtake their rival? The key feature of the English nation for many eighteenth-century French commentators was its emphasis on liberty. French interest in English liberty stimulated calls for France to be transformed into a constitutional monarchy on the English model, but it also prompted French interest in seventeenth-century England, since this was seen as the cradle of English liberty.[40]

Seventeenth-century English republican works became known in France via translations, and articles in French-language newspapers, produced by Huguenots in Holland. The *Memoirs* of Edmund Ludlow (first published by Toland in 1698–9) and Sidney's *Discourses* were translated into French in the early years of the eighteenth century; and both Ludlow and Sidney, along with Milton and Harrington, were the focus of articles in the Huguenot press.[41] In 1774 the Chevalier d'Eon de Beaumont published a translation of Marchamont Nedham's *The excellencie of a free state* in his magisterial *Les Loisirs du chevalier d'Eon de Beaumont*.[42] Several works by eighteenth-century British commonwealthmen were also translated into French. Most of the works of Henry St John, viscount Bolingbroke, were translated during the 1750s, and various of those of John Trenchard and Thomas Gordon appeared during the 1750s and 1760s.[43]

---

[40] On the use of the English constitutional model see J. O. Appleby, 'America as a model for the radical French reformers of 1789', *WMQ* (1971), 267–86; E. Dziembowski, 'The English political model in eighteenth-century France', *Historical Research* lxxiv (2001), 151–71.

[41] E. Ludlow, *Les Mémoires d'Edmond Ludlow*, . . . *contenant ce qui s'est passé de plus remarquable sous le règne de Charles I jusqu'à Charles II* . . . *traduit de l'anglois*, Amsterdam 1699; A. Sidney, *Discours sur le gouvernement, par Algernon Sidney*, . . . *publiez sur l'original manuscrit de l'auteur, traduits de l'anglois par P. A. Samson*, The Hague 1702, repr. 1755; J. Bernard (ed.), *Nouvelles de la république*, Amsterdam 1700: 'Discourses concerning government by Algernon Sidney' (mars–mai 1700), 243–69, 426–56, 553–79; 'Harrington's *Oceana* and other works by Toland' (sept. 1700), 243–63; *Histoire des ouvrages des savans par Monsr B*** docteur en droit*, Rotterdam 1702: (1698) xv. 271 and (1699) xv. 521–33 (Ludlow); (1699) xvi. 78–88 and (1699) xvi. 242–48 (Milton); (1702) xix, 63–75 (Sidney); P. Kemp and others (eds), *Bibliothèque britannique*, The Hague 1737: '*Oceana* and other works of Harrington by Toland plus an appendix containing those works omitted by Toland' (juill.–sept. 1737), 408–30. On the French-language Huguenot press see H. J. Reesink, *L'Angleterre dans les périodiques français de Hollande, 1684–1709*, Paris 1931. On the Huguenots and their connections with the English republican tradition see M. C. Jacob, *The radical Enlightenment: pantheists, freemasons, and republicans*, London 1981.

[42] D'Eon de Beaumont, *Les Loisirs du chevalier d'Eon de Beaumont ancien ministre plénipotentiaire de France, sur divers sujets importans d'administration, &c. pendant son séjour en Angleterre*, Amsterdam 1774, vi. 137–399. On d'Eon de Beaumont and this translation see chapter 2 below.

[43] Bolingbroke lived in France between 1715 and 1725 and again between 1735 and 1744, which helps to explain why so many of his works were translated and reviewed in the French language press. There are too many translations to list them all here, but on Bolingbroke's reputation in France see D. J. Fletcher, 'The fortunes of Bolingbroke in

It has recently been suggested that English republicanism influenced a number of key figures in pre-revolutionary France.[44] Boulainvilliers's account of the corruption in contemporary French society – which he blamed on the replacement of the values of 'birth', 'virtue' and 'merit' by those of 'wealth', 'favour' and 'ambition'[45] – offers a striking parallel to the critiques of British society produced by the eighteenth-century commonwealthmen. Harold Ellis has described Boulainvilliers as an anglophile, but Wright goes further in insisting that 'Boulainvilliers . . . made clear his debt to English commonwealth thought, the likely proximate source and inspiration for his civic humanism'.[46] Montesquieu's debt to the commonwealth tradition has also been explored in some detail. As Wright has demonstrated, Montesquieu also engaged in the debate over France's ancient constitution, and his ambivalent account of the English constitution in The spirit of the laws is again typical of the commonwealth tradition.[47] Moreover, Robert Shackleton has suggested that Montesquieu's thought, and particularly his notion of the 'separation of powers', owed something to Bolingbroke.[48] Mably made use of a British commonwealthman 'Milord Stanhope', as an interlocuter, in his Des Droits et des devoirs du citoyen.[49] 'Stanhope' sets out the British commonwealth case in his conversations with an anonymous Frenchman and succeeds in convincing him. Baker and Wright also speculate that Mably may have been inspired by Sidney's Discourses and Gordon's Discourses on Tacitus; and

France in the eighteenth century', in T. Besterman (ed.), Studies on Voltaire and the eighteenth century, Geneva 1966, 207–32, and Sonenscher, 'Republicanism', 277–82. T. Gordon, Discours historiques, critiques et politiques sur Tacite [trans. P. Daudé], Amsterdam 1742 (repr. 1749, 1751), and Discours historiques et politiques sur Salluste; par feu Mr Gordon, traduits de l'Anglois, par un de ses amis [P. Daudé], Paris 1759; [Baron P. H. D. von Holbach], L'Esprit du clergé, ou le christianisme primitif vengé des entreprises & des excès de nos prêtres modernes, traduit de l'anglois, London [Amsterdam] 1767.

44 M. Sonenscher, Work and wages: natural law, politics and the eighteenth-century French trades, Cambridge 1989, 333–61. This point is also made in all three of the articles discussed above: Baker, 'Transformations of classical republicanism'; Wright, 'Republican constitution'; Sonenscher, 'Republicanism'.

45 H. A. Ellis, Boulainvilliers and the French monarchy: aristocratic politics in early eighteenth-century France, Ithaca 1988, 69. On Boulainvilliers see also F. Furet and M. Ozouf, 'Two historical legitimations of eighteenth-century French society: Mably and Boulainvilliers', in F. Furet, In the workshop of history, trans. J. Mandelbaum, Chicago–London 1984, 125–39; Wright, 'Republican constitution', 292.

46 Ellis, Boulainvilliers and the French monarchy, 166; Wright, 'Republican constitution', 292.

47 Wright, 'Republican constitution', 292–94. See also J. Dedieu, Montesquieu et la tradition politique anglaise en France, Geneva 1971 (repr. of 1909 edition).

48 R. Shackleton, 'Montesquieu, Bolingbroke, and the separation of powers', French Studies iii (1949), 25–38. See also his 'Montesquieu and Machiavelli: a reappraisal', Comparative Literature Studies i (1964), 1–13.

49 G. B. Mably, Des Droits et des devoirs du citoyen, ed. J. L. Lecercle, Paris 1972. On the model for 'Milord Stanhope' see Wright, Classical republican, 71; Sonencher, 'Republicanism', 278.

Sonenscher convincingly demonstrates his debt to Bolingbroke.[50] Another figure of particular interest is Jean Paul Marat. In 1774, during his stay in England, Marat published a work entitled *The chains of slavery*, which was written in the context of the forthcoming British election.[51] In that work Marat employed the language of classical republicanism in an attempt to persuade the English people to use the election to end the corruption of the House of Commons by placemen. Though the English version was published anonymously, Marat did admit his authorship of the French version, which he published in 1793.[52]

With the onset of Revolution in 1789, French interest in the writings of English republican authors increased.[53] Works that had already been translated were republished, including Bolingbroke's *The idea of a patriot king*, Sidney's *Discourses concerning government* and Gordon's *Discourses on Tacitus and Sallust*.[54] The revolutionary orator and leader Honoré-Gabriel Riqueti, comte de Mirabeau, showed considerable interest in Milton in the early years of the Revolution, and produced French versions of both *Areopagitica* and *A defense of the people of England*.[55] Though Mirabeau himself did not emphasise

[50] Baker, 'A script for a French Revolution', 241–2, 248–9; Wright, *Classical republican*, 80; Sonencher, 'Republicanism', 277–82.

[51] [J. P. Marat], *The chains of slavery: a work wherein the clandestine and villainous attempts of princes to ruin liberty are pointed out, and the dreadful scenes of despotism disclosed, to which is prefixed, an address to the electors of Great Britain, in order to draw their timely attention to the choice of proper representatives in the next parliament*, London 1774. See Baker, 'Transformations of classical republicanism', 43–7.

[52] J. P. Marat, *Les Chaînes de l'esclavage, ouvrage destiné à développer les noirs attentats des princes contre les peuples; les ressorts secrets, les ruses, les menées, les artifices, les coups d'état qu'ils emploient pour détruire la liberté, et les scènes sanglantes qui accompagnent le despotisme*, Paris l'an I [1793]. There is a recent edition that usefully includes both the English and the French versions: J. P. Marat, *Les Chaînes de l'esclavage 1793; The chains of slavery 1774*, ed. C. Goëtz and J. De Cock, Brussels 1995.

[53] In France several articles have been produced on this subject: O. Lutaud, 'Des Révolutions d'Angleterre à la Révolution française: l'exemple de la liberté de presse ou comment Milton "ouvrit" les etats-généraux', *Colloque international sur la Révolution française*, Clermont Ferrand 1986, 115–25 (my thanks to Professor Lutaud for providing me with a copy of this paper), and 'Emprunts de la Révolution française à la première révolution anglaise', *Revue d'histoire moderne et contemporaine* xxxvii (1990), 589–607; A. Thomson, 'La Référence à l'Angleterre dans le débat autour de la république', in M. Vovelle (ed.), *Révolution et république: l'exception française*, Paris 1994, 133–44.

[54] Henry St John, viscount Bolingbroke, *Des Devoirs d'un roi patriote, et portrait des ministres de tous les temps: ouvrage traduit de l'anglois de Bolingbroke*, Paris 1790; A. Sidney, *Discours sur le gouvernement, par Algernon Sidney, traduits de l'anglais par P. A. Samson: nouvelle édition conforme à cette de 1702*, Paris 1794; T. Gordon, *Discours historiques, critiques et politiques de Thomas Gordon sur Tacite et sur Salluste, traduits de l'anglois* [by P. Daudé], nouvelle édition, corrigée, Paris l'an II [1794].

[55] H. G., comte de Mirabeau, *De la Liberté de la presse: imité de l'anglais de Milton*, Paris 1788. The 1792 second edition of this translation has recently been reproduced in C. Tournu, *Milton et Mirabeau: rencontre révolutionnaire*, n.p. 2002, 55–92; H. G., comte de Mirabeau, *Théorie de la royauté après la doctrine de Milton*, Paris 1789. On Mirabeau and his circle see J. Bénétruy, *L'Atelier de Mirabeau: quatre proscrits génevois dans la tourmente*

the republican implications of these works, they were made evident when his translation of *A defense of the people of England* was republished in 1792, by the council of the département of Drôme, in the context of the debates over what should be done with Louis XVI.[56] Mirabeau also oversaw the production of a five-volume translation of Catharine Macaulay's republican *History of England*.[57] The works of Harrington were also translated into French. The year 1795 witnessed two separate translations of works by him.[58] Beyond the translations, a number of works appeared that drew on English republican texts and ideas. Sidney was invoked in an anonymous work of 1789, while in 1794 a history of the English republic appeared that was explicitly based on Ludlow's *Memoirs*.[59] Interest did not come to an end with Napoleon Bonaparte's *coup d'état*: Bertrand Barrère translated Walter Moyle's common-wealth work on the government of Rome in 1801.[60] Moreover, English republican and British commonwealth ideas appear to have provoked interest among a wide cross-section of revolutionaries. In addition to Mirabeau's interest in Milton and Macaulay, and Barrère's translation of Moyle, there has been some speculation as to the influence of the ideas of Harrington on the *abbé* Sieyès.[61]

révolutionnaire, Paris 1962. Milton's influence on Mirabeau has also received some atten-tion from anglophone scholars: D. M. Wolfe, 'Milton and Mirabeau', *Publications of the Modern Languages Association of America* xlix (1934), 1116–28; 'Mirabeau', in W. B. Hunter and others (eds), *Milton encyclopedia*, Lewisburg 1978–83, v. 148; T. Davies, 'Bor-rowed language: Milton, Jefferson, Mirabeau', in D. Armitage, A. Himy and Q. Skinner (eds), *Milton and republicanism*, Cambridge 1995, 254–71.

56 *Défense du peuple anglais sur la jugement et la condamnation de Charles premier, roi d'Angleterre: par Milton: ouvrage propre à éclairer sur la circonstance actuelle où se trouve la France, réimprime aux frais des administrateurs du Département de la Drôme*, Valence 1792. This translation also appears in Tournu, *Milton et Mirabeau*, 93–158.

57 H. G., comte de Mirabeau, *Histoire de l'Angleterre, depuis l'avènement de Jacques Ier jusqu'à la révolution, par Catharine Macaulay Graham, traduit en français et augmentée d'un discours préliminaire, contenant un précis de l'histoire de l'Angleterre jusqu'à l'avènement de Jacques I, et enrichie de notes*, Paris 1791–2. On Macaulay herself see B. Hill, *The republican virago: the life and times of Catharine Macaulay, historian*, Oxford 1992.

58 J. Harrington, *Oeuvres politiques de James Harrington*, trans. P. F. Henry, Paris l'an III [1795]; *Aphorismes politiques*, trans. P. F. Aubin, Paris 1795.

59 *Lettre de felicitation de milord Sidney aux parisiens et à la nation françoise: ou résurrection de milord Sidney second coup de griffe aux renards de toute couleur*, Paris 1789; *Histoire de la republique d'Angleterre d'après les Mémoires d'Edmond Ludlow l'un des principaux chefs des républicains anglais: contenant la narration des faits qui ont précédé accompagné et suivi ces momens lucides de la nation anglaise, par un républicain*, Paris l'an II [1794].

60 [W. Moyle], *Essai sur le gouvernement de Rome, traduit de l'anglois* [by B. Barrère de Vieuzac], Paris 1801.

61 On Harrington's influence on Sieyès see J. H. Clapham, *The abbé Sieyès*, Westminster 1912; H. Russell-Smith, *Harrington and his Oceana*, Cambridge 1914, 205–15; 'Introduc-tion' to S. B. Liljegren (ed.), *A French draft constitution of 1792 modelled on James Harring-ton's Oceana*, Lund 1932, 44–79; D. Trevor, 'Some sources of the constitutional theory of the *abbé* Sieyès: Harrington and Spinoza', *Politica* (1935), 325–42; M. Forsyth, *Reason and revolution: the political thought of the abbé Sieyès*, Leicester 1987.

While the wide range of French revolutionaries who showed an interest in and made use of English republican ideas certainly demonstrates their importance at the time, it also presents a problem of coherence. These ideas were made use of by all kinds of revolutionaries, in diverse ways, to justify a wide variety of political positions. There was, however, one group of revolutionaries – associated with the radical, Paris-based Cordeliers Club – that made extensive, and surprisingly consistent, use of a substantial number of English republican texts during the French Revolution. They did so in order to develop, support and justify their own distinctive version of French revolutionary republicanism. This republicanism, which they developed in opposition to the modern republicanism of the Brissotins, was extremely democratic in nature. It thus adds a new dimension to our understanding of republicanism in late eighteenth-century France.

This account of the English-inspired republicanism of members of the Cordeliers Club comprises three parts. The first (chapter 1) introduces the Cordeliers Club and some of its members. It deals with the Cordeliers District, which was in many ways a forerunner to the club, as well as with the origins of the club itself. It also examines the republican and democratic ideas of members of the club. A second section (chapters 2–4) details the uses made of seventeenth-century English republican ideas by several members of the Cordeliers Club between 1790 and 1792. It examines translations (both acknowledged and unacknowledged) of the works of Nedham and Harrington, as well as references to, and borrowings from, their writings and those of their contemporaries. This section demonstrates how the Cordeliers drew on English ideas in order to develop and justify the building of a democratic republic in late eighteenth-century France. It also traces the ways in which the Cordeliers developed and adapted the original English ideas so as to make them better suited to their own circumstances and concerns. The final section (chapter 5) takes the story on to 1793 and 1794. It shows how, under the very different circumstances of the first French republic and the Terror, one leading member of the Cordeliers Club – Camille Desmoulins – returned to English republican sources in an attempt to revive and reassert the old Cordeliers principles against those of the revolutionary government.

1

The Cordeliers Club and the Idea of a Democratic Republic

The Cordeliers Club is often seen as the poorer cousin of the more well-known and influential Jacobin Club. As a body the Cordeliers certainly never achieved the fame of the Jacobins, nor did individual club members infiltrate the offices of power to anything like the same extent. Indeed, members of the Cordeliers Club were more likely to find themselves on the wrong side of both municipal and national authority. None the less, the extent to which the Cordeliers have been neglected within the historiography of the French Revolution is unjustified.

Some work was done on the club by the French historians Alphonse Aulard and Albert Mathiez early in the twentieth century.[1] However, their accounts were affected by their disagreement as to whether Georges Jacques Danton or Maximilien Robespierre had been the more important revolutionary figure.[2] Mathiez's work was also heavily influenced by his Marxist approach to the Revolution, which led him to emphasise social and economic factors at the expense of politics and ideas. More recent general works include George Robertson's unpublished doctoral thesis (1972) and Jacques De Cock's *Les Cordeliers dans la Révolution française* (2001).[3] The latter not only provides an account of the club, its origins and its actions, but also painstakingly details the surviving documentary evidence relating to the Cordeliers. While both works add greatly to our understanding of the Cordeliers, neither is concerned with their political thought.[4] Some research has

---

1 A. Aulard, 'Danton au district des Cordeliers et à la commune de Paris' and 'Danton au club des Cordeliers et au département de Paris', in A. Aulard (ed.), *Études et leçons sur la Révolution française*, 4th ser. Paris 1904, 90–127, 128–52; A. Mathiez, *Le Club des Cordeliers pendant la crise de Varennes et le massacre sur le Champ de Mars: documents en grande partie inédits*, Paris 1910. See also A. Bougeart, *Les Cordeliers: documents pour servir à l'histoire de la Révolution française*, Caen 1891.
2 On the dispute between Aulard and Mathiez itself see J. Friguglietti, *Albert Mathiez historien révolutionnaire (1874–1932)*, Paris 1974.
3 G. M. Robertson, 'The society of the Cordeliers and the French Revolution, 1790–1794', unpubl. PhD diss. Wisconsin 1972; J. De Cock, *Les Cordeliers dans la Révolution française*, I: *Lineaments*, Lyon 2001. Unfortunately the second volume of De Cock's work did not appear in time for it to be made use of here.
4 Given that a general trend within the historiography of the French Revolution in recent years has been to focus on the intellectual history, and especially the political thought, of the Revolution, this neglect is particularly significant. The one exception is

been done on the later years of the club's existence (1793–4) and, in particular, on the *Enragés* and *Hébertists* who came to dominate the club during this period.[5] Much less attention has, however, been given to the earlier years of the club's existence. One practical reason for the neglect of the Cordeliers club by scholars is that many of the documents relating to it were destroyed in a fire in the archives of the Paris Prefecture de Police in May 1871. None the less, sufficient information has survived in official records, published petitions and pamphlets to recreate some sense of the club and, particularly, its intellectual dimension.

The Cordeliers District

Any account of the Cordeliers Club must begin with some discussion of the eponymous district that prefigured it. The origins of the sixty districts of Paris lay in the *Réglements royaux* of 13 April 1789, which set out the rules by which the Paris elections to the estates-general were to be conducted.[6] The estates-general, which had been summoned to meet at the beginning of May in order to deal with the financial crisis facing the nation, had not been called since 1614. The electoral process was complex. The elections of representatives of the three estates were to be carried out separately, each on the basis of a two-stage process: the citizens would gather to choose their electors and then the electors would gather, in electoral assemblies, to choose the Paris deputies to the estates-general. For the purposes of choosing the electors for the third estate, the city was divided into sixty electoral wards or districts.[7]

The district assemblies met for the first time on 21 April 1789 mostly in churches or other religious buildings within their localities. It was from these meeting places that many of the districts derived their official titles. From their first meeting some of the district assemblies already displayed the spirit of independence that was to characterise their existence. Some shunned official control and instead asserted their right to choose their own president and officers. Others even went so far as to produce their own individual *cahiers des*

Patrice Gueniffey's article, which does offer some discussion of the political thought of the club: 'Girondins and Cordeliers: a prehistory of the republic?', trans. L. Mason, in Fontana, *Invention of the modern republic*, 86–106.

5 R. B. Rose, *The Enragés: socialists of the French Revolution?*, Melbourne 1965; M. Slavin, *The Hébertists to the guillotine: an anatomy of a 'conspiracy' in revolutionary France*, Baton Rouge–London 1994; J. Guilhaumou and R. Monnier, 'Les Cordeliers et la république de 1793', in Vovelle, *Révolution et république*, 200–12; R. Monnier, 'Cordeliers, sans-culottes et Jacobins', *AHRF* (1995), ii. 249–60.

6 On the electoral and administrative systems of Paris during the early years of the French Revolution see M. Genty, *L'Apprentissage de la citoyenneté: Paris, 1789–1795*, Paris 1987.

7 The electoral divisions for the two other estates were completely separate. For the elections of the first estate (clergy) the city was divided into fifty-two parishes and for the elections of the second estate (nobility) it was split into twenty departments.

doléances.[8] Amid the popular mobilisation following Louis XVI's dismissal of Jacques Necker as finance minister on 11 July 1789, which culminated in the storming of the Bastille on the 14th, many of the districts began to sit permanently. At the same time they were invited to form and organise branches of the national guard within their localities. As a result they moved beyond their original electoral role and became one of the central, albeit unofficial, branches of the new, provisional government of the capital. In this role they became involved in a three-way power struggle with the mayor and the *assemblée générale des représentants de la commune* (communal assembly).[9]

On 15 July 1789 the assembly of electors of Paris, surrounded by a crowd of Parisians, declared one of the Paris deputies to what was now the National Assembly, Jean Sylvain Bailly, mayor of the city.[10] At the same time, the marquis de Lafayette was proclaimed *commandant général* of the new national guard. These positions were subsequently confirmed by the districts.[11] It was up to the new mayor to organise a provisional system of municipal authority and to arrange for the establishment of a more permanent municipal constitution. Despite the popular nature of his rise to power, Bailly's views on the formation of the new municipal government were strongly anti-democratic. In his opinion, the mayor was the one true representative of the commune. On this basis he favoured a centralised administration with executive power and legislative initiative being held in the hands of the mayor.

A week later, on 23 July, Bailly instructed each of the sixty districts to elect two deputies to form an assembly charged with drawing up a new municipal constitution and also with administering the city in the interim. This elected

8   Genty, *L'Apprentissage*, 21–2. The districts had been granted rights of discussion and deliberation in order to contribute to the *Cahier général de la ville*. However, in producing their own individual cahiers they were going beyond their remit. See *Actes de la commune de Paris pendant la Révolution*, ed. S. Lacroix, 1st ser., Paris 1894–8, repr. New York 1974, i, pp. vi–vii.

9   On the power struggle within the municipality see H. E. Bourne, 'Improvising a government for Paris in July, 1789', *AHR* x (1905), 280–308, and 'Municipal politics in Paris in 1789', *AHR* xi (1906), 263–86; R. B. Rose, 'How to make a revolution: the Paris districts in 1789', *Bulletin of the John Rylands University Library of Manchester* lix (1977), 426–57; M. Genty, 'Pratique et théorie de la démocratie directe: l'exemple des districts parisiens (1789–1790)', *AHRF* cclix (1985), 8–24; K. Tønnesson, 'La Démocratie directe sous la Révolution française: le cas des districts et sections de Paris', in C. Lucas (ed.), *The French Revolution and the creation of modern political culture*, II: *The political culture of the French Revolution*, Oxford 1988, 295–306; and De Cock, *Les Cordeliers*, 51–61. As these works testify, the politics of the capital was of huge importance, particularly during the early months of the Revolution. The debates over the drawing up of a municipal constitution paralleled and played into the simultaneous debates concerning the creation of a national constitution. Moreover, many figures who played a key role on the national stage, were also deeply engaged in the politics of Paris.

10   As president of the third estate, Bailly had played a key role in both the adoption of the title National Assembly on 17 June 1789 and the swearing of the tennis court oath three days later.

11   *Actes de la commune*, 1st ser., i, pp. xiii–xiv, 407n.

body of 120 members met for the first time at the *hôtel de ville* on 25 July. The writer and journalist Jacques Pierre Brissot was elected to this assembly, by the district of Filles-Saint-Thomas, and became one of its leading members. Brissot and his colleagues criticised Bailly's view as to where power should lie and insisted instead that it should be vested in the communal assembly. To support their claim to power, they advocated a theory of representative government, presenting the communal assembly as the representative body within the capital. The title they adopted, *assemblée générale des représentants de la commune*, reflected this claim. However, almost from its inception, the communal assembly's assumption of representative status was challenged by some of the districts.

These districts insisted that sovereignty should be held and exercised by the citizens gathered in their district assemblies. In their view, the communal assembly should be nothing more than a federative association of district leaders who should be personally accountable to the districts. As the members of the assembly did not appear to share their view, the districts began to take action to undermine some of the functions that the assembly saw as its own. They began to communicate directly with the mayor and his assistants and they also established the practice of sharing their decisions and ideas with one another. From the end of July they extended their co-operation through their organisation of a *comité central de correspondence* based at l'Archevêque.[12] It was designed to make it easier for the districts to communicate with each other and to harmonise their work. They also occasionally called *ad hoc* assemblies to deal with particular issues. Central among the militant districts was the Cordeliers District headed by Danton.[13]

The Cordeliers District took its name from the old Cordeliers convent, a Franciscan monastery, founded in 1230, which was situated at its heart.[14] The area had a reputation for free thinking and radical ideas. The café Procope at 13 rue de l'Ancienne Comédie-Française, reputedly the world's oldest coffee house, had long been a meeting place for radical writers and thinkers. Camille Desmoulins, a local inhabitant, was explicit about the connections between the long-standing reputation of the locality and the aims and activities of the district:

[12] The communal assembly expressed its concern about the existence of this assembly as early as 28 July 1789: ibid. i. 30, 33–6, 591.

[13] Alphonse Aulard did much to clarify the precise role played by Danton among the Cordeliers. He challenged Alfred Bougeart's claim that Danton had been president of the Cordeliers District from the beginning. The first mention of Danton as president, he insisted, was to be found on an insurrectional manifesto dated 4 October 1789. Danton was, however, subsequently re-elected as Cordeliers president four times: Aulard, *Études et leçons*, 90–127.

[14] On the convent, and the use of its buildings prior to and during the Revolution, see De Cock, *Les Cordeliers*, 25–46.

The Cordeliers district is delightful . . . It is clear that this district feels the effects of being in the neighbourhood of the café Procope. . . . It is true that one no longer has the pleasure of hearing Piron, Voltaire, Jean-Baptiste Rousseau, but the patriots sustain its reputation still. . . . It has the unique fame that the language of servitude has never been heard there; that the royal patrols have never entered there; and it is the only sanctuary where liberty has not been violated.[15]

According to an account given by Danton on 19 August 1792, the Cordeliers district had played a key role on 14 July 1789 and it had begun meeting at 9 a.m. every morning from that date.[16] During its short existence the district pursued two main policies. First, it provided a safe haven for individuals who were being persecuted by the authorities. Secondly, it was at the forefront of the campaign, within the municipality, to counter the representative claims of both the communal assembly and mayor Bailly.

The most famous recipient of Cordeliers protection was the radical journalist Jean Paul Marat.[17] Marat had originally faced charges in the autumn of 1789 for allegedly having provoked the popular march to Versailles of the 5 and 6 of October and for his attacks against the communal authorities and Necker.[18] An arrest warrant (*décret de prise de corps*) was issued against him from Châtelet (the focus of royal civil and criminal jurisdiction within the city) and Marat was forced into hiding.[19] In the midst of all this, Marat turned to the Cordeliers District for protection. In response to his request, the district declared that it would protect all authors within its jurisdiction.[20] Despite already being in a dangerous position, Marat continued to provoke the authorities. His *L'Ami du peuple* did not appear for almost a month after 8 October, but when it started up again on 5 November he was as vitriolic as ever in his attacks on the National Assembly, the municipal authorities and

---

[15] 'C'est un charmant district que les Cordeliers. . . . On voit que ce district se ressent du voisinage du café Procope. . . . On n'a plus, il est vrai, le plaisir d'entendre Piron, Voltaire, Jean-Baptiste Rousseau, mais les patriots soutiennent encore sa reputation. . . . Il a la gloire unique que jamais le langage de la servitude n'a osé s'y faire entendre; que jamais les patrouilles royales n'ont osé y entrer; et c'est le seul asile où la liberté n'ait pas été violée': quoted in Aulard, *Études et leçons*, 117.

[16] Ibid. 115. See also 'Extrait du procès-verbal de l'assemblée du district des Cordeliers: du mardi 14 juillet 1789', repr. in De Cock, *Les Cordeliers*, 49–50.

[17] The key documents from the Marat Affair were collected together and published as *Pièces justificatives: exposé de la conduite et des motifs du district des Cordeliers concernant le décret de prise de corps prononcé par le Châtelet contre le sieur Marat, le 8 octobre 1789 et mis à exécution le 22 janvier 1790*, Paris [1790].

[18] The accusations against Marat primarily concerned material that appeared in his newspaper *L'Ami du peuple*: J. P. Marat, *Marat dit l'Ami du peuple*, Tokyo 1967, nos viii–xxviii, 75–243.

[19] The arrest warrant itself is reprinted as the fourth item in *Pièces justificatives*, 9–10.

[20] District des Cordeliers, 'Extrait du registre des délibérations du district des Cordeliers, 7 octobre 1789'. See also De Cock, *Les Cordeliers*, 141.

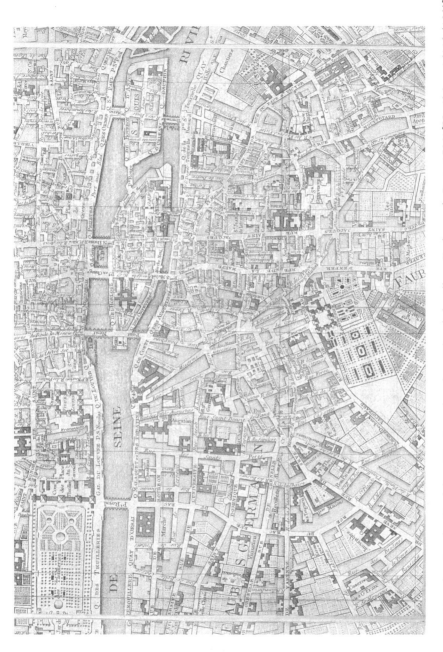

Plate 1a. Map showing the Cordeliers District, taken from 'Plan de la ville et Faubourg de Paris, 1790' [BL, *Maps 16110.(180)]. Reproduced by permission of the British Library

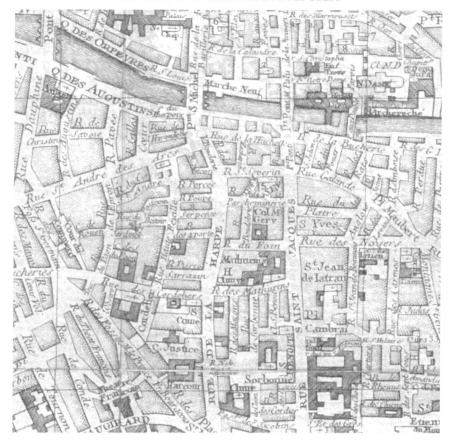

Plate 1b. Detail of the map of the Cordeliers District.

Necker. The authorities finally caught up with him on 12 December and he was taken before the *comité des recherches* and questioned by Lafayette.[21] He was subsequently released, and by the following week was again producing *L'Ami du peuple*. In January 1790 the old arrest warrant was revived and again Marat appealed to the Cordeliers District for support.[22] Their response was immediate. On 11 January they agreed that the district itself should be directly involved in all arrests made within its boundaries.[23] At their meeting of 19 January the Cordeliers confirmed their decree of the 11th and named several commissioners (*commissaires conservateurs de la liberté*) whose respon-

---

[21] Marat, *L'Ami du peuple*, no. xxi, 432–6.
[22] Ibid. nos xxiii–xcvi, 607–35; no. c, 665–8.
[23] For the decree issued by the Cordeliers District on 11 January 1790 see *Actes de la commune*, 1st ser., iii. 521–2. For Marat's account, which differs slightly in its wording from the Cordeliers decree, see Marat, *L'Ami du peuple*, nos xciii, xcv, xcvi, ci, ciii.

sibility it would be to oversee the procedure and to authorise arrests within the district.[24] Three days later the promises made by the Cordeliers were put to the test when soldiers from the national guard invaded the Cordeliers District and surrounded the building, on the rue de l'Ancienne Comédie-Française, in which Marat was living and from where he published his *L'Ami du peuple*.[25] That same day the Cordeliers District sent a delegation to the National Assembly.[26] They appealed to the assembly, referring to the recent laws reforming the criminal justice system (8 and 9 October 1789), which had rendered illegal precisely this kind of arbitrary arrest. On these grounds, the Cordeliers presented themselves as adhering to and upholding the laws of the National Assembly in acting to ensure that the warrant against Marat was not carried through. Whilst the Cordeliers did gain support from certain deputies in the discussion that ensued, the general feeling was that the Cordeliers had been wrong in assuming that the recent laws could be applied retrospectively to earlier arrest warrants, such as that against Marat.[27] The following day a deputation of Cordeliers, led by Danton, went before the communal assembly.[28] The assembly was informed of the recent events involving Marat, and of the response of the Cordeliers District to them. As a result of his attempt to intervene, Danton himself became the subject of a Châtelet *décret de prise de corps* several weeks later.[29] However, it was not until 18 May that the question of Danton's arrest was brought before the National Assembly.[30] The charges against him were dropped at this point but, according to Aulard, the Marat affair was used in September 1790 as a reason for excluding Danton from the communal assembly.[31]

The attempt by the districts to counter the representative claims of the communal assembly and mayor Bailly found focus in discussions on the form that was to be taken by the future municipal constitution. At its first meeting, on 25 July 1789, the communal assembly had established a committee of sixteen of its members charged with drawing up a plan for the future munic-

---

24 District des Cordeliers, 'Extrait des registres des délibérations de l'assemblée du district des Cordeliers, du 19 janvier 1790', *Pièces justificatives*, 1–4.

25 *Moniteur universel: réimpression de l'ancien Moniteur; seule histoire authentique et inaltéré de la Révolution française; depuis la réunion des états-généraux jusqu'au consulat (mai 1789 – novembre 1799)*, Paris 1847–79, iii. 183 (23 Jan. 1790).

26 *Archives parlementaires, 1787–1860*, ed. M. Madival and E. Laurent, 1st ser. Paris 1879–1914, xi. 287–8.

27 Ibid. xi. 288. For the decree of the National Assembly on this issue and the president's letter to the Cordeliers District informing them of the National Assembly's decision see *Pièces justificatives*, 16–18.

28 *Actes de la commune*, 1st ser., iii. 528–30.

29 District des Cordeliers, 'Extrait des registres des délibérations de l'assemblée du district des Cordeliers, du 18 mars 1790', Paris 1790. See also GRANDE *motion sur le* GRAND *forfait du* GRAND M. DANTON, *perpétré dans le* GRAND *district des* GRANDS CORDE-LIERS, *et sur les* GRANDES *suites d'icelui*, repr. in Aulard, *Études et leçons*, 130–2.

30 *Archives parlementaires*, xv. 583.

31 Aulard, *Études et leçons*, 134.

ipal organisation of the city. That committee met for the first time the following day.[32] Though not chosen as a committee member, Brissot very quickly took the constitutional task, delegated to the communal assembly, into his own hands.[33] The *Plan de municipalité*, which he produced in early August, embodied the notion of representative government that was favoured by him and many of his colleagues.[34] It prioritised the role of the communal assembly at the expense of that of the districts. The districts were to be limited to electing their representatives, the mayor and *commandant général*, and their district officials; executing the decisions of the municipal authorities within their locality (to be carried out by the *comité* of each district); and discussing issues set before them by the communal assembly. Though the *comité* of each district would meet regularly, the district assemblies could only meet once a year (for the purpose of elections) or at the will of the communal assembly. Moreover, once elected, the representatives were not to be subject to their particular district: 'Each representative belongs to the whole commune, none of them can be revoked by the assemblies of the districts.'[35] According to Brissot, his plan was well received both by the constitutional committee, which used it as the basis of its constitutional plan, and by the communal assembly as a whole.[36] On 12 August M. Fondeur, one of the members of the constitutional committee, read a report to the communal assembly detailing the work that the committee had done so far.[37] It was decided that three hundred copies of the *Projet du plan de municipalité* would be produced. On 20 August Brissot himself addressed the communal assembly, offering some explanation of the motives behind the *Projet*.[38] Copies of this speech were printed, accompanied by the *Projet* itself. The communal assembly also agreed that it would work through the document article by article.

Throughout the summer of 1789 mayor Bailly repeatedly expressed his concern at the slow rate of progress being made in the constitutional task.[39] On 30 August he wrote to the districts explaining that the communal assembly urgently needed to hear their responses to the *Projet du plan de*

---

[32] *Actes de la commune*, 1st ser., i. 10–11, 22.

[33] Ibid. i. 383.

[34] J. P. Brissot de Warville, *Motifs des commissaires, pour adopter le plan de municipalité, qu'ils ont présenté à l'assemblée générale des représentans de la commune: lues à l'assemblée-générale, par J. P. Brissot de Warville, représentant de la commune: suivis du projet du plan de municipalité*, Paris 1789. See also *Actes de la commune*, 1st ser., i. 195–200.

[35] 'Chaque représentant appartenant à toute la commune, aucun ne pourra être révoqué par les assemblées de districts': Brissot de Warville, *Projet*, 8.

[36] Idem, *Le Patriote français: journal libre, impartial et national*, Frankfurt-am-Main 1989, i, no. xvi, 3–4 (14 Aug. 1789). See also *Actes de la commune*, 1st ser., i. 185.

[37] *Actes de la commune*, 1st ser., i. 185.

[38] Ibid. i. 283.

[39] Ibid. i. 148, 196, 259, 397, 403. The Communal Assembly began discussing the plan on 20 August 1789 but its discussions were constantly interrupted by more pressing issues: ibid. i. 284, 380, 385–6.

municipalité.[40] He also invited them to support his own recommendation, designed to ease the situation, that certain clauses of the plan be implemented immediately. Mayor Bailly's letter was endorsed by the communal assembly. In their meeting of 30 August they stated the need for certain representatives to devote themselves solely to examining and amending the *Projet du plan de municipalité* and they asked that the districts agree to part of the plan being put into operation immediately.[41]

A number of districts responded over the next few days.[42] The more militant among them saw Brissot's plan as a direct attempt to curb their powers and accused him of threatening the popular sovereignty that had so recently been won. They objected, in particular, to the proposal that the districts should no longer sit permanently but should be used primarily for the purpose of elections; to the suggestion that the president of each district be selected from among the members of the communal assembly – a measure aimed at ensuring that the assembly would be in a position to maintain a tight reign over the activities of the districts; and to the recommendation that each district representative to the assembly was a representative of the commune as a whole and could not, therefore, be recalled by his district. The Cordeliers District was one of those that opposed Brissot's plan. According to Sigsmund Lacroix, they debated the issue on 3 September 1789 and decided that they were not prepared to implement any part of the *Projet* without judging the whole.[43] Against it they continued to advocate a more democratic form of municipal government centred on the districts themselves. They insisted that the communal assembly should take orders from the district assemblies and that the independence of deputies should be severely restricted. In practice, this would involve the deputies polling their local assembly before voting on important issues, and being made subject to recall by their constituents.

Despite their concerns, the districts did accept the replacement of the original communal assembly by a larger body. This second communal assembly, which met for the first time on 19 September 1789, was composed of 300 members (five deputies from each of the sixty districts). It was to be divided, with a proportion of its members taking on the administration of the city, while the rest focused their attentions on examining and modifying the *Projet du plan de municipalité*. The new assembly included many of the members of its predecessor and its position on the question of municipal

---

40 Bailly's letter is reprinted ibid. i. 392–4.
41 Assemblée des représentans de la commune de Paris, *Extrait du procès-verbal de l'assemblé des représentans de la commune de Paris, du 30 août 1789*, Paris 1789.
42 For a list of the districts that did respond see *Actes de la commune*, 1st ser., i. 590–1.
43 Ibid. i. 483, 489, 590. See also *Pièces qui établissent l'illégalité de l'arrêté des mandataires provisoires de l'Hôtel-de-Ville, relativement aux cinq mandataires particuliers du district des Cordeliers (12 septembre–22 novembre 1789)*, Paris [1789], 3–5.

organisation remained the same. Consequently the conflict between the communal assembly and the districts continued.

A declaration by the communal assembly dated 28 September declared: 'attempts have been made to establish the principle that, henceforth, the districts no longer have any rights over their deputies to the commune. That all their control ceased from the moment that their deputies were admitted to the general assembly of the representatives of the commune'.[44] For its part the Cordeliers District continued to correspond with the other districts on particular issues (thus by-passing the communal assembly) and kept up its protests against certain of the decisions made by that assembly.

By late October the communal assembly was plainly irritated by the behaviour of the Cordeliers District.[45] On the 29th of that month they issued a statement complaining about the constant interference of the Cordeliers in administrative business, their attempts to unite with other districts and their references to the idea of binding mandates (*mandats imperatives*).[46] They also took the opportunity to reaffirm their authority over the districts and their independence from them. The Cordeliers District offered an immediate response four days later. They insisted on strict limits to the authority of the communal assembly: 'That the representatives of the commune hav[e] no other powers than those necessary to govern provisionally and to propose a plan of municipal organization, to be sanctioned by the districts.'[47] They also defended their right to bind their deputies with a mandate and to communicate with other districts on particular issues. The full response of the Cordeliers District, however, came a few days later. On 11–12 November it set out an oath that its deputies to the communal assembly were to take:

WE SWEAR AND PROMISE to oppose, as much as we are able, all that the representatives of the Commune may undertake that is harmful to the general rights of our constituents.

WE SWEAR, moreover, to conform scrupulously to all the particular mandates of our constituents, and to protest against all establishments, whether civil or military, made or to be made, which have not been sanctioned by the majority of the districts.

---

[44] 'on avait cherché à y faire passer pour maxime que les districts n'avaient plus, dès ce moment, aucuns droits sur leurs députés à la Commune, que même toute leur autorité avait cessé du moment où leurs députés avaient été admis à l'Assemblée générale des représentants de la Commune': quoted in Genty, *L'Apprentissage*, 40–1.

[45] On the increasing tensions between the communal assembly and the Cordeliers District in late October 1789 see *Actes de la commune*, 1st ser., ii. 642.

[46] Ibid. ii. 463–4. See also *Pièces qui établissent*, 11–15.

[47] 'Que les représentans de la Commune n'ayant d'autres pouvoirs que ceux nécessaires pour régir provisoirement & proposer à la sanction des districts un plan d'organisation municipale': District des Cordeliers, 'Extrait des registres des délibérations de l'assemblée du district des Cordeliers, du 2 Novembre 1789', repr. in *Pièces qui établissent*, 7.

WE ACKNOWLEDGE, that we are revocable at the will of our District, after three assemblies, held consecutively for this purpose, whatever the rules to the contrary that the representatives attempt to make.[48]

Of the five Cordeliers representatives to the communal assembly, two agreed to take the oath while the other three refused and resigned. The district accepted the resignations and appointed three replacements in fresh elections, insisting that their binding mandate was justified. The two original and three new deputies turned up to the meeting of the communal assembly on 16 November.[49] The assembly, under the leadership of the marquis de Condorcet, interrogated the Cordeliers deputies. As a result, one of them agreed to resign, but the others stood their ground. The communal assembly decided by 31 votes to 20 to annul the oath, the resignation of the original three Cordeliers deputies and the election of their replacements. It described the oath as 'detrimental to the true rights of the representatives of the commune' ('attentatoire aux véritables droits des représentants de la commune') and reasserted its belief 'that the deputies of a district, from the moment that they become representatives of the commune, no longer belong to their district in particular but to the commune as a whole'.[50] Both sides appealed to the National Assembly, which promised to consider the issue.[51] The committee delegated by the National Assembly to do so produced a report, which was presented on 23 November.[52] This largely supported the communal assembly in questioning the legitimacy of the Cordeliers oath, but warned the assembly that it had exceeded its functions in denying the right of the Cordeliers to choose three new deputies to replace those who had resigned. Undeterred, and alongside other districts that supported them on this point, the Cordeliers continued to express their view that the deputies to the communal assembly should be seen as *mandataires*.[53] An *arrêt* of 17 December 1789 explained:

[48] 'NOUS JURONS ET PROMETTONS de nous opposer, autant qu'il sera en nous, à tout ce que les représentans de la Commune pourroient faire de préjudiciable aux droits généraux des citoyens constituans. /NOUS JURONS, en outre, de nous conformer scrupuleusement à tous les mandats particuliers de nos constituans, & de protester contre toutes les formations, soit civiles, soit militaires, faites ou à faire, qui n'ont pas eu, ou n'auroient pas la sanction de la majorité des districts. /NOUS RECONNOISSONS, que nous sommes révocables, à la volonté de notre District, après trois assemblées, tenues consécutivement pour cet objet, quels que soient les réglemens à ce contraires, que les Représentans généraux tenteroient de faire': District des Cordeliers, 'Extrait des registres des délibérations de l'assemblée des Cordeliers, du 17 novembre 1789', repr. in *Pièces qui établissent*, 16–17.

[49] *Actes de la comumune*, 1st ser., ii. 637–43.

[50] 'que les députés d'un district, du moment où ils sont devenus les Représentans de la Commune, n'appartiennent plus à leur district en particulier, mais à la Commune entière': ibid. ii. 639.

[51] *Archives parlementaires*, x. 82–3, 144–5. See also *Pièces qui établissent*, 22–30.

[52] *Archives parlementaires*, x. 229–30.

[53] On the use of the terms 'mandataires' and 'représentans' and their significance see

they must wait for the view of their constituents in order to have a legal opinion on the decisions of the districts, and . . . after the voicing of this opinion,
each provisional delegate of the commune must espouse it and maintain it . . .
and the general assembly of these delegates [will] reveal the majority opinion
of the true commune, and [will] have no other opinion than that of this majority, however contrary it might be to the private intentions of the delegates of
the commune.[54]

In January 1790 the Cordeliers voted to replace all their deputies to the
communal assembly, with Danton himself being among those elected.[55]

The new municipal plan was finally voted by the National Assembly on
21 May 1790 and sanctioned by the king on 27 June. As a result of the pressure exerted by the communal assembly it was decided that the sixty districts
were to be replaced by forty-eight sections, the functions of which would be
electoral and judicial, and which would not sit permanently. It was explicitly
stated that the sections were not to concern themselves 'with any other business than that of elections and of the swearing of the civic oath'.[56] Following
the sanctioning of the plan by the king, the convocation of the citizens of
Paris into sections began. However, some were unwilling to embrace the new
system. On 28 June, concerned by the decision to replace the districts with
sections and by the speed with which action was being taken, the Cordeliers
called on the other districts to demand that no action be taken to reorganise
the municipality of Paris until after 30 July.[57] They received significant
support from the other districts, but the municipal and national authorities
were unwilling to listen.

The victory of Brissot and his associates in the communal assembly over
the districts was short-lived, since they were not subsequently re-elected to
the communal assembly. None the less, this episode marked the beginning
rather than the end of the involvement of both the Cordeliers and Brissot
and the other members of the communal assembly in revolutionary politics.

M. Genty, 'Mandataires ou représentants: un problème de la démocratie municipale à
Paris, en 1789–1790', AHRF ccvii (1972), 1–27.
54 'c'est à eux d'attendre le voeu de leurs commettants pour avoir même une opinion légale
sur les arrêtés des districts, et . . . après l'émission de ce voeu, chaque mandataire provisoire
de la Commune doit l'épouser et le maintenir, chacun relativement à son district, et
l'Assemblée générale de ces mandataires manifester la majorité des voeux de la vraie
Commune, et n'avoir point d'autre opinion que celle de cette majorité, quelque contraire
qu'elle puisse être aux intentions privées des mandataires provisoires de la Commune':
quoted in Genty, L'Apprentissage, 52.
55 Aulard, Études et leçons, 140–1.
56 'd'aucune autre affaire que des élections et des prestations du serment civique': quoted in
Genty, L'Apprentissage, 68.
57 District des Cordeliers, Extrait des registres des délibérations de l'assemblée du district des
Cordeliers, du 28 juin 1790, Paris 1790. See also District des Cordeliers, Extrait des registres de
l'assemblée générale du district des Cordeliers, du premier juillet mil sept cent quatre-vingt-dix,
Paris 1790.

Cordeliers ideas survived both in the séction du Théâtre Française, which covered much of the territory originally within the Cordeliers District, and in the Cordeliers Club.[58]

The establishment of the Cordeliers Club

In an 'Adresse aux parisiens', written in August 1791 the Cordeliers Club provided its own account of its origins:

> It is to the dissolution of the Cordeliers District that the Society of the rights of man and of the citizen owes its origin. It was natural that citizens who since the revolution had been meeting daily to watch over the public good, and who had contracted in these assemblies the habit of seeing each other, of closely observing each other, and of esteeming each other: it was natural, I say, to these fellow citizens to reunite under another name; they agreed therefore to substitute for the word District, which they could not keep, that of Cordeliers Club.[59]

Aulard, drawing on this document, linked the establishment of the Cordeliers Club directly to the abolition of the Cordeliers District. He insisted that it was when the districts were abolished that 'Danton and his friends founded the celebrated popular society which called itself the *Cordeliers Club, Society*

---

58   The séction du Théâtre Français was made up of the old Cordeliers District plus the eastern end of the district of l'Abbaye-Saint-Germain-des-Près and the northern part of the district of Saint-André-des-Arts as well as a small fragment of the district of Carmes. The reorganisation was said to have been deliberately aimed at diluting the militancy of the Cordeliers District: Genty, *L'Apprentissage*, 143. Genty has emphasised the extent to which the sections continued to uphold the idea of democracy originally advocated by the districts. More specifically there does seem to have been a particularly close connection between the séction du Théâtre Français and the Cordeliers District (and later the club). In October 1790 the séction du Théâtre Français began meeting in the Cordeliers convent, the former meeting place of the district. Thus between then and May 1791 the section and the club shared their meeting place. In May 1791 both groups were evicted by the authorities. The Cordeliers eventually found a permanent home in the Musée, Hôtel de Genlis, 105, rue Dauphine. The séction du Théâtre Français, however, was able to return to the Cordeliers convent on 15 June 1791. As well as sharing a meeting place the district, the section and the club also shared many of the same members. A list of the electors of the séction du Théâtre Français was printed in the *Journal du Club des Cordeliers* in July 1791. The list included many who had been involved in the district (and a number who were also members of the Cordeliers Club) including Danton, Boucher Saint-Sauveur, Momoro and Desmoulins: A. F. Momoro (ed.), *Journal du Club des Cordeliers*, Paris 1791, 26.
59   'C'est à la dissolution du district des cordeliers, que la société des droits de l'homme et du citoyen doit son origine. Il étoit naturel que des citoyens qui depuis la révolution s'étoient journellement assemblés pour surveiller la chose publique, et qui avoient contracté dans ces assemblées l'habitude de se voir, de s'étudier, et de s'estimer; il étoit naturel, dis-je, à ces con-citoyens de se réunir sous une autre dénomination; ils convinrent donc de substituer au mot District qu'ils ne pouvoient pas conserver, celui de club des cordeliers': 'Adresse aux parisiens', repr. in Momoro, *Journal du club*, 87–8.

of the friends of the rights of man and of the citizen'.[60] Mathiez, while not denying some connection between the Cordeliers District and the Société des amis des droits de l'homme et du citoyen, none the less chided Aulard for assuming the connection to be quite so direct.[61] He pointed to an announcement, dated 27 April 1790, which had appeared in *Le Moniteur* on 5 May.[62] This came from the 'Club des droits de l'homme' which Mathiez claimed was an earlier embodiment of the Cordeliers Club. As Jacques De Cock has noted, this was at precisely the time when Danton was in trouble for his involvement in the Marat Affair and when the municipality was threatening to abolish the districts and replace them with sections. De Cock links the creation of the Club des droits de l'homme directly to this situation.[63] There are certainly some grounds for accepting the idea that the Club des droits de l'homme was an early embodiment of the Cordeliers Club; indeed, there are several clues that point in this direction in the announcement itself. The description of the main aim of the club fits with Cordeliers concerns: 'to denounce to the court of public opinion the abuse of various powers and all attacks on the rights of man'.[64] The announcement goes on to invite citizens to inform the club of any examples of oppression or injustice of which they were aware. In turn the club would publicise these offences in the hope that it could: 'prevent any undertakings against common liberty and against particular rights'.[65] Letters detailing acts of oppression and injustice were to be sent to 'M. Dulaure, rue du Jardinet, opposite that of l'Eperon'.[66] Significantly, rue du Jardinet was itself at the heart of the Cordeliers District and, according to the list drawn up by Robertson, Dulaure was later a member of the Cordeliers Club.[67] None the less, it seems likely that the abolition of the districts gave a new impetus to the recently formed club and prompted their adoption of the Cordeliers title.

Whilst the connections between the municipal reorganisation within Paris and the establishment of the Cordeliers Club remain somewhat obscure, it would appear that this reorganisation did inspire the municipal opponents of the Cordeliers to establish their own society. At the last session of the communal assembly an announcement was made that the ousted municipal politicians would regroup as the 'Société fraternelle des anciens représentants

---

60 'Danton et ses amis fondèrent la célèbre Société populaire qui s'appela *Club des Cordeliers, Société des amis des droits de l'homme et du citoyen*': Aulard, *Études et leçons*, 229.
61 Mathiez, *Le Club des Cordeliers*, 1–2.
62 *Moniteur universel*, iv. 279.
63 De Cock, *Les Cordeliers*, 57–61.
64 'de dénoncer au tribunal de l'opinion publique les abus des différents pouvoirs et toute espèce d'atteinte aux droits de l'homme': *Moniteur universel*, iv. 279.
65 'prévenir plusieurs entreprises contre la liberté commune et contre les droits particuliers': ibid.
66 Ibid.
67 Robertson, 'The society of the Cordeliers', appendix A, 277.

de la commune de Paris'.[68] This organisation did not last, but was taken over by the *Confédération des amis de la vérité*, which comprised many of the same people.[69] The first meeting of the *confédération* took place on 13 October 1790 at the Palais Royal, with an estimated 4,000 people listening to the *abbé* Fauchet's opening address.[70] On 22 October the *confédération* chose Goupil de Préfeln as its president. From then on the club met every Friday afternoon at 5 p.m. The avowed aim of the *confédération* was to speculate on political principles and to unite the political and social ideas of the *philosophes* with the interests of the Third Estate. To this end they undertook a detailed analysis of Rousseau's *Social contract*.[71] The *confédération* was headed by the directoire du Cercle Social, which described its key aim as being to decipher the 'will of the people'.[72] One way in which it sought to do this was through the *Journal du Cercle Social*, which had been established in January 1790. An iron box (*bouche de fer*) was erected at the headquarters of the Cercle Social and members of the public were invited to place ideas and comments in the box for inclusion in the journal. Against the background of the controversy within the municipality, the *bouche de fer* can be seen as a means of bridging the gap between constituents and their representatives, whilst maintaining representative government. In 1791 the Cercle Social launched a new journal entitled *La Bouche de fer*, edited by Nicolas Bonneville, which was directly linked to the *confédération*.

Mathiez drew a direct contrast between the *confédération* and the Cordeliers Club. He described the former as a political academy, the main aim of which was to provide public instruction in preparation for future political change. The Cordeliers Club, by contrast, was described by him as a society of action and combat, the preoccupations of which were practical and directly connected to the needs and concerns of the ordinary people.[73]

The distinctiveness of the Cordeliers Club *vis-à-vis* both the *confédération* and the Jacobin Club cannot be explained, as has sometimes been suggested, simply with reference to the composition of the three societies. The Cordeliers Club certainly does appear to have been more open than either the *confédération* or the Jacobin Club. Both passive citizens and women were allowed to attend the meetings and the membership fee was set at two *sols* per month, placing it well within the means of small townsmen.[74] None the less, the club tended to be dominated by the financially better off and many of its leaders were also members of other political clubs, including both the

---

[68] *Actes de la commune*, 1st ser., vii. 443, 444–52.
[69] On the *confédération* see G. Kates, *The* Cercle Social, *the Girondins and the French Revolution*, Princeton 1985.
[70] Ibid. 77–8.
[71] Ibid. 80–1.
[72] Ibid. 56.
[73] Mathiez, *Le Club des Cordeliers*, 5–7. Bougeart also offered a similar comparison: *Les Cordeliers*, 69.
[74] I. Bourdin, *Les Sociétés populaires à Paris pendant la Révolution*, Paris 1937, 175.

confédération and the Jacobin Club.[75] While the composition of the key political societies of the early 1790s did not vary dramatically, their aims and activities were, as Mathiez suggested, fundamentally different. It is the principles, objectives and actions of the Cordeliers Club that served to differentiate it from its counterparts.

The driving force behind the creation of the Cordeliers Club ('Société des amis des droits de l'homme et du citoyen') in the spring of 1790 was the belief that the Revolution, and the liberty it promised, were being halted far short of the goals that had been laid down in the *Declaration des droits de l'homme et du citoyen* of 26 August 1789.[76] The club's members saw that document as 'democratic' in the sense that it granted certain freedoms, and gave the right to vote and to hold office, to all citizens. Yet they were concerned that in practice the promises were not being fulfilled. This belief was acted upon, by the members of the club, in two ways. First, they presented themselves as a body of surveillance (the emblem of the club was an open eye) the task of which was to keep watch over authorities at all levels and to publicise and take a stand against any encroachments on the rights of man as laid down in the *Declaration des droits*. Secondly, they provided support and relief for the victims of oppression and injustice. The words of the 'Adresse aux parisiens' summarised the club's self-perception of this aspect of its work:

> Each and every day the members of this society are active, some visiting the prisons and consoling the unfortunate, others defending them in the courts, others appealing in their favour before the committees of the national assembly . . . and . . . in [addition] all members take part in acts of charity through frequent financial contributions.[77]

During the first few months of the club's existence, the Cordeliers became involved in a number of controversies concerning the illegal and arbitrary arrest of citizens, the exercise of political rights – including the right of petition – and the bearing of arms. In these actions there would seem to be a very definite connection back to the role played by the Cordeliers District. Moreover, it was not just in their commitment to watching over the authorities and defending the victims of persecution and oppression that the Cordeliers Club appeared to be continuing a tradition originally established by the

---

75 Our knowledge of the membership and procedures of the Cordeliers Club is limited owing to the loss of crucial documents in the fire of 1871. In his PhD thesis, 'The society of the Cordeliers', Robertson did his best to reconstruct some sense of this aspect of the club from the available material.

76 Each club meeting began with the reading of the minutes of the previous meeting and of the *Déclaration des droits* itself: Momoro, *Journal du club*, 11.

77 'c'est cette société dont les membres sont journellement occupés, les uns à visiter les prisons, et à consoler les malheureux, d'autres à les défendre dans les tribunaux, d'autres à solliciter en leur faveur dans les différens comités de l'assemblée nationale, ou chez les ministres, et dont en général tous les membres concourent par des contributions fréquentes à des actes de bienfaisance': 'Adresse aux parisiens', ibid. 88.

district. The club also endorsed the democratic practices that had been upheld by the district in its confrontation with the communal assembly. Moreover, members of the club also proposed the extension of such democratic practices beyond the municipality of Paris to the realm of national politics.[78] The first step towards this end, according to many leading club members, was the abolition of the French monarchy and its replacement by a republic.

Republicanism in late eighteenth-century France

It was Montesquieu and Rousseau who essentially set the terms in which republicanism was understood and discussed in late eighteenth-century France.[79] Both thinkers described their understanding of republican government in great detail and seemed to view it, at least in theoretical terms, as the best form of government. According to Montesquieu's typology, republics were to be distinguished from monarchies and despotisms:

> *republican government is that in which the people as a body, or only a part of the people have sovereign power; monarchical government is that in which one alone governs, but by fixed and established laws; whereas, in despotic government, one alone, without law and without rule, draws everything along by his will and his caprices.*[80]

In contrast, Rousseau drew a distinction between sovereignty (the making of the laws) and government (the executing of the laws). His understanding of a republic was of a state in which sovereignty lay with the people – though within a republic government could be exercised as a monarchy, an aristocracy or a democracy:

> I therefore call Republic any State ruled by laws, whatever be the form of administration: for then the public interest alone governs, and the public thing counts for something. Every legitimate Government is republican*.[81]

* By this word I understand not only an Aristocracy or a Democracy, but in general any government guided by the general will, which is the law. To be legitimate, the Government must not be confused with the Sovereign, but be its minister: Then monarchy itself is a republic.

---

[78] For a similar argument concerning the extension of democratic practices from the local to the national level, this time in early modern England see M. Goldie, 'The unacknowledged republic: officeholding in early modern England', in T. Harris (ed.), *The politics of the excluded*, c. *1500–1850*, Basingstoke 2001, 153–94.

[79] Shklar, 'Montesquieu and the new republicanism', 265.

[80] Montesquieu, *The spirit of the laws*, ed. A. Cohler, B. Miller and H. Stone, Cambridge 1989, 10.

[81] J. J. Rousseau, *The social contract and other later political writings*, ed. V. Gourevitch, Cambridge 1997, 67.

Yet despite their praise for republics in theory neither Montesquieu nor Rousseau believed such a form of government to be suited to the states of the modern world – least of all France. A key reason for this was that republics were thought to be applicable only in relatively small nations. As Montesquieu explained:

> It is in the nature of a republic to have only a small territory; otherwise, it can scarcely continue to exist. In a large republic, there are large fortunes, and consequently little moderation in spirits: the depositories are too large to put in the hands of a citizen; interests become particularised; at first a man feels he can be happy, great, and glorious without his homeland; and soon, that he can be great only on the ruins of his homeland.

> In a large republic, the common good is sacrificed to a thousand considerations; it is subordinated to exceptions; it depends upon accidents. In a small one, the public good is better felt, better known, lies nearer to each citizen; abuses are less extensive there and consequently less protected.[82]

Rousseau also believed a true republic only to be possible in a small state – one in which the whole population could gather together on a regular basis: 'The Sovereign, having no other force than the legislative power, acts only by means of the laws, and the laws being nothing but the authentic acts of the general will, the Sovereign can only act when the people is assembled.'[83] As far as Rousseau was concerned representative government was not an acceptable solution to this problem:

> Sovereignty cannot be represented for the same reason that it cannot be alienated; it consists essentially in the general will, and the will does not admit of being represented: either it is the same or it is different; there is no middle ground. The deputies of the people therefore are not and cannot be its representatives, they are merely its agents; they cannot conclude anything definitively. Any law which the People has not ratified in person is null; it is not a law. The English people thinks it is free; it is greatly mistaken, it is free only during the election of Members of Parliament; as soon as they are elected, it is enslaved, it is nothing. The use it makes of its freedom during the brief moments it has it fully warrants its losing it.[84]

Another obstacle to the establishment of republics in the modern world that was highlighted by both Montesquieu and Rousseau was their reliance on civic virtue. For Montesquieu virtue was the principle of republican (and particularly democratic) government.[85] Rousseau also emphasised the impor-

---

82 Montesquieu, *Spirit of the laws*, 124.
83 Rousseau, *Social contract*, 100.
84 Ibid. 114. Nevertheless, in his *Considerations on the government of Poland* Rousseau did offer some kind of solution for larger states, in the use of delegates who would be subject to binding mandates: *Social contract*, 177–260.
85 Montesquieu, *Spirit of the laws* 22. For Montesquieu's definition of virtue see the 'Author's foreword' at pp. xli–xlii.

tance of civic virtue and insisted on the need to instill in the population the appropriate manners, virtues and customs for the form of government.[86] However, he feared that the establishment of virtuous manners was an impossibility in an old nation, where customs were already in place and prejudices deep-rooted, and especially one in which commerce and luxury had already taken hold.[87] On this basis he denied that the French were capable of the required regeneration.

Advocates of republicanism during the French Revolution were well aware of the views of Montesquieu and Rousseau on republican government. And all sought to deal with, and overcome, the obstacles that they had described.

It has often been suggested that calls for the establishment of a French republic only began to emerge in 1791.[88] This view is certainly borne out if one focuses solely on the Jacobins.[89] In any clear sense Jacobin republicanism only came into existence following Louis XVI's flight to Varennes in June 1791. Initially the Jacobins blamed ministers and the queen, rather than Louis XVI himself, for the problems faced by the nation. Moreover, members of the Jacobin Club generally sought to disassociate themselves from republicans.[90] Indeed, Michael Kennedy, in his three-volume work on the Jacobin Clubs, described the prototypical club member as 'a staunch monarchist [with] a high regard for Louis XVI'.[91] Even after the king's flight to Varennes the Jacobin shift towards republicanism was gradual. Between 23 June and 15 July 1791 few of the Paris Jacobins openly espoused republicanism, although they were more explicitly anti-royalist than before. A similar picture is evident in the provinces. Following the Varennes incident, the club at Montpellier circulated a petition calling for an end to the monarchy, but

---

86 Rousseau, Social contract, 81.

87 Ibid. 72–3.

88 'No one on the eve of the Revolution had ever dreamed of the establishment of a republic in France': A. Aulard, The French Revolution: a political history, 1789–1804, trans. B. Miall, London 1910, i. 125; 'prior to June 1791, not even the radicals desired a republic. All were content with a very limited role for the King. It was the King's aborted attempt to flee which changed attitudes towards the role of the monarchy': L. Whaley, Radicals: politics and republicanism in the French Revolution, Stroud 2000, 37–8. In addition to Aulard and Whaley see J. M. Goulemot, 'Du Républicanisme et de l'idée républicaine au XVIIIe siècle', in Furet and Ozouf, Le Siècle de l'avènement républicain, 25–56, in which the idea that revolutionary republicanism emerged out of the Enlightenment is comprehensively rejected.

89 On the Jacobins see C. C. Brinton, The Jacobins: an essay in the new history, New York 1961; M. L. Kennedy, The Jacobin clubs in the French Revolution: the early years, Princeton 1982; F. Fehér, The frozen revolution: an essay on Jacobinism, Cambridge 1987; M. L. Kennedy, The Jacobin clubs in the French Revolution: the middle years, Princeton 1988; L. Jaume, Le Discours jacobin et la démocratie; Paris 1989; P. Higonnet, Goodness beyond virtue: Jacobins during the French Revolution, Cambridge, Mass. 1998; and M. L. Kennedy, The Jacobin clubs in the French Revolution, 1793–1795, New York–Oxford 2000.

90 Brinton, The Jacobins, 266.

91 Kennedy, The middle years, 239.

only two other clubs responded positively.[92] Louis XVI became more unpopular with his use of the royal veto on 12 November 1791 and his expulsion of Jean-Marie Roland, Étienne Clavière and Joseph Servan from his ministry on 13 June 1792. The latter event no doubt helped to inspire the invasion of the Tuileries on 20 June. With the failure of this *journée*, the Jacobins turned more explicitly to the question of dethronement. On 3 August Jérôme Pétion, a member of the Jacobin Club and mayor of Paris, delivered a petition to the Legislative Assembly calling for the removal of the king. A week later a second popular invasion of the Tuileries resulted in Louis XVI's suspension and the decision to establish a republic.

Robespierre embodied the views of the Jacobins on this issue. He had originally been impressed by the 'monarchical republic' that Rousseau had proposed for Poland, and had urged the Constituent Assembly to adopt this model.[93] He failed, but he did not immediately change his opinions. Even after Varennes he remained sceptical about the possibility of establishing a non-monarchical system of government in France. In May 1792 he was involved in a campaign to prevent the overthrow of the monarchy in the face of war. And in the first issue of his 'Défenseur de la constitution', which appeared in the same month, he set out an exposition of his principles and clarified his own rather tame definition of republicanism:

> I am a republican! yes, I wish to defend the principles of equality and the exercise of sacred rights that the constitution guarantees to the people against the dangerous systems of schemers who regard it only as the instrument of their ambition. I would rather see a popular representative assembly and citizens who are free and respected under a king, than a people enslaved and degraded under the stick of an aristocratic senate and a dictator. I like Cromwell no better than Charles I, and I can support the yoke of the Decemvirs no more than that of Tarquin. Is it in these words of *republic* or of *monarchy* that the solution to the great social problem rests? Is it these definitions invented by diplomats to class the diverse forms of government which determine the happiness and the misfortune of nations, or the combination of laws and of institutions which constitute real happiness?[94]

---

[92] Ibid.

[93] J. Ramaswamy, 'Reconstituting the "liberty of the ancients": public credit, popular sovereignty and the political theory of the Terror during the French Revolution, 1789–1794', unpubl. PhD diss. Cambridge 1995, 150.

[94] 'Je suis républicain! oui, je veux défendre les principes de l'égalité et l'exercice des droits sacrés que la constitution garantit au peuple contre les systèmes dangereux des intrigans qui ne le regardent que comme l'instrument de leur ambition; j'aime mieux voir une assemblée représentative populaire et des citoyens libres et respectés avec un roi, qu'un peuple esclave et avili sous la verge d'un sénat aristocratique et d'un dictateur. Je n'aime pas plus Cromwel que Charles 1er; et je ne puis pas plus supporter le joug des Décemvirs que celui de Tarquin. Est-ce dans les mots de *république* ou de *monarchie* qui réside la solution du grand problème social? Sont-ce les définitions inventées par les diplomates pour classer les diverses formes de gouvernement qui font le bonheur et le malheur des nations, ou la combinaison des lois et des institutions qui en constituent la véritable nature?': M. Robespierre, 'Exposition de

Yet, if one looks beyond the Jacobin Club it is clear that republican senti-ments were being expressed well before 1792.[95] Even before the Revolution, during the 1780s, Brissot and Clavière had been exploring republican ideas.[96] Moreover, the Brissotins were not the only advocates of republican govern-ment prior to 1791.

As Gary Kates has recognised, Camille Desmoulins's pamphlet *La France libre*, which appeared in July 1789, can be seen as 'the first truly republican manifesto of the revolutionary era'.[97] In that work Desmoulins was unequiv-ocal in his opposition to monarchy: 'Do the facts not cry out that Monarchy is a detestable form of government?'[98] By contrast, he described popular government as 'the only one which suits men, and moreover the only one that is wise'.[99] Moreover, for Desmoulins it was not simply a matter of the fail-ings of this particular king: 'I like Louis XVI himself, but Monarchy is no less odious to me.'[100]

In spite of Desmoulins's activities it is only from late 1790 that one can truly speak of the existence of a republican faction. At this early stage repub-licanism took a predominantly literary form. The autumn of 1790 witnessed the appearance of several republican works including *Du Peuple et des rois* by Louis de la Vicomterie de Saint-Samson, and Pierre François Joseph Robert's *Républicanisme adapté à la France*.[101] These writers were just as vehement in their anti-monarchical sentiments as Desmoulins:

> any institution other than republicanism is a crime of *lèze-nation* . . . the apos-tles of royalty are either traitors or men stupidly misled which society must regard as its enemies.

> It is said at this time that France is free; what France is free! and a monarchy? We must not deceive ourselves; if France is free, she is not a monarchy, and if a monarchy, she is not free.[102]

mes principes', in *Oeuvres*, IV, V: *Les Journaux: lettres à ses commettants*, ed. G. Laurent, Gap 1961, iv. 9.
95   See R. Monnier, *L'Espace public démocratique: essai sur l'opinion à Paris, de la Révolution au Directoire*, Paris 1994; Gueniffey, 'Girondins and Cordeliers'.
96   R. Whatmore and J. Livesey, 'The democratic republicanism of the Girondins', unpubl. paper (I am grateful to Richard Whatmore for allowing me to see a copy of this paper); Whatmore, *Republicanism and the French Revolution*; Livesey, *Making democracy*, 20–87.
97   G. Kates, 'Introduction' to C. Desmoulins, *Les Révolutions de France et de Brabant*, ed. G. Kates, Frankfurt-am-Main 1989, i, p. iii.
98   'Les faits ne crient-ils pas que la Monarchie est une forme de gouvernement détestable?': C. Desmoulins, *La France libre*, Paris 1789, 38.
99   'le seul qui convienne à des hommes, est encore le seul sage': ibid. 45.
100   'J'aimois personnellement Louis XVI, mais la Monarchie ne m'étoit pas moins odieuse': ibid. 44.
101   L. de La Vicomterie de Saint Samson, *Du Peuple et des rois*, Paris 1790; F. Robert, *Le Républicanisme adapté à la France*, Paris 1790.
102   'toute autre institution que le Républicanisme est un crime de lèze-nation . . . et que les apôtres de la royauté sont ou des traîtres ou des hommes imbécilement égarés, que la société

It is undoubtedly significant that Desmoulins, La Vicomterie and Robert were all members of the Cordeliers Club.[103]

Camille Desmoulins

Lucie Simplice Camille Benoît Desmoulins had been born at Guise in Picardie on 2 March 1760. The eldest son of a local public official, he was educated alongside Robespierre at the *collège* of Louis-le-Grand in Paris. He trained as a lawyer and became an advocate of the *parlement* of Paris. Desmoulins put himself forward for election as a deputy of the third estate in his native Guise – but he was not elected. None the less, he did succeed in finding other ways of influencing the course of events.

On 12 July 1789, following Louis XVI's dismissal of Necker, Desmoulins made a speech at the Café de Foy in the Palais Royal which aroused the crowd and has been described as one of the events that provided the impetus behind the storming of the Bastille on 14 July.

At the time of his speech Desmoulins had already written *La France libre*, which, finally printed by Antoine Momoro (another future member of the Cordeliers Club), was ready for sale by 18 July.[104] The pamphlet was just as inflammatory and radical as the speech. In it Desmoulins declared that the French nation was just beginning to recover its liberty. He attacked the first two orders (the clergy and the nobility) as well as the monarchy itself. In place of these institutions of the *ancien régime* he proposed a democratic government complete with a National Assembly, a national treasury and a national militia.

From the beginning of the Revolution Desmoulins had close Cordeliers connections. He lived at 22 rue de l'Odéon in the heart of the Cordeliers District and just a few minutes walk from the Cordeliers convent. Moreover, he must have frequented the convent regularly; first as a citizen of the District and later as a member of the club.[105]

---

doit regarder comme ses ennemis./On dit dans ce moment que la France est libre: quoi la France est libre! et c'est une monarchie? Il ne faut pas nous abuser; si la France est libre, elle n'est pas une monarchie; et si elle est une monarchie, elle n'est pas libre': Robert, *Républicanisme*, 1–2.

[103] De Cock rejects the idea of the Cordeliers Club as the mouthpiece of a republican party on the grounds that it was individual club members, rather than the club as a body, who took this stance: *Les Cordeliers*, 69–78. While not denying De Cock's point, my interest lies in looking at those individuals and their ideas. The fact that so many of the republicans of this period were members of the club seems to me to be of interest in itself.

[104] J. Janssens, *Camille Desmoulins: le premier républicain de France*, Paris 1973, 123. According to Janssens, the work had initially been submitted to a printer on 20 June 1789, but Desmoulins had trouble getting anyone to agree to print it.

[105] For Desmoulins's own account of becoming a member of the district see his *Révolutions de France et de Brabant*, Paris 1789–91, i, no. xiv, 20. The 'Histoire de Paris' plaque, which currently stands outside the remains of the Cordeliers convent on the rue de l'École de Médecine, claims that Desmoulins founded the Cordeliers Club. However, I have found no evidence to support this claim. None the less, Desmoulins was certainly involved with the

Between 1789 and 1791 Desmoulins edited his own newspaper which was entitled *Révolutions de France et de Brabant*.[106] Its purpose was to provide readers with relevant news and comment not only on France itself but also Brabant 'and the other Realms which embrace the cockade and demand a National Assembly'.[107] As in *La France libre* Desmoulins continued to express his preference for republican over monarchical government:

> I have wished to employ all my powers to assist the progress of philosophy and to work to foster this sublime experiment. To discover the solution to the problem: *whether the government that I call a republic – that is to say equality, the brotherhood of men, and the monarchy of the law – is an illusion.*[108]

Moreover, the kind of republic he favoured was one that involved everybody:

> An old sage, the philosopher Heraclitus, said: *the most beautiful science, the only art which is worthy of the name of politics, is the art of* GOVERNING ALL BY ALL. This maxim must be written, in letters of gold, on the door of the national assembly, of all the directories of the departments and districts, and of all the municipalities[109]

Desmoulins remained a radical to the end of his short life. While he is often presented as a Jacobin, his foremost allegiance throughout his revolutionary career was to the principles and ideals of the Cordeliers of 1789–91.[110]

Louis de La Vicomterie

Louis de la Vicomterie de Saint-Samson was born in 1732 at Saint-Samson de Bonfossé.[111] Prior to the Revolution he had lived in Paris as a, largely

club from an early stage and his name does appear on Robertson's list of club members: 'The society of the Cordeliers', appendix A, 277.

[106] This was also the period in which his pamphlet *Discours de la lanterne aux parisiens* appeared. Though it was published anonymously in 1789 Desmoulins's authorship was widely recognised.

[107] '& les autres Royaumes, qui, aborant la cocarde & demandant une Assemblée Nationale': Desmoulins, *Révolutions de France et de Brabant*, prospectus.

[108] 'j'ai voulu employer toutes mes forces à seconder les impulsions de la philosophie, et à concourir à cette expérience sublime et à la solution de ce problème: *Si le gouvernement, que j'appelle une république, c'est-à-dire, l'égalité, la fraternité des hommes et la monarchie de la loi n'étoit pas une chimère*': ibid. iii. 345.

[109] 'Un ancien sage, le philosophe Héraclite disoit: *la plus belle science, le seul art qui soit digne du nom de politique*, est l'art de GOUVERNER LE TOUT PAR LE TOUT. Cette maxime devroit être écrite, en lettres d'or, sur la porte de l'assemblée nationale, de tous les directoires de départemens et de districts, et de toutes les municipalités': ibid. vi. 125–6.

[110] On Desmoulins's allegiance to Cordeliers ideals through to 1794 see chapter 5 below.

[111] Although La Vicomterie does not appear on Robertson's list of Cordeliers Club members he was certainly close to other Cordeliers, held similar political views to them and was probably a club member himself. Mathiez certainly seems to have believed this to be the case: *Le Club des Cordeliers*, 35. Raymonde Monnier provides a discussion of La Vicomterie in her article 'Républicanisme et revolution française', 110–15.

unsuccessful, writer. He was an enthusiastic supporter of the French Revolution and wrote his own commemorative ode to the events of 1789 entitled *Liberté*.

Though it was not his first work, *Du Peuple et des rois* was La Vicomterie's first notable success. In it he argued that historians had distorted reality in presenting kings as inherently good. He urged the incompatibility of liberty and monarchy (hereditary monarchy in particular) and insisted, against much contemporary opinion, that France could become a republic, indeed a democracy. La Vicomterie followed *Du Peuple et des rois* with a number of other works – most notably *Des Crimes des rois de France depuis Clovis jusqu'à Louis seize* and *Les Droits du peuple sur l'assemblée nationale* both of which appeared in 1791.[112] In these works too La Vicomterie attacked the monarchy and argued in favour of its replacement by a republic. As he explained in the latter: 'In *Les Crimes des rois*, I attacked tyranny and hereditary despotisms. I shook their hideous altars. In this work I attack the oppressors of [the last] two years, who wish to reaffirm by their so-called laws the cause of twenty centuries of attacks.'[113]

In 1792 La Vicomterie was elected to the Convention and was among those who supported the execution of the king. It was also in that year that he published another important work, his *République sans impôt* in which he again insisted on the necessity of a French republic.[114] He later became a member of the *Comité de sûreté générale*. After 9 Thermidor he escaped the guillotine only due to the amnesty law and he died in Paris in 1809.

Pierre François Robert

Born on 21 January 1763 at Gimnée near Givet in the Ardennes, Robert had trained and practised as a lawyer prior to the Revolution.[115] In 1789 he was named commander of the national guard of Givet. It was in this role that he was sent to Paris to settle a disagreement between the new municipality and the commune of Givet. He chose to remain in the capital and became involved in events there.

Robert soon established himself as a well known and imposing figure. The

---

112 L. de La Vicomterie de Saint Samson, *Des Crimes des rois de France depuis Clovis jusqu'à Louis seize*, Paris 1791, and *Les Droits du peuple sur l'assemblée nationale*, Paris 1791.

113 'Dans *les Crimes des Rois*, j'ai attaqué la tyrannie, le despotisme héréditaire. J'ai ébranlé leurs affreux autels. J'attaque dans cet ouvrage des oppresseurs de deux années, qui veulent raffermir par de prétendues loix la cause de vingt siècles d'attentats': idem, *Les Droits du peuple*, p. xxix.

114 Idem, *République sans impôt*, Paris 1792.

115 On Robert and Keralio see L. Antheunis, *Le Conventionnel belge François Robert (1763–1826) et sa femme Louise de Keralio (1758–1882 [sic recte 1822])*, Wetteren 1955; G. Mazel, 'Louise de Kéralio et Pierre François Robert: précurseurs de l'idée républicain', *Bulletin de la Société de l'histoire de Paris et de l'Ile-de-France*, Paris 1990, 163–237; C. Hesse, *The other Enlightenment: how French women became modern*, Oxford–Princeton 2001, 81–103.

soldier Charles Dumouriez described him as a 'small man with black hair, as wide as he was high!', while Madame Roland presented him as having 'a fat face, wide, shining with health and with contentment at himself'.[116] His first political pamphlet, which appeared in 1790, set forth the argument that it was the nation as a whole, rather than any particular individual (not least the monarch), that held the right of declaring war and making peace.[117]

During 1790 Robert became a member of both the Jacobin and the Cordeliers Clubs. His connections with the latter were particularly strong. By the summer of 1791 he was living on the rue de Condé, in the heart of the former Cordeliers District and very close to where the club met. He led a number of Cordeliers campaigns and even acted as club president for a time during 1791. It was also from his base within the Cordeliers Club that Robert organised the *comité central des sociétés patriotiques*. This committee, which he established in May 1791, was aimed at uniting the various patriotic societies or popular clubs that had appeared in the early months of the Revolution.[118] Initially the *comité* met in the same room as the Cordeliers in the convent. But after just a few weeks both groups were banished from there by the authorities and so the *comité* was forced to meet elsewhere. Among the Cordeliers, Robert was said to be a particularly close friend of Desmoulins.[119] Following Danton's appointment as minister of justice in August 1792 both Desmoulins and Robert acted as his secretaries.

In 1791 Robert married Louise de Keralio who was already a prolific writer in her own right. She was the daughter of Louis Félix Guinement de Keralio – a soldier, scientist and man of letters. She had been born in Paris in 1758 and prior to the Revolution had already published several works including a history of Elizabeth I of England and a number of translations of English and Italian texts. With the outbreak of Revolution Keralio was not afraid to express her political views. She produced a pamphlet entitled 'Observations sur quelques articles du projet de constitution de M. Mounier' in which she apparently insisted that the actions of the king should be submitted to the approbation of the Assembly.[120] Robert joined his wife in editing the newspaper *Mercure national, ou journal d'état et du citoyen*. Interestingly Keralio was also the author of what was presumably a companion piece to one of La Vicomterie's works, *Les Crimes des reines de France*.[121] The connection between La Vicomterie and the Roberts was evidently close and by 1791 they

---

116 'petit homme à tête noire, aussi large qu'il a de hauteur!' 'à face de chanoine, large, brillante de santé et de contentement de soi-même': M. Roland, *Mémoires de Madame Roland*, ed. S. A. Berville and J. F. Barrière, 2nd edn, Paris 1821, ii. 174, 169.
117 F. Robert, *Le droit de faire la paix et la guerre appartient incontestablement à la nation*, Paris 1790.
118 On the popular clubs see Bourdin, *Les Sociétés populaires*.
119 Bourdin said of Robert that he 'faithfully frequented the salon' ('fréquentait assidûment le salon') of Desmoulins: ibid. 164.
120 Antheunis, *Le Conventionnel belge*, 13.
121 [L. Keralio], *Les Crimes des reines de France, depuis le commencement de la monarchie*

were good friends. Reviewing *Des Crimes des rois de France* in *Mercure national* Louise Robert declared: 'today we are connected by ties of friendship to him'.[122]

Robert's pamphlet *Républicanisme adapté à la France* is a prime example of republican propaganda designed to help its readers overcome the psychological barriers to imagining a French republic. It was divided into three parts. In the first, Robert argued that contemporary French opinion was not an obstacle to the destruction of royalty, and he used a fictional dialogue between a country priest and a parishioner to convey this idea. In the second part of the work he discussed the various ways in which monarchy, as it existed in France following the Revolution, was incompatible with liberty. In the third and final part Robert presented his own proposal for a republican system of government. Robert, like La Vicomterie, survived the Revolution, although he did not escape entirely unscathed. He was involved in the *journée* of 10 August 1792 and was subsequently elected, along with Desmoulins and La Vicomterie, to the Convention. He sat with the Montagnards, initially supporting Danton and later Robespierre. Like Desmoulins and La Vicomterie, he was particularly vocal in calling for the trial and execution of Louis Capet. However, under the Terror, Robert's actions were limited and he repeatedly faced financial problems. In later years he focused his attentions on trade rather than politics, but he was none the less exiled as a regicide in 1815. He died, in Belgium, in 1826 four years after his wife.

The republicanism of the ancients and the republicanism of the moderns

Members of the Cordeliers Club demonstrated an interest in and respect for the republican models of classical antiquity. In both official and unofficial publications by members of the club, ancient references and examples abound and the ancient republics are presented as the paradigms of republican government. As Desmoulins lamented in *La France libre*, 'For many years, I have searched everywhere for republican souls, I despair at not having been born Greek or Roman.'[123] Moreover, these writers often drew a parallel between the citizens of the Roman republic and their own compatriots in the early 1790s. Robert's *La Républicanisme adapté à la France* opened as follows: 'That your voice is the oracle of France; that France is a republic, and that finally my patrie says, in considering the annals of free Rome, *and I too may*

---

jusqu'à la mort de Marie Antoinette: avec pièces justicatives, Paris 1791. The pamphlet appeared, not under Keralio's name but under that of the publisher Prudhomme.
[122] 'aujourd'hui nous sommes liés d'amitié avec lui': L. Keralio, *Mércure national et révolutions de l'Europe: journal démocratique*, Paris 1791, iii. 135.
[123] 'Il y a peu d'années, je cherchois par-tout des ames républicaines, je me désespérois de n'être pas né Grec ou Romain': Desmoulins, *La France libre*, 50.

name Brutus as one of my children.'[124] Similarly, in the Cordeliers 'Petition à l'assemblée nationale dite des cent' we read:

> When the Romans, this first free people, saw the *patrie* to be in danger and it was a question of ruling in the interests of all, they assembled as a People. The Senators came to take in [the views of] their assemblies and the spirit of their deliberations. The Senate never pronounced alone on such important interests.

> The present citizens display a character that they draw from the Romans. [On the basis of] this character of liberty, which they defend to the death, [they] demand that the representatives of the Nation make no definitive ruling on the fate of Louis XVI until the opinion of the communes of France has been made manifest, until the voice of the mass of the People has been heard.[125]

This emphasis on ancient models served to distinguish the Cordeliers from the other main advocates of republican government at the time – the former members of the communal assembly, and in particular Brissot.

According to Brissot the ancient models were not applicable to the circumstances of late eighteenth-century France. He described his preferred form of republican government as follows: 'I understand, by republic, *a government in which all the powers are, 1. delegated or represented; 2. elective among and by the people, or its representatives; 3. temporary or removable.'*[126] None of the ancient republics, Brissot noted, had managed to combine these three requirements within a single system. Rome had had an hereditary senate, Sparta hereditary kings and Athens had been a pure democracy without any form of representation. There was, Brissot asserted, a fundamental difference between ancient and modern republics. Brissot assured the moderates that French republicans did not want the pure democracy of Athens, and that consequently their ideas did not threaten to reintroduce the problems that had arisen in the ancient world.[127] Brissot's rejection of the ancient models was shared by many of his republican friends and associates.

---

[124] 'Que ta voix soit l'oracle de la France; que la France soit une république, et qu'enfin ma patrie dise, en considérant les fastes de Rome libre, *et moi aussi, j'ai des Brutus parmi mes enfans*': Robert, *Républicanisme*, preface 'Aux Manes de Brutus'.

[125] 'Lorsque les Romains, ce premier Peuple libre, voyoient la Patrie en danger et qu'il s'agissoit de statuer sur les intérêts de tous, ils se rassembloient comme Peuple, les Sénateurs venoient prendre dans leurs assemblées l'esprit des délibérations qu'ils dictoient et jamais le Sénat ne prononçoit seul sur des intérêts aussi importans. / Les citoyens présens viennent donc, avec ce caractère qu'ils tiennent des Romains, avec ce caractère de liberté qu'ils conserveront jusqu'à la mort, demander aux représentans de la Nation, de ne rien statuer en définitif sur le sort de Louis XVI, avant que le voeu des communes de France ne se soit manifesté, avant que la voix de la masse du Peuple ne se soit fait entendre': 'Pétition à l'Assemblée Nationale dite des cent', repr. in Mathiez, *Le Club des Cordeliers*, 113.

[126] 'J'entends, par république, *un gouvernement où tous les pouvoirs sont, 1. délégués ou représentatifs; 2. électifs dans et par le peuple, ou ses représentans; 3. témporaires ou amovibles*': Brissot de Warville, *Le Patriote français*, no. 696, 19.

[127] Ibid.

For example, Jean Henri Bancal des Issarts, a pamphleteer and publicist who had worked for Brissot, also noted the differences between ancient and modern societies and on this basis rejected the use of ancient models in relation to France.[128]

In seeking to develop a form of republicanism that would be applicable to the circumstances of the modern world, Brissot and his friends were forced to address the two key obstacles described by Montesquieu and Rousseau: the large size of modern states and the need to inculcate republican virtue. They also addressed the question of how republican government could be made compatible with commercial society. Their solution to these problems, which drew on the ideas and practices of the city-state of Geneva and of the new United States of America, involved a representative form of government that would obviate the size problem; the reinforcement of republican manners among the population by various means – notably education; and an emphasis on Montesquieu's 'commerce d'économie'.[129]

In his newspaper Le Patriote français, Brissot made frequent reference to the ideas and writings of Desmoulins, La Vicomterie and Robert. In each case he expressed a certain degree of respect for their ideas, but went on to criticise many of their opinions and conclusions. In the case of La Vicomterie he declared, in a rather patronising fashion

> I do not know this author personally, but I wager, on the basis of the spirit of his ideas and the intemperance of his Patriotism, that he is young, but that he is honest and true. He heartily detests royalty and ministerial corruption, but he does not have enough respect for the work of the national assembly.[130]

Brissot also chided Robert for not being adequately aware of the many obstacles that remained to the establishment of republican government in France:

> In spite of my fondness for republicanism, I do not believe that M. Robert has completely proved that the circumstances in which we live lend themselves to the establishment of this form [of government]. – There is in France so much ignorance and corruption, too many towns and factories, too many men and

---

128 J. H. Bancal des Issarts, Secondes Réflexions sur l'institution du pouvoir exécutif: lues à la Société des amis de la constitution de Clermont-Ferrand, le 3 juillet 1791, Clermont-Ferrand 1791, 5.

129 On the political economy of the Brissotins see R. Whatmore, 'Commerce, constitutions, and the manners of a nation: Étienne Clavière's revolutionary political economy, 1788–93', History of European Ideas xxii (1996), 351–68. For more detail see Whatmore, Republicanism and the French Revolution.

130 'Je ne connois point personnellement cet auteur; mais je parierois, à la fougue de ses idées, et à l'intempérence de son patriotisme, qu'il est jeune, mais qu'il est honnête et vrai. Il déteste cordialement la royauté, la gangrène ministérielle; mais il ne respecte pas assez les travaux de l'assemblée nationale': Brissot de Warville, Le Patriote français, no. 670, 638–9. In fact Brissot's assumptions were mistaken. La Vicomterie had been born in 1732 making him 18 years older than Brissot himself.

not enough land, etc. and I hardly believe that republicanism can sustain itself in the face of these causes of degradation.[131]

Despite Brissot's accusations, the Cordeliers were not ignorant of the problems of trying to establish a republic in the modern world. However, the solutions they adopted were very different from those of the Brissotins. The Cordeliers showed little interest in the problem of making republicanism compatible with commercial society. Their emphasis was on politics rather than political economy. Moreover, when they did discuss economic matters their preference was for an agricultural, rather than a commercially driven, society.[132]

Of greater interest to the Cordeliers was the problem of the large size of modern states. Desmoulins was least concerned by this issue. In *Révolutions de France et de Brabant* he sought to down-play the obstacles to the establishment of a republic in late eighteenth-century France:

> he supports the thesis that I have upheld many times, that republican government is the form that best suits France. [This claim] is supported by the experience of all time. It proves that the size and the population of France, far from being an obstacle to this form of government, favours it and even necessitates it. [Experience] refutes all imaginary objections to which hatred of liberty, or at least habit and weakness, have given birth.[133]

Similarly, in *La France libre* he had insisted that a large republic would be more successful than a small one. Indeed, in his view the problem with republics such as Geneva and Venice was that they were too small:

> If America has need of the barriers of the ocean to defend itself, it is a proof that the small size of a state, far from being favourable to republican government, will rather be detrimental to it; since the smaller it is, the easier it is to invade. A large country, such as France, constituted as a republic, would have no need of either the barriers of the sea, or the boulevard of the Alps; liberty would be invincible there.[134]

---

131 'Malgré mon penchant pour le républicanisme, je ne crois pas que M. Robert ait complettement prouvé que toutes les circonstances où nous sommes se prêtent à l'établissement de cette forme. – Il y a en France beaucoup d'ignorance, de corruption, de villes, de manufactures, trop d'hommes et trop peu de terres, etc. et j'ai peine à croire que le républicanisme se soutienne à côté de ces causes de dégradation': ibid. no. 498, 3.

132 On the political economy of the Cordeliers see chapter 3 below.

133 'il soutient enfin la thèse que j'ai soutenue tant de fois, que le gouvernement républicain est celui qui convient le mieux à la France; c'est avec l'expérience de tous les tems, c'est en prouvant que l'étendue, que la population de la France, loin d'être un obstacle à ce gouvernement, le favorisent et même; le nécessitent, qu'il réfute toutes les objections imaginaires que la haine de la liberté, ou du moins l'habitude et la foiblesse ont fait naître': Desmoulins, *Révolutions de France et de Brabant*, v. 282.

134 'Si l'Amérique a besoin des barrieres de l'Océan pour se défendre, c'est une preuve que la petitesse d'un Etat, loin d'être favorable au gouvernement républicain, lui seroit plutôt contraire, puisque plus il est petit, plus il est facile à envahir. Un grand pays comme la

It was a combination of a free press and local assemblies, according to Desmoulins, that would guarantee the success of a republic in a state such as France. A free press would ensure that news of political issues would quickly be available to all citizens: 'But the discovery of the printing press, the liberty of the press – the marvellous immediate circulation of ideas in a vast country – has resolved the problem of large republics.'[135] Local assemblies, like those that had existed in the districts of Paris, were required as a forum in which citizens could voice their opinions and participate in decision-making.

Robert was less optimistic than Desmoulins:

> But, it is known that perfect democracy is only possible in a very small state. It would be physically impossible for the 25 million men who make up France to gather in a single place to make their will heard and to have it drawn up; one would be foolish to propose such a mode of government.[136]

While accepting that perfection could not be achieved, Robert insisted that one should not reject the idea of democracy altogether. On the question of representation, Robert referred back to Rousseau's negative opinions; but he then went on to draw a distinction between England 'where the representatives are absolute legislators as soon as they are named' and a system 'where the representatives are only representatives and cannot make laws without or against the will of those they represent'.[137] As this statement suggests, the Cordeliers rejected the form of representative government advocated by the Brissotins in favour of what they described as 'democracy'.

The democratic republicanism of the Cordeliers

As early as 1789 Desmoulins was not shy to admit: 'I loudly declare myself to be in favour of democracy.'[138] It is no coincidence that among the ancient city-states Desmoulins favoured Athens, conventionally seen as the most democratic of them all.[139] Similarly, La Vicomterie, writing in 1790, sought

France, constitué république, n'auroit besoin ni de la barriere des mers, ni du boulevard des Alpes; la liberté y seroit invincible': idem, *La France libre*, 47.

135 'Mais la découverte de l'imprimerie, la liberté de la presse, cette merveilleuse circulation de la pensée en un moment dans un vaste empire, a résolu le problème des grandes républiques': idem, *Révolutions de France et de Brabant*, i. 361.

136 'Or, on sait que la démocratie parfaite n'est possible que dans un très-petit état? Il seroit physiquement impossible que les 25 millions d'hommes qui composent la France s'assemblassent en un même lieu, se fissent entendre et rédigeassent leur volonté: il faudroit être fou, pour proposer un pareil mode de gouvernement': Robert, *Républicanisme*, 87.

137 'ou les représentans sont législateurs absolus dès qu'ils sont nommés . . . où les représentans ne fussent que représentans, et ne pussent faire des loix sans, et contre la volonté des représentés': ibid. 89.

138 'Je me déclare donc hautement pour la démocratie': Desmoulins, *La France libre*, 46.

139 Desmoulins was very unusual in this respect. See Vidal-Naquet, *Politics ancient and modern*, esp. chs iii, v.

to defend democracy against its critics: the agents of tyranny, he admitted, had declared democracy to be the worst form of government, but, he explained, 'They confound confusion or anarchy with the power of the people duly represented in the exercise of its rights.'[140]

In fact, the Cordeliers advocated a mixture of delegate and semi-direct democracy.[141] They sought various means by which the actions and decisions of the deputies or representatives could be placed under the control of the people. Binding mandates and short terms of office were two obvious possibilities. Desmoulins spoke in favour of the idea of binding mandates in his newspaper *Révolutions de France et de Brabant*: 'it must be admitted that the powers of our legislative body are only the powers of delegates, of representatives, and that the eternal rules of mandates are in this question the essence of the matter'.[142] On the question of short terms of office Robert explained that by allowing the representatives to hold power for only a short period of time their decisions would automatically be controlled through their knowledge that they themselves would have to live under the laws that they had made. But the Cordeliers also went beyond delegate democracy in suggesting that the people themselves should vote to accept or reject every law. Responding to the conventional objection of size in relation to this point, Robert argued that with the division of France into departments, districts, cantons, municipalities and sections it would be no more difficult to assemble people for the purposes of sanctioning laws then it was to assemble them to name their representatives:

> From this point of view, I say that there is nothing easier than to make all French citizens take part in the making of the law, as they take part in the nomination of their representatives, and if they once take part in making the laws, they are free, and France is happily transformed into a republic.[143]

---

[140] 'Ils confondent volontairement la confusion, l'anarchie, avec la puissance du Peuple duement représenté, avec l'exercice de ses droits': La Vicomterie, *Du Peuple et des rois*, 23.

[141] Delegate democracy refers to a system in which elected deputies act as delegates – controlled by binding mandates and permanently subject to recall by their constituents – rather than as independent representatives. The Swiss apparently adopted the term semi-direct democracy to describe a system that relied on extensive use of referendum and initiative: J. Steinberg, *Why Switzerland?*, Cambridge 1976, 56, 74–6. I have discussed these different forms of democracy at length with Ian Bullock and on this I am indebted to him. On the use of 'democracy' and the existence of 'democratic' practices across the centuries see J. Dunn (ed.), *Democracy: the unfinished journey, 508BC–AD1993*, Oxford 1992.

[142] 'il faut donc avouer que les pouvoirs de notre corps législatif ne sont que les pouvoirs de mandataires, de représentans, et que les règles, éternelles de mandats, sont dans cette question les principes de la matière': Desmoulins, *Révolutions de France et de Brabant*, vii. 109.

[143] 'Ceci posé, je dis qu'il n'y a rien de plus aisé que de faire concourir tous les citoyens français à la confection de la loi, comme ils concourent à la nomination de leurs représentans; et si une fois ils concourent à faire la loi, ils sont libres, et la France est heureusement changée en république': Robert, *Républicanisme*, 88, and see also pp. 93–4.

The popular sanctioning of laws was another point on which Brissot had attacked both Desmoulins and La Vicomterie in the pages of Le Patriote français. In a reference to Desmoulins's Les Révolutions de France et de Brabant, Brissot declared: 'and that one is surprised to find in the newspaper of M. Desmoulins, who carries the sovereignty of the people much further, since he wishes to make them ratify all the acts of the legislative power'.[144] In the conclusion to his work Les Droits du peuple sur l'assemblée nationale, La Vicomterie had listed as the first 'power' of the people 'Ratification by them of projects of law given to them, which, in case of emergency have a provisional execution.'[145] Responding to this work, in an article in Le Patriote français, Brissot questioned the efficacy of La Vicomterie's proposals:

> M. la Vicomterie has not given a clear idea of the sovereignty of the people. This ardent apostle of the people does not know that according to his system he is its most cruel enemy. Because if there is a means of having neither law, nor liberty, it is by wishing to have all the laws ratified by the six thousand primary assemblies.[146]

In his reply, which appeared in a later issue of the newspaper, La Vicomterie defended his original position against Brissot's assertion that he was confounding constitutive and legislative power:

> I ask you, sir, whether one can ratify [the constitution] without being free to change it? . . . I avow that I have not enough shrewdness to conceive how this could be done and why the projected laws that follow, which are necessary links in this constitutional chain, could not as easily be ratified by the people as the constitution itself, which you agree yourself must be done.[147]

The most detailed call for the ratification of laws by the citizens was Réné Girardin's Discours sur la nécessité de la ratification de la loi, par la volonté générale.[148] This speech was given by Girardin to the Cordeliers Club on

---

[144] 'et qu'on est surpris de retrouver dans le journal de M. Desmoulins, qui porte encore bien plus loin la souveraineté du peuple, puisqu'il veut lui faire ratifier tous les actes du pouvoir législatif': Brissot de Warville, Le Patriote français, no. 586, 285.

[145] 'Ratification par lui des projets de loix qu'on lui donne, qui, dans les cas urgens, aurant une exécution provisoire': La Vicomterie, Les Droits du people, 177.

[146] 'M. la Vicomtérie ne s'est pas fait une idée nette de la souveraineté du peuple. Cet apôtre ardent du peuple ne sait pas qu'avec son système, il en est le plus cruel ennemi. Car s'il est un moyen de n'avoir ni loi, ni liberté, c'est de vouloir faire ratifier toutes les lois par les six mille assemblées primaires': Brissot de Warville, Le Patriote français, no. 670, 639.

[147] 'Je vous demande, monsieur, si on peut la ratifier sans être libre de la changer? . . . j'avoue que je n'ai pas assez de sagacité pour concevoir comment cela peut s'opérer, et pourquoi les projets de lois qui suivront, qui sont des anneaux nécessaires de cette constitution, ne pourroient pas être aussi aisément ratifié par le peuple que la constitution même, que vous convenez d'abord qui le doit être': ibid. no. 683, 695–6. La Vicomterie was still upholding the idea of the popular ratification of laws in his République sans impôt of 1792.

[148] R. Girardin, Discours de Réné Girardin sur la nécessité de la ratification de la loi, par la volonté générale, Paris [1791]. Girardin, who was also a member of the Cordeliers Club, had

7 June 1791. Girardin was unequivocal in demanding the ratification of laws and presented it as necessary to the fulfilment of the Cordeliers's sacred document, the *Déclaration des droits*:

> in order for the law really to be the practical expression [of the general will], it is necessary that all the citizens can take part in its formation, following their inalienable right and solemnly proclaimed by article 6 of the declaration of the rights of man and of the citizen.
>
> This precious right is, both the essence, and the existence itself of sovereignty; the nation cannot therefore lose it, nor delegate it, without relinquishing its sovereignty too.
>
> The necessity of the ratification of the laws by the general will is, therefore, such a crucial point that it is precisely, gentlemen (if you will allow me to use here a word which is of great effect since it is the title of the march of liberty) that it is absolutely the *ça ira* of the declaration of the rights of man and of the citizen.[149]

He went on to draw the Rousseauean distinction between sovereignty (constitution essential) and government (constitution administrative) and urged the need to make the notion that sovereignty resides in the nation a reality. Referring explicitly to Rousseau, he criticised representative government, quoting the key passages on this issue from the *Social contract*. In the second half of his speech Girardin turned to the practical application of popular ratification. He firmly rejected the arguments of those who believed France to be too large for anything but representative government and he set out his own system which, as he explained, exploited recent advances in printing, the liberty of the press and the postal service. Two copies of all laws decreed by the National Assembly would be sent to each municipality. The citizens of the nation would be called to meet on the same day (which would be a Sunday) in their respective communes in order to ratify the laws. The president of each local assembly would make a speech on the proposed law(s), each article would then be read out and discussed separately before being put

---

an interesting background. As Réné Louis, marquis de Girardin, he had been a friend of Rousseau. It was he who offered Rousseau a retreat on his land at Ermenonville and it was also Girardin who, after his friend's death, set about producing an edition of his collected works. Girardin survived the Revolution and died in 1808.

[149] 'pour que la loi puisse en être réellement l'expression pratique, il faut que tous les citoyens puissent concourir à sa formation, suivant le droit imprescriptible, et solennellement proclamé par l'article 6 de la déclaration des droits de l'homme et du citoyen. /Ce droit précieux est, et l'essence, et l'existence même de la souveraineté; la nation ne peut donc le perdre, ni le déléguer, sans se déssaisir aussi-tôt de la souveraineté. /La nécessité de la ratification de la loi par la volonté générale est donc un point si capital, qu'il est précisément, Messieurs, (qu'il me soit permis de me servir ici d'un mot d'un grand effet puisqu'il est le mot de la marche de la liberté) qu'il est absolument *le ça ira* de la déclaration des droits de l'homme et du citoyen': ibid. 4.

to a yes/no vote. The decision taken on each article would be marked in the margin of both copies of the laws; one of which would remain in the commune while the other would be returned to the National Assembly to be counted with all the rest. All articles and laws rejected by the majority could be rewritten and sent again for ratification: 'It is thus that each citzen without altering their condition, can take part personally in the law, and that it will be ratified by *the people in person*; it is thus that the law will be known by all, that it will be truly sacred, respectable and respected by all, because it will be the work of all.'[150] Girardin also insisted that, while the process of ratification should not be complicated by amendments, the right of petition was fundamental to the success of the system, making it possible for individuals or groups to comment on the laws once in place.[151] Girardin ended by proposing that several commissioners be nominated to draw up an address to the patriotic societies and primary assemblies, inviting them to comment and express their views on the popular ratification of the laws, the right of petition and the necessity of establishing a constitution which would conform to the *Déclaration des droits*.

The club decided that Girardin's speech should be printed and sent to the patriotic societies. Moreover, they also published their own opinions on the issues raised by Girardin. They strongly supported his call for the ratification of laws by the citizens gathered in their local assemblies:

That it is an eternal truth that a law, when it has only been proposed by a national council composed of delegates of a people, is not yet a law; that is to say that it can be counted only as the object and matter of the law; that it can only become and only really becomes a finished and complete law when, by virtue and by the effect of the ratification of the people, it finds itself converted from a simple proposition of the delegates into its own clear, formal, and explicit will.[152]

The popular ratification of laws was also openly expressed in the discussions concerning the club's 'profession of faith' in their meeting of 4 August 1791:

[150] 'C'est alors que chaque citoyen sans se déplacer, pourra concourir personnellement à la loi, et qu'elle sera ratifiée par *le peuple en personne*; c'est alors que la loi sera connue de tous, qu'elle sera véritablement sacrée, respectable et respectée de tous, parce qu'elle sera l'ouvrage de tous': ibid. 23.
[151] The right of petition was a topical issue when the speech was given. On 18 May 1791 the national assembly had forbidden the submission of collective petitions. This particularly affected the Cordeliers Club, which had made much use of petitions.
[152] 'Qu'il est d'éternelle vérité qu'une loi, lorsqu'elle n'a encore été que proposée par un conseil national, composé des mandataires d'un peuple, n'est point encore une loi: c'est-à-dire qu'elle ne peut être censée que l'objet et la matiere de la loi; qu'elle ne peut devenir et ne devient réellement loi finie et complette, que lorsque, en vertu et par l'effet de la ratification du peuple, elle se trouve convertie de simple proposition de ses délégués, en sa propre volonté éclairée, formelle, et explicite': Girardin, *Discours de Réné Girardin*, 26.

Another object of [our] profession of faith concerns the right of the people to sanction the laws. . . .

The law is the expression of the general will. This will, though supposed to be expressed through the organ of the representatives of the people, must still be made manifest by the people itself.[153]

The same idea can also be seen to lie behind the Cordeliers insistence, following Louis XVI's flight to Varennes, that it was the people gathered in their local assemblies, and not the representatives gathered in the National Assembly, who should judge the king.[154]

The flight to Varennes and the massacre on the Champ de Mars

In spite of their differences, Brissotin and Cordeliers republicans were briefly brought together by the events of June and July 1791.[155] On the night of 20 to 21 June Louis XVI, together with his wife and family, fled Paris for the border, where royalist forces were allegedly waiting for them. They did not succeed in their flight. Louis and his entourage were stopped in the small town of Varennes after the town officials had informed the Parisian authorities of the new arrivals. The escapees were returned to Paris under an armed guard and Louis was provisionally suspended from the exercise of power. The king's flight gave hope to the republicans. With Louis having proved himself to be untrustworthy, they saw a possibility of convincing the rest of the French population of the advantages of republican government. With this aim in mind, Brissotins and Cordeliers united and members of both groups revived and reiterated the republican ideas that they had been voicing for some time.

As soon as news of the king's flight reached the Cordeliers Club they took action. On the evening of 21 June the club modified the formula of its civic sermon to remove the promise of fidelity to the king. The club also declared itself to be in permanent session (day and night).[156] At the same time, Robert

---

[153] 'Un autre objet de la profession de foi portoit sur le droit de sanctionner les loix par le peuple. . . . La loi est l'expression de la volonté générale. Cette volonté quoique censée exister par l'organe des représentans du peuple, doit encore se manifester particulierement par lui': Momoro, *Journal du club*, 87.

[154] See 'Pétition de la Société des amis des droits de l'homme et du citoyen aux Réprésentants de la Nation', 21 juin 1791, and 'Pétition des 30,000', 24 juin 1791. Both are reprinted in Mathiez, *Le Club des Cordeliers*, 45–7, 53–4.

[155] The grounds for this collaboration had clearly been prepared during the debates concerning popular sovereignty and the constitution in the spring of 1791. See R. Monnier, 'Paris au printemps 1791: les sociétés fraternelles et le problème de la souveraineté', *AHRF* (1992), 1–16; 'L'Invention de la république et la dynamique culturelle démocratique', *History of European Ideas* xx (1995), 243–52; and ' "Démocratie representative" ou "république démocratique": de la querelle des mots (république) à la querelle des anciens et des modernes', *AHRF* (2001), 1–21.

[156] Momoro, *Journal du club*, 2.

drew up a Cordeliers petition to the National Assembly which expressed strongly republican views and insisted that no decision should be made as to what should be done with the king until the will of the French people, gathered in their departments and primary assemblies, had been established:

> You have consacrated tyranny, in declaring the king irremovable, inviolable, and hereditary; you have consacrated the slavery of the French, in declaring France a monarchy. . . .

> Penetrated by the truth, by the grandeur of these principles, it can no longer be concealed that royalty, that hereditary royalty above all, is incompatible with liberty. . . .

> And after this [the flight of the king], we beseech you in the name of the patrie, to declare straight away that France is no longer a monarchy, that she is a republic.[157]

The petition was immediately printed by the Cercle Social publishing house. Robert was sent, together with two other Cordeliers, to take the petition to the Jacobin Club. On his way, he came across members of the National Guard arresting a number of citizens for posting up copies of the Cordeliers petition. Robert intervened and was himself arrested. He was, however, released later that day – largely due to the intervention of the Jacobin Club.[158] In spite of this he continued in his campaign. He set himself to work re-editing his earlier pamphlet *Le Républicanisme adapté à la France* to suit the new circumstances, under the timely title *Avantages de la fuite de Louis XVI.*[159] It was also in the immediate aftermath of the king's flight to Varennes that the Cordeliers Club began producing its own *Journal du Club des Cordeliers*, edited by club members Sentier and Momoro.[160] The newspaper, which was explicitly aimed at countering libellous accusations made against the club, was

---

157 'Vous aviez consacré la tyrannie, en l'instituant Roi inamovible, inviolable, et héréditaire; vous aviez consacré l'esclavage des françois, en déclarant que la France étoit une monarchie. . . . Pénétrée de la vérité, de la grandeur de ces principes, elle ne peut donc plus se dissimuler que la royauté, que la royauté héréditaire sur-tout est incompatible avec la liberté. . . . Et d'après cela, nous vous conjurons, au nom de la patrie, ou de déclarer sur-le-champ que la France n'est plus une monarchie, qu'elle est une république': repr. ibid. 3–5.
158 A. Aulard, *La Société des Jacobins: recueil de documents pour l'histoire du club des Jacobins de Paris*, Paris 1889–97, ii. 541–2. Despite their intervention many of the Jacobins did not approve of the content of Robert's petition. It was described by one Jacobin as villainous ('scélératesse') and another demanded that no deputation of Cordeliers be admitted to a Jacobin meeting until they had retracted their republican petition.
159 F. Robert, *Avantages de la fuite de Louis XVI, et nécessité d'un nouveau gouvernement: second édition du Républicanisme adapté à la France*, Paris 1791.
160 The first issue appeared on Tuesday 28 June 1791. However, it had been planned prior to the king's flight. The undated prospectus suggests that the first issue was supposed to appear on Thursday 23 June: A. F. Momoro, *Prospectus: Club des Cordeliers, Société des droits de l'homme et du citoyen*, Paris 1791, 6.

largely taken up with accounts of club meetings.[161] The focus throughout the short life of the paper (the last issue appeared in August 1791) was the king's flight to Varennes and the responses to it. However, both the prospectus, and the details of club meetings in the paper itself, also indicate the continued commitment of the club to the defence and protection of the victims of oppression and injustice.

Brissotin republicans, and others associated with the Cercle Social, proved just as active as their Cordeliers counterparts. Nicolas Bonneville immediately wrote an article for *La Bouche de fer* that included a discussion of republican government under the heading 'Point des rois' ('No more kings').[162] On 3 July Bancal des Issarts proposed to the Jacobins of Clermont-Ferrand that the French monarchy should be replaced by a republic.[163] This idea had already been set down in the meeting of the *Confédération des amis de la vérité* for 1 July, which was dominated by speeches calling for a republic based on universal suffrage. On 8 July Condorcet made a speech at the *confédération* entitled 'De la republique ou un roi est-il nécessaire à la liberté?'. He declared the French monarchy to be corrupt and called for the establishment of an elected national convention with the authority to transform France into a republic.[164] On 11 July *La Bouche de fer* included a petition on behalf of the Cercle Social that demanded the abolition of the monarchy.

Perhaps the most well known republican work of this period was the newspaper *Le Républicain*. On 1 July Achille Duchastelet, a *colonel de chasseurs*, posted up his placard around Paris which was entitled: 'Trente millions à gagner. Avis aux français'. It was designed to serve as a prospectus to the newspaper *Le Républicain: ou le défenseur du gouvernement représentatif* which Duchastelet was to edit, together with Condorcet and Thomas Paine, between 2 and 23 July.[165] Both the placard and the newspaper used the king's flight to Varennes to justify opposition to monarchical government. The history of France, the placard explained, offered undeniable evidence of the misfortunes of the French people that had resulted directly from the actions of their kings. Louis XVI's recent addition of treason to the list of offences meant that such a system of government should no longer be tolerated. Indeed it was suggested that the French would be better off without a king: '[these] are unequivocal signs, that the absence of a king is better than his presence, and that he is not only superfluous in politics, but moreover a heavy

[161] Ibid. 1.
[162] N. Bonneville, *La Bouche de fer*, Paris 1791, no. lxxi, 3–6 (23 June 1791).
[163] Bancal des Issarts, *Secondes Réflexions*.
[164] Condorcet, 'De la République ou un roi est-il nécessaire à la liberté?', repr. in *Archives parlementaires*, xxviii. 336–8.
[165] A. Duchastelet, 'Trente millions à gagner', repr. in *Actes de la commune de Paris pendant la Révolution*, ed. S. Lacroix, 2nd ser., Paris 1900–14, v. 376–7; *Le Républicain: ou le défenseur du gouvernement représentatif, par un société de républicains*, Paris 1791. On Achille Duchastelet and *Le Républicain* see E. Dumont, *Souvenirs sur Mirabeau et sur les deux premières assemblées législatives*, Paris 1832, chs xiii, xvi.

burden weighing on the whole of the nation'.[166] In this context, the aim of the newspaper was described as being to 'enlighten spirits' on republicanism and on the inutility, vices and abuses of royalty.

The unified Brissotin–Cordeliers republican campaign did not last long. Division re-emerged with the ill-fated demonstration on the Champ de Mars in early July.[167] The demonstration was prompted by the National Assembly's announcement on 15 July that Louis XVI was considered to be personally inviolable and that he had not fled the capital on 20 June – but had been kidnapped. On receiving this news a plan was made to hold a meeting on the Champ de Mars on 17 July to sign a petition asking the National Assembly to revoke their decision. A joint Brissotin–Cordeliers petition, drawn up by a committee led by Brissot, was approved by the Jacobins on the morning of 16 July and then carried to the Champ de Mars. However, members of the Cordeliers Club expressed their unhappiness with the petition. As it was being read out Cordeliers are alleged to have called out 'No more monarchy! No more tyrants!'[168] They objected to the sentence which stated that Louis XVI would be replaced 'by constitutional means'. According to them, this would simply result in the replacement of one 'tyrant' by another. What was required instead was constitutional change. The Cordeliers alternative, which was entitled 'Pétition à l'assemblée national rédigée sur l'autel de la patrie le 17 juillet 1791' and was drafted by Robert, was much more radical and proposed the repudiation of the Constitution of 1791.[169] It was rejected by the Brissotins and by the Jacobin Club.

On 17 July a crowd of unarmed Parisians gathered peacefully on the Champ de Mars to sign the petition. Following some minor disturbances, the national guard arrived, surrounded the crowd, and opened fire. As many as fifty people may have been killed. In the words of the *Journal du Club des Cordeliers*: 'Betrayed shamefully by their brothers in the national guard, the citizens are ruthlessly massacred.'[170]

Following the massacre the gap between the Brissotins and Cordeliers grew even wider. The Brissotins took note of the restrained popular response to the events of June and July 1791 and to Cordelier calls for a republic. The *confédération* did not reopen its doors. Instead the Brissotins allied themselves

---

166 'sont des signes non équivoques, que l'absence d'un roi vaut mieux que sa présence, et qu'il n'est pas seulement une superfluité politique, mais encore un fardeau très-lourd qui pèse sur toute la nation': Duchastelet, *Le Républicain*, 3.
167 On the Champ de Mars massacre see D. Andress, *Massacre at the Champ de Mars: popular dissent and political culture in the French Revolution*, Woodbridge 2000.
168 'Plus de monarchie! Plus de tyran!': Robertson, 'The society of the Cordeliers', 46.
169 'Petition à l'assemblée nationale', repr. in Mathiez, *Le Club des Cordeliers*, 135–6. The constitution of 1791, which was still being drawn up, was eventually ratified by the king on 13 September. It established a constitutional monarchy.
170 'Trahis indignement par leurs freres de la garde nationale, les citoyens sont impitoyablement massacrés': Momoro, *Journal du club*, 70. For details of the prosecutions against Cordeliers Club members see Mathiez, *Le Club des Cordeliers*.

with the Jacobins and retreated into the modest position of concentrating on educating the people on the subject of republicanism before trying to bring it about. Clavière is said to have commented 'that *Le Républicain* was abandoned, and that the idea of a republic no longer existed; that in the aftermath monarchy was entirely favoured, that the Assembly itself appeared to work for the counter-revolution, and that the merest suspicion of republicanism was an odious mark'.[171] By contrast the Cordeliers, unwilling to pass up the opportunity, continued to oppose the Constitution of 1791 and to push for an immediate end to monarchy in France. After a short suspension 'to let our tears fall on the precious ashes of the new martyrs to liberty' ordinary meetings resumed on 25 July.[172] Moreover, the Cordeliers were keen to make public their continued existence. An extract from the register of the club for 28 July read: 'Following the reading of the minutes of the previous meeting, the society sent a deputation to the municipality, to inform it that the society is continuing to hold its meetings at the musée, rue Dauphine.'[173] And in the account of the meeting of 31 July it was stated that 'The society has decided to insert in the patriotic journals a note aimed at making known to all citizens that the society has never been dissolved and that it continues to hold its meetings at the musée rue dauphine.'[174]

Not only did republicanism exist in France prior to the king's flight to Varennes in June 1791, but there co-existed two distinct republicanisms – that of Brissot and the Brissotins and that of the members of the Cordeliers Club. In the Brissotin case an emphasis on the need to create a successful republican system that could function in the large, commercial societies of the modern world resulted in their advocating a representative system of government and in their deep concern for the morality of the populace – and particularly of those chosen to act as representatives. The Cordeliers, by contrast, rejected representative government and instead advocated a mixture of delegate and semi-direct democracy. They proved far less concerned about either the need to make republicanism compatible with commercial society or the importance of morality.

To support their form of modern republicanism, the Brissotins drew on the

---

[171] 'que le *Républicain* était abandonné, et que l'idée de la république n'existait plus; que le reflux actuel était tout entier en faveur de la monarchie; que l'assemblée même semblait travailler à la contre-révolution, et que le seul soupçon de républicanisme était une tache odieuse': quoted in Dumont, *Souvenirs sur Mirabeau*, 333–4.

[172] 'pour arroser de ses larmes les cendres précieuses des nouveaux martyrs de la liberté': Momoro, *Journal du club*, 75.

[173] 'A la suite de la lecture du procès-verbal de la séance précédente, la société a députe à la municipalité, pour la prévenir qu'elle continuoit ses séances au musée, rue Dauphine': ibid. 76.

[174] 'La société a arrêté de faire insérer dans les journaux patriotiques un avis tendant a faire connoitre aux citoyens que la société n'avoit jamais été dissoute et qu'elle continuoit ses séances au musée rue dauphine': ibid. 78.

recent experiences of the city-state republic of Geneva and the new republic of the United States of America. The experiences of these demonstrated the possibility of a modern republic and the means by which such a system could be achieved. In holding various positions of power at both a local and national level the Brissotins were at a distinct advantage in relation to the Cordeliers. Members of the Cordeliers Club rarely attained office beyond the radical political clubs of the capital. They therefore needed to find a model that would convince the French public that – contrary to what the Brissotins claimed – a form of classical democratic republicanism was applicable to the large nations of the modern world, and that modern republicanism, with its need for representation and its unrealistic emphasis on morality, was not the only option.

Some prominent members of the Cordeliers Club did succeed in finding the required model and propounded it from 1790 onwards. It was provided by seventeenth-century English republican writers, who just over a century earlier had themselves been engaged in attempts to establish a form of classical republicanism in another large European nation.

2

Théophile Mandar, Marchamont Nedham and The Excellencie of a Free State

From this day [14 July 1789], my friend, I devoted myself more than ever to the reading of works that have contributed towards enlightening men on their interests. The first to which I gave my attention was that of Needham.[1]

Théophile Mandar, a future member of the Cordeliers Club, wrote these words to his friend Guillaume Tibbatts on 2 September 1790. Mandar had been so struck by the importance of the republican ideas of the seventeenth-century English journalist Marchamont Nedham, and by their relevance to revolutionary France, that he had decided to produce a French translation of Nedham's *The excellencie of a free state*. To render himself more familiar with the English language, in preparation for this task, he had produced French translations of several works of English travel literature, including *Voyage en Suisse* by William Coxe (1790) and *Voyages dans les montagnes de l'Ecosse et dans les isles Hébrides*, by John Knox.[2] Mandar's translation of *The excellencie of a free state*, enriched with notes drawn from a variety of French and English writers, was published in 1790 under the title *De la Souveraineté du peuple, et de l'excellence d'un etat libre*.

Marchamont Nedham and *The excellencie of a free state*

Nedham's *The excellencie of a free state* had already had a controversial life in England.[3] Born in 1620, Nedham had received a classical education typical of

---

[1] 'Depuis ce jour, mon ami, je me suis livré, plus que jamais, à la lecture des ouvrages qui ont contribué à éclairer les hommes sur les intérêts. Le premier auquel je donnai mes veilles, fut celui de Needham': Théophile Mandar to Guillaume Tibbatts, 2 Sept. 1790, repr. in T. Mandar, *De la Souveraineté du people, et de l'excellence d'un état libre, par Marchamont Needham, traduit de l'anglais, et enrichi de notes de J. J. Rousseau, Mably, Bossuet, Condillac, Montesquieu, Letrosne, Raynal, etc. etc. etc.*, Paris 1790, ii. 228. Mandar consistently spells Marchamont Nedham's surname as Needham. I will use the commonly accepted spelling Nedham when referring to him myself, but I will retain Mandar's spelling in all quotations.

[2] Ibid.

[3] See Worden, 'Marchamont Nedham', and ' "Wit in a Roundhead": the dilemma of Marchamont Nedham', in S. Dwyer Amussen and M. A. Kishlansky (eds), *Political culture and cultural politics in early modern England*, Manchester 1995, 301–37.

the time. In 1634 he went up to All Souls College, Oxford, where he gained his degree three years later. He worked at Merchant Taylor's School in London, and as a clerk at Gray's Inn, before taking up a career as a writer.[4] Employed as a journalist throughout the period of the English Civil War, Nedham changed his attitude – and his allegiance – as the circumstances dictated. During the 1640s he produced works on behalf of both the Long Parliament and King Charles I; and he successively welcomed, and celebrated, the downfall of, each of the regimes established during the turbulent period of the 1650s (the Rump Parliament, the 'Barebone's Parliament' and the Cromwellian Protectorate). In 1660 he hailed the Restoration and the triumphant return of Charles II.[5]

It was in June 1650, under the Rump Parliament, that Nedham began to produce the weekly newspaper *Mercurius politicus*. The prospectus for the paper claimed that it would be written 'in defence of the commonwealth, and for the Information of the People'.[6] In October 1651 Nedham began a series of editorials in the newspaper in which he turned to history in an attempt to demonstrate, by means of evidence as well as reason, the advantages of a free state. It was five years later, in 1656, that the printer Thomas Brewster (who was also responsible for publishing works by James Harrington) published an anonymous pamphlet entitled *The excellencie of a free state*. This work constituted a republication of most of the editorials of *Mercurius politicus* that had been produced between 1651 and 1652. There is no reference in *The excellencie of a free state* to the earlier version of the work. Rather, the preface simply suggests that it was a reply to a section from *Some sober inspections* by the royalist James Howell.[7] The original target of Nedham's editorials had been the Rump Parliament of 1651–2. Republishing the work as a monograph in 1656, his target shifted to the Cromwellian Protectorate. The content, however, remained much the same.

Unlike the writings of other seventeenth-century English republicans, Nedham's *The excellencie of a free state* was not republished at the turn of the century. Owing in part to this neglect, the work did not receive the attention of the francophone Huguenots in the early eighteenth century that other English republican works enjoyed. However, a new edition of Nedham's work, edited by Richard Baron, appeared in 1767 (and was reprinted in 1774). Thomas Hollis, a republican who spent much of his fortune publishing and distributing seventeenth-century English republican treatises in Europe and America, and American writings in England, sent a copy of the 1767

---

4 Idem, ' "Wit in a Roundhead" ', 305.
5 Idem, 'Marchamont Nedham', 60.
6 This is quoted in J. Frank, *Cromwell's press agent: a critical biography of Marchamont Nedham, 1620–1678*, n.p. 1980, 88.
7 M. Nedham, *The excellencie of a free state*, London 1767, pp. v–vii.

version of Nedham's text to America where it was widely read.[8] The work was translated into French in 1774 by the chevalier d'Eon de Beaumont.[9]

The chevalier d'Eon de Beaumont and *De l'Excellence d'un état libre*

Charles Geneviève Louis Auguste André Timothée d'Eon de Beaumont (1728–1810) was a complex and colourful character.[10] He was a well-known diplomat, a military hero and a prolific writer. His translation of Nedham's text appeared in the sixth volume of *Les Loisirs*, an ambitious thirteen-volume work, which was published in 1774 when he was living as an exile in England.[11] D'Eon had originally been sent to London in 1762 as secretary to the duc de Nivernois, who led the delegation charged with drawing up a peace treaty with the British. Perhaps owing to his role as a spy, as part of Louis XV's 'secret du roi', d'Eon chose to remain in England after the treaty had been concluded – despite being officially recalled to France in October 1763.[12] His refusal to return, together with his publication in March 1764 of *Lettres, mémoires, et négociations particulières* – which included private correspondence concerning the negotiations surrounding the Treaty of Paris, resulted in him being declared an outlaw and stripped of his official diplomatic functions (although he appears to have continued to operate as a spy). D'Eon used his free time to produce his *Les Loisirs*:

> As the title suggests, it is a collection of materials on all sorts of aspects of public administration that I hurriedly gathered together in the course of my travels and my political activities; [and] that I have sought to turn into a published work, with as much care as I could, during my, often troubled, spare time in England.[13]

---

8 On Hollis see Robbins, 'The strenuous Whig', and P. D. Marshall, 'Thomas Hollis (1720–74): the bibliophile as libertarian', *Bulletin of the John Rylands University Library of Manchester* lxvi (1984), 246–63.

9 Interestingly, d'Eon's French translation was probably also sent to America by Hollis. Caroline Robbins listed the chevalier d'Eon de Beaumont as one of the writers whose works 'stand on the Harvard shelves as gifts of Hollis': 'Library of liberty – assembled for Harvard College by Thomas Hollis of Lincoln's Inn', in Taft, *Absolute liberty*, 219n.

10 For a recent account of some of the more colourful aspects of his life see G. Kates, *Monsieur d'Eon is a woman: a tale of political intrigue and sexual masquerade*, New York 1995, and 'The transgendered world of the chevalier/chevalière d'Eon', *JMH* lxvii (1995), 558–94.

11 D'Eon de Beaumont, *Les Loisirs*, vi. 137–399.

12 Kates, *Monsieur d'Eon is a woman*, 91–2.

13 'Le titre annonce suffisament que c'est une union de matériaux sur toutes sortes d'objets concernant l'administration publique, rassemblés à la hâte pendant le cours de mes voyages & de mes occupations politiques, que j'ai tâché de mettre en oeuvre avec le plus de soin que j'ai pu pendant mes loisirs souvent fort agités en Angleterre': D'Eon de Beaumont, *Les Loisirs*, i. 12.

During his stay in England d'Eon became interested in the Wilkes Affair (which was paralleled, by contemporaries, with his own misfortunes).[14] He came to know both John Wilkes and also the historian Catharine Macaulay, who sent him a copy of her *History* in 1768.[15] It was perhaps through Macaulay that d'Eon came across Richard Baron's 1767 edition of Nedham's text.

There has been some speculation as to why d'Eon decided to translate Nedham's work. In her article comparing d'Eon with Wilkes, Anna Clark suggests that d'Eon may have identified with Nedham: 'Nedham switched sides in the English civil war several times, much as d'Eon himself spied for the French while defending English liberties.'[16] In fact, Clark's subsequent suggestion, that Nedham's ideas were not all that different from d'Eon's own, seems a more likely explanation. D'Eon appears to have been attracted to the notion of a free state in which the liberties of individuals would be protected and in which politics would be directed towards the public good.[17] He did not even shy away from the kind of anti-monarchical republican ideas that were expressed in Nedham's work:

> Lies, calumny, and iniquity appear . . . to constitute the essence of a monarchi-cal ministry and even more so that of a despotic ministry. In a republic, although human nature is the same, if the ministry appears more virtuous it is because of the necessity of obeying the laws that constrain it; and its enlight-ened conduct makes it fear the censure of patriots, of its rivals or of its ene-mies.[18]

In his 'Avis du traducteur' (translator's note) to Nedham's text d'Eon referred to the importance of liberty in England and the various English writings on how to secure the liberty of the people. He believed the lessons of such works to be relevant not just to the English, but much more widely:

> It is this general advantage that made me decide to translate one of the boldest works on this subject that has been produced in England. . . . [Nedham] dis-cusses with depth and solidity an important question. This is sufficient to com-pensate my work.[19]

---

14 On the comparisons between d'Eon and Wilkes see A. Clark, 'The chevalier d'Eon and Wilkes: masculinity and politics in the eighteenth century', *Eighteenth-Century Studies* xxxii (1998), 19–48.

15 Kates, *Monsieur d'Eon is a woman*, 197.

16 Clark, 'The chevalier d'Eon and Wilkes', 35.

17 See d'Eon's 'Discours préliminaire', to *Les Loisirs*, i. 7–36.

18 'La mensonge, la calomnie et l'iniquité semblent, . . . constituer l'essence d'un ministre monarchique & bien plus encore celle d'un ministre despotique. Dans une république, quoique la nature humaine soit la même, si le ministre paroît plus vertueux, c'est que la nécessité d'obéir aux loix l'y contraint, & que sa conduite toujours éclairée, lui fait redouter la censure des patriots, de ses rivaux ou de ses enemis': ibid. i. 20–1.

19 'C'est cet avantage général qui m'a déterminé à donner la traduction d'un des ouvrages

Yet even in England, d'Eon claimed, Nedham's work had not received the attention it deserved. He hoped to raise awareness of it in France by translating and publishing it.

Mandar presumably did not know about d'Eon's translation. Moreover, it was his view that Nedham's work was still neglected in France in 1790; and, in the context of the early months of the Revolution, he came to believe that this neglect should not be allowed to continue. It was for this reason that he too decided to translate Nedham's work himself.

Théophile Mandar

Michel-Philippe, commonly known as Théophile, Mandar was born in Marines, a village north west of Paris close to Pontoise, on 19 September 1759.[20] He survived the Revolution and died in Paris on 2 May 1823. During his life he travelled extensively in America, Spain and England. Like Camille Desmoulins, Mandar was said to have been one of the orators who encouraged the people to resist in early July 1789.[21] Indeed, on the 13th of that month he was allegedly instrumental in making it possible for the crowd to seize arms from the Hôtel des Invalides. His involvement in the Revolution continued – Albert Mathiez described him as having 'joua un certain role' [played an important role].[22] He is recorded as a citizen of the section du Temple in Paris,[23] and was described at the time as a soldier, a publicist and a municipal politician. Most significantly, during the early 1790s Mandar was a key member of the Cordeliers Club.

As a soldier, Mandar was among those camped on the Champ de Mars during July 1789; although, as he explained in his letter to Guillaume Tibbats, he was not actually at the Bastille on the 14th.[24] Mandar's role as a publicist began with his French translations of English travel literature and of Nedham's *The excellencie of a free state*. Yet, these works were by no means his last. Over the course of the next thirty years Mandar produced an eclectic range of works. These included his *Des Insurrections: ouvrage philosophique et*

les plus hardis que l'Angleterre ait produits sur ce sujet . . . il discute avec profendeur & solidité une question importante, c'est assez pour compenser mon travail': ibid. vi. 138.

20 The name Théophile is of Greek origin meaning 'divinely loved'. In 1796 a group calling themselves *Théophilantropes* and advocating *Théophilanthropie* was established. Their ideas were deistic in nature. Mandar appears to have been involved with this group: A. Mathiez, *La Théophilanthropie et le culte décadaire (1796–1802): essai sur l'histoire religieuse de la Révolution*, Paris 1904.

21 *Biographie universelle ancienne et moderne*, ed. J. F. Michaud, Paris 1843–65, xxiv. 320.

22 Mathiez, *La Théophilanthropie*, 85n.

23 In September of 1792 he held the position of vice-president of the section du Temple. In 1793 he gave his address as 'ma thébaïde [solitary retreat], *rue de Malthe, marais du Temple*'.

24 Mandar, *De la Souveraineté*, ii. 201–31.

politique sur les rapports des insurrections avec la prospérité des empires, funeral orations to French generals and various sacred works.

Much of Mandar's political activity during the early 1790s was conducted from his standpoint as a member of the Cordeliers Club. He appears to have belonged to the club almost from the time of its inception and he acted as club secretary during 1791.[25] In this role he signed a number of important Cordeliers documents. These included the petition against the *marc d'argent* – the silver mark worth fifty-two livres that was proposed in 1789 as the level of taxation required of all deputies. The petition was drawn up by Nicolas Bonneville, on behalf of the fraternal societies and the Cordeliers Club, and was delivered to the National Assembly by Mandar on 14 June 1791.[26] Most significant was Mandar's keen involvement in the protests that followed the king's flight to Varennes. Not only was Mandar a signatory to the 'Pétition des 30,000' of 26 June, which insisted that the representatives of the nation should take no decision on what was to be done with Louis XVI without consulting the eighty-three departments, but he actually led the deputation of commissioners who presented it to the National Assembly.[27] On discovering that the petition had not been read to the Assembly Mandar appealed to the president, Alexandre de Beauharnais, asking that the petition be given a proper hearing.[28] Beauharnais responded in reassuring tones but Mandar remained dissatisfied. His signature appears again on a Cordeliers petition dated 9 July, which referred back to the neglect of earlier demands, and again insisted that it was the nation that should judge Louis XVI and his violation of the constitution that he was supposed to defend.[29] In addition, it may have been as a result of his position within the Cordeliers Club that Mandar became involved in the insurrections of 20 June and 10 August 1792, which resulted in the fall of the French monarchy and paved the way for the declaration of the first French republic on 25 September of that year. Following the *journée* of 10 August, Mandar acted as secretary to the *jury spécial d'accusation du tribunal*, which met for the first time on 17 August to hear and discuss the cases of those accused of committing crimes against 'la sûreté, la liberté, et le bonheur de la nation française' during it.[30] Whatever his involvement in the summer of 1792, Mandar's *De la Souveraineté* reveals that he was a strong advocate of republican government more than a year earlier and prior to the king's flight to Varennes.

---

[25] Mathiez, *Le Club des Cordeliers*, 11n.
[26] Ibid. 53n.
[27] Momoro, *Journal du club*, 7–8, repr. in Mathiez, *Le Club des Cordeliers*, 52–4.
[28] *Actes de la commune*, 2nd ser., v. 37.
[29] Mathiez, *Le Club des Cordeliers*, 86–7.
[30] 'The safety, the liberty, and the happiness of the French nation': 'Ordre du jury spécial d'accusation du tribunal du 17 août', AN, C158, no. 332 (46); C192, no. 160 (19).

De la Souveraineté du peuple, et de l'excellence d'un état libre

The main body of Mandar's *De la Souveraineté* is dominated by his French translation of *The excellencie of a free state*. As in Nedham's original, the work begins with an introduction and is then divided into four parts. In the first, the reader is presented with fourteen arguments in favour of a free state. The second is designed to refute the objections to the establishment of such a state. Part three asserts the idea that the people are the source of all legitimate power, and the fourth and final part describes errors of policy, in an attempt to 'strip tyranny of its charms'.[31]

Mandar saw his task as being not simply to translate Nedham's work but to present it, in as accessible a way as possible, to his eighteenth-century French audience. At several points towards the end of his preface, Mandar explicitly urged the French people to secure and protect their liberty. He reminded them of their role as a model for other European nations, and he emphasised to them the relevance of Nedham's work to their own situation. The climax of these calls came with Mandar's explanation that he was dedicating his translation of Nedham's work to the French revolutionaries:

> WISE LEGISLATORS, and you FRENCH MEN, BROTHERS IN ARMS, oh my fellow citizens! it is to you that I dedicate this work.
>
> You [will] find collected together in it, all the rights of a people to liberty, independence, and prosperity. These rights are inseparable from its greatness; they are inherent in all that ensures the duration of empires. These rights are as inviolable as your promises and as eternal as your glory. Because of you, FRENCH MEN, the century in which we live will be, for future races, the era of liberty and of laws; as it is of enlightenment, philosophy, and the triumph of man over tyranny and despotism.[32]

Mandar was clearly aware of the problems that his readers might face in coming to an understanding of Nedham's text, and he therefore adopted various measures aimed at making that task easier. One of these was his addition of prefatory material, quotations and even other works of his own to the text, with the aim of enhancing and enriching it. In the forty-three-page preface which opens the work Mandar provided his readers with his views on the background, structure and key points of Nedham's text, as well as offering

---

[31] Mandar, *De la Souveraineté*, ii. 28.

[32] 'SAGES LÉGISLATEURS, et vous FRANÇAIS, FRERES D'ARMES, ô mes concitoyens! c'est à vous que je dédie cet ouvrage./Vous y trouverez rassemblés tous les droits d'un peuple à la liberté, à l'indépendance, et à la prospérité. Ces droits sont inséparables de sa grandeur; ils sont inhérens à tout ce qui peut assurer la durée des empires. Ces droits sont, comme vos promesses, inviolables; éternels comme votre gloire. Et par vous, FRANÇAIS, le siècle où nous vivons sera, pour les races futures, l'ère de la liberté et des loix, comme il l'est des lumières, de la philosophie, et du triomphe de l'homme sur la tyrannie et sur le despotisme': ibid. i, pp. xlii–xliii.

some explanation for his decision to translate it. Mandar set Nedham's ideas in their seventeenth-century context, both by providing his audience with some sense of the politics of mid seventeenth-century England and by associating Nedham's ideas with those of others of the time. In the course of the preface he likened Nedham's thought to that of both Milton (p. x) and Sidney (p. xxvii), suggesting an awareness of the notion of a tradition of seventeenth-century English republican thought. In addition he attempted to draw connections between Nedham's ideas and those of writers who would have been more familiar to his audience. He did so by linking the seventeenth-century English republicans with eighteenth-century British thinkers, including Earl Stanhope and Richard Price, to whom he addressed various comments towards the end of the preface; and, more especially, with French thinkers: 'In modern times, Milton, Algernon Sidney, Marchamont Nedham, and more recently, the divine Fénélon, Hume, Mercier, Raynal, Mably, Mirabeau, Peyssonel, Letrosne! . . . Such are, o people! the men who have sacrificed themselves for the cause of liberty, and who have thwarted all the tricks of tyranny.'[33]

Quotations drawn from a variety of anglo- and francophone thinkers of the seventeenth and eighteenth centuries pepper both Mandar's preface and the text itself. He justified his addition of these quotations as follows:

I have gathered together notes on the most celebrated authors, such as Montesquieu, J. J. Rousseau, Bossuet, Letrosne, l'abbé de Mably, M. de Peyssonel, etc. etc., whose writings are as a monument, repeating to our descendants that which we have done, the point from which we set out, the march of enlightenment – its dramatic rise and its effects.

These notes come to the support of my author – they prove what he has only indicated, and they affirm his reports. If I have recourse too often to the evidence of these writers, I will be pardoned without doubt on the basis of the sublime nature of their expressions, the justice of their thoughts, and the perspicacity of their judgement.[34]

---

[33] 'Dans les siècles modernes, Milton, Algernon Sydney, Marchamont Needham, et plus récemment, le divin Fènelon, Hume, Mercier, Raynal, Mably, Mirabeau, Peyssonel, Letrosne! . . . Tels sont, ô Peuple! les hommes que se sont sacrifiés pour la cause de la liberté, et qui ont déjoué toutes les ruses de la tyrannie': ibid. i, pp. xxviii–xxix. Mandar sometimes spells Algernon Sidney's surname Sydney. I will use the commonly accepted spelling Sidney when referring to him myself, but I will retain Mandar's spelling in all quotations.
[34] 'J'ai recueilli des notes dans les auteurs les plus célèbres, tels que Montesquieu, J. J. Rousseau, Bossuet, Letrosne, l'abbé de Mably, M. de Peyssonel, etc. etc., dont les écrits, comme autant de monumens, rediront à nos neveux ce que nous fûmes, le point d'où nous sommes partis, la marche des lumières, leur explosion et leurs effets. / Ces notes viennent à l'appui de mon auteur; elles prouvent ce qu'il n'a fait qu'indiquer, elles affirment ce qu'il rapporte; et s'il m'arrive d'avoir trop souvent recours au témoignage de nos auteurs, on me le pardonnera sans doute en faveur de la sublimité de leurs expressions, de la justesse de leurs pensées, et de la perspicacité de leur jugement': ibid. i, pp. xv–xvi.

At the end of his preface Mandar explained that, in addition to incorporating quotations within the text, he had also added an appendix to each volume of his translation containing one or two chapters from works by other writers that he believed to be illuminating in relation to Nedham's text. The appendix to the first volume consisted of two chapters taken from *The prince* by Niccolo Machiavelli, which were used to support Mandar's point on the extent to which the politics of princes differs from that of a free people as described by Nedham. The appendix to the second volume contained a chapter from Jean Jacques Rousseau's *Social contract*, intended to demonstrate the similarities between the ideas of Nedham and those found in Rousseau's work.

Furthermore, the editor of Mandar's translation also made his own additions to the work. On page 200 of the second volume he explained his inclusion of the letter written by Mandar in September 1790 to his friend Guillaume Tibbatts:

> The letter that follows, by M. Théophile Mandar, appears to us to contain details and thoughts relevant to the maintenance of zeal and love of liberty in the hearts of citizens. At the same time this letter contains a faithful account of the truly patriotic actions of M. Mandar towards the general who commanded the camp on the Champ de Mars, on the 14 July 1789. His departure for England (where he is now) has provided us with the liberty to insert it at the end of this second volume.[35]

The editor also included *Observations sur le commerce et l'esclavage des nègres* which Mandar had written in December 1788, supposedly in response to some questions by B. S. Frossard which had appeared in the *Journal de Paris*.[36] Mandar's purpose in the work was to point out that slavery and the slave trade are incompatible with the practices of a free state and should therefore be shunned by the French.

Mandar's interest in Nedham's work appears to have been derived from what he believed to be its central theme: liberty. In his preface Mandar praised Nedham as a man who had proclaimed 'the inalienable right of man to liberty'.[37] Moreover, Mandar believed Nedham's ideas to be capable of practical application: 'few men have, before him (if we except Milton), united more happily the love of liberty with the desire to render it common to

---

[35] 'La lettre suivante, de M. Théophile Mandar, nous ayant paru contenir des détails et des réflexions propres à entretenir dans le coeur des citoyens le zèle et l'amour de la liberté, en même tems que cette lettre contient le récit fidèle de la démarche véritablement patriotique de M. Mandar auprès du général qui commandoit le camp du champ de Mars, le 14 juillet 1789, nous avons profité de la liberté qu'il nous a laissée en partant pour l'Angleterre (où il est maintenant), de l'insérer à la fin de ce second volume': ibid. ii. 200.
[36] Ibid. ii. 277. As is explained in the text, B. S. Frossard was the author of *La Cause des noirs, portée au tribunal de l'humanité, et de la justice, et de la religion*.
[37] 'le droit inaliénable de l'homme à la liberté': Mandar, *De la Souveraineté*, i, p. xxiii.

their fellow creatures'.[38] Similarly, in his letter to Guillaume Tibbatts, Mandar explained that Nedham was regarded by the English as 'one of the most daring geniuses who has written on the liberty of the people'.[39] Mandar himself evidently rated the importance of liberty very highly, and he was keen to stress its importance to the French: 'CITIZENS! without liberty, there is for you no asylum where you can say with truth: here I am protected from the attacks of the authorities. Without liberty all your pleasures will be precarious.'[40]

For Mandar, the events of July 1789 had marked 'the rising of the sun of liberty' in France.[41] What was important a year later was that that liberty should not be lost. This required vigilance on the part of the French people: 'People! never forget that kings are passionate and skilful at profiting from the first moments of drowsiness and indolence to which you might succumb, [in order] to enslave you.'[42] The dangers of not watching over liberty were evident from the English example. In his preface Mandar described the mid-seventeenth century as a time when the English had seized, and become better acquainted with, their rights, when they had examined the authority of kings and, on this basis, had advanced from tyranny, via anarchy, to liberty: 'One saw little by little, and as minds calmed themselves, men enlightened by the fire of civil dissension; [and yet] still ill at ease about the storms which precede the return of liberty for a people debased over the centuries and who have languished under a raging despotism.'[43] Yet, despite believing that the English had become free in the 1640s, Mandar was under no illusions as to the position of eighteenth-century England:

(If we consider now what is the liberty of our neighbours, the English; will we not be forced to cry out in seeing that the people the most proud and the most active, the most clear as to their interests, and altogether the most rich, remain bent under the triple yoke of a government, which no longer has vigour?)

(The advantages of the British constitution are balanced by much abuse!)[44]

---

38 'peu d'hommes ont, avant lui (si nous en exceptons Milton), réuni plus heureusement l'amour de la liberté, au désir de la rendre commune à leurs semblables': ibid. i, p. x.

39 'un des génies les plus hardis qui aient écrit sur la liberté des peuples': ibid. ii. 228.

40 'CITOYENS! sans la liberté, il n'est pour vous aucun asyle où vous puissiez dire avec vérité: Ici je suis à couvert des attentats de l'autorité. Sans la liberté, toutes vos jouissances seroient précaires': ibid. ii. 208.

41 Ibid. ii, p. xxxv.

42 'Peuples! n'oubliez jamais que les rois sont ardens et habiles à profiter des premiers momens de sommeil et d'indolence auxquels vous pourrez vous livrer, pour vous asservir': ibid. ii. 202–3.

43 'On vit peu à peu, et à mésure que les esprits se calmèrent, les hommes éclairés par le feu des dissentions civiles, encore mal rassurés contre les orages qui précèdent le retour de la liberté chez un peuple avili pendant des siècles, et qui a langui sous un despotisme dévorant': ibid. i, p. iii.

44 '(Si nous considérons maintenant quelle est la liberté de nos voisins, les Anglais; ne

Neither Mandar's own favouring of liberty, nor his perception of *The excellencie of a free state* as a book which was ultimately about liberty, are particularly striking or unusual. It is well known that liberty was the clarion call of the French Revolution. Revolutionaries of all shades articulated their aims in the language of liberty and adopted the concept as their own. Nor was Mandar the first French revolutionary to associate the concept of liberty with the English. The early months of the Revolution had witnessed the rise of a group of anglophiles known as the *monarchiens*.[45] This group, which included Jean Joseph Mounier (1758–1806), Trophime Gérard, de Lally Tollendal (1751–1830), Pierre Victor Malouet (1740–1814) and Nicolas Bergasse (1750–1832), emphasised the need to establish a French constitution. Aware of the English system through their reading of the works of eighteenth-century writers (not least Montesquieu's *Spirit of the laws* and J. L. Delolme's *Constitution de l'Angleterre*) and parliamentary debates, as well as through correspondence with English friends, they advocated the construction of a similar model in France. In particular, they called for the introduction of a bicameral legislative system and sought to protect the powers of the king through the imposition of an absolute royal veto. Mounier, Lally Tollendal and Bergasse were all appointed in the summer of 1789 to the *comité de constitution* where they advocated their English bicameral model against the unicameral system favoured by the *abbé* Sieyès and others. The decisions of the National Assembly in early September against the bicameral system and in favour of a suspensive veto were a blow to the *monarchiens* and their influence declined from this point. While Mandar and the *monarchiens* both celebrated the ideal of liberty, and while both associated that concept with England and the English, their ideas were very different. What was distinctive about Mandar's view was the particular definition of liberty that he adopted, and his ideas about what this entailed and how it could best be secured.

Mandar's definition of liberty was typical of that of the Cordeliers more generally. Liberty was one of the key rights of man that they celebrated and sought to defend. As was typical of the time, they contrasted liberty with tyranny and despotism. In his account of *The excellencie of a free state* Mandar described Nedham as having 'torn away the veil which covered the mysteries

---

serons-nous pas forcés de gémir, en voyant que le peuple le plus fier et le plus actif, le plus éclairé sur ses intérêts, et tout ensemble le plus riche, reste courbé sous le triple joug de son gouvernement, qui n'en impose plus?) / (Les avantages de la constitution Britannique sont balancés par tant d'abus!)': ibid. i, pp. xii–xiii.

45 On the *Monarchiens* see J. Egret, *La Révolution des notables: Mounier et les monarchiens, 1789*, Paris 1950; R. Griffiths, *Le Centre perdu: Malouet et les 'monarchiens' dans la Révolution française*, Grenoble 1988; and F. Furet and M. Ozouf (eds), *Terminer la Révolution: Mounier and Barnave dans la Révolution française*, Grenoble 1990. On the use of the term 'monarchien' see Griffiths, *Le Centre perdu*, 13.

of tyranny'.[46] However, Mandar extended the meaning of the term to include imperial and monarchical rule generally: 'It is easy to judge with what audacity, with what blind fury, the people have been governed by these revered tyrants, known under the name of emperors, of kings, denounced as bishops, and inquisitors.'[47] His argument was not simply that there was a danger of monarchy declining into tyranny, but that in fact monarchical government (understood as the permanent rule of one) was *per se* opposed to liberty. In speaking, in his preface, of Nedham's work Mandar declared:

> In the first two parts, he attacks the enemies of the liberty of the people. It is clear that all the efforts by which one would attempt to confirm power in the hands of one person could only render it legitimate and reasonable if the person to whom it had been entrusted could only obtain its prolongation by the free consent of the people, represented in their formal and successive assemblies.[48]

In the second part the contrast is constantly drawn between the benefits of a free state and the evils of a monarchy, or indeed any form of permanent power. For example, Mandar quoted Mably on the fact that the rewards offered under a free state are much better for the state than the gifts of money and power offered under a monarch.[49] A few paragraphs later he suggested that the actions of Alexander the Great in the ancient world demonstrated the 'perfidy of kings'.[50] Moreover, Mandar had no qualms about the idea of the people judging their king. In the fourth part, in the midst of a discussion on the importance of educating the youth of a free state in the principles of liberty, Mandar inserted a footnote in which he suggested that children must be taught to disobey their king where this is necessary to secure liberty. Following this he spoke directly to the French people (implying the relevance of this point to them) and criticised Louis XVI for the crimes committed in his name.[51] Similarly a little later, Mandar insisted that the execution of a king is sometimes necessary. Again, he followed this with an appeal to the French people and advocated the establishment of a tribunal of citizens to judge a king who had transgressed the laws of the state.[52]

---

46 'déchire le voile qui couvroit les mystères de la tyrannie': Mandar, *De la Souveraineté*, i, p. xxi.

47 'Il est facile de juger avec quelle audace, quelle aveugle fureur, les peuples ont été gouvernés par ces tyrans révérés, connus sous le nom d'empereurs, de rois, denonces, d'évêques, et d'inquisiteurs': ibid. i, p. xxiii.

48 'Il attaque les ennemis de la liberté du peuple, dans les deux premières parties; et l'on reconnoît que tous les efforts par lesquels on tenteroit d'affermir le pouvoir dans les mains d'un seul, ne pourroient le rendre légitime et raisonnable, si celui auquel il auroit été confié n'en obtenoit la prolongation par le consentement libre du peuple, réprésenté dans ses assemblés solemnelles et successives': ibid. i, p. xviii.

49 Ibid. i. 68.

50 Ibid. i. 70.

51 Ibid. ii. 81.

52 Ibid. ii. 101–2.

Like Nedham, Mandar was, in a very real sense, anti-monarchical. However, neither Mandar nor Nedham was so simple-minded as to assume that the removal of monarchy would of itself produce liberty. Nedham's introduction to his work was concerned precisely with the question of what constituted a 'free state', and was designed to demonstrate that it could not simply be understood as a nation without a king. Following Nedham, Mandar referred back to Roman history to prove the point:

> It was not sufficient for the Romans to abolish the name of king, to obtain the full enjoyment of their rights and their privileges . . .

> When all was in the hands of the senate, the nation was regarded as free, because it was not subject to the will of a single man; but it was only free in practice when no-one could impose any laws upon it without the free consent of the people, obtained in its great assemblies.[53]

For Mandar, as for Nedham, only the people themselves could secure their liberty. Therefore what was required was popular sovereignty. Following Nedham, Mandar insisted that this could only be achieved under a form of government in which authority lay in popular assemblies elected on a frequent and regular basis by the people. In its emphasis on the role played by the people the form of republicanism presented by Mandar in his translation of Nedham was typical of what was being advocated by his fellow Cordeliers Club members. Moreover, like them, Mandar also looked to ancient models and examples.

Early in his preface, Mandar explained that one of the great advantages of Nedham's work was that it was based on a study of the history of ancient principles. The text was indeed peppered with references to, and parallels drawn from, the practices of the ancient city-state republics. Mandar reinforced the ancient bias with the quotations that he inserted into the text. Some of these affirmed the idea of the ancient world as a source of information on the government of free states. For example, Mandar quoted Bossuet who had argued that in Rome liberty was a treasure preferred to all the riches of the universe.[54] Several other quotations dealt with the similarities and differences between the ancients and the moderns. Early in his translation, Mandar quoted a passage from Joseph Cerutti to this effect:

> 'Different from modern republics, where one speaks only of the arts, of commerce, or riches; in the ancient republics [people] spoke, above all things, of government, of legislation, of the patrie – this word [that is] so touching, so

---

[53] 'Il n'a pas suffi aux Romains d'abolir le nom de roi, pour obtenir la jouissance entière de leurs droits et de leurs privilèges; . . . lorsque tout étoit dans les mains du sénat, la nation étoit regardée comme libre, parce qu'elle n'étoit point sujette à la volonté d'un seul homme; mais elle ne le fut en effet que lorsqu'on ne put lui imposer aucunes loix sans le libre consentement du peuple, obtenu dans ses grandes assemblées': ibid. i. 16, 20.
[54] Ibid. i. 4.

expressive, so dear for whoever has a heart – and of liberty, this word almost forgotten elsewhere. Athens and Rome, in engraving it in all hearts, ensured it was kept in all quarters. It presided over all feasts – even those of combat – over games as well as over business. In the public places it assembled and delighted the multitude; in the private houses, it created all delights and, as the principal treasure of each family, one heard it there more often even than father, son and spouse. The child stammered it from the cradle; the old man pronounced it with warmth on his death bed; it was, so to speak, the cry of the state. After the name of the gods, it was the best known and the most revered.'
M. CERUTTI.[55]

Similarly, later in the translation, Mandar inserted a quotation from the *abbé* Mably that focused on the passions that favour despotism in contrast to those that favour liberty.[56] Those in the former category included fear, idleness, avarice and love of dignities and luxury. Those in the latter included courage, modesty, frugality and regard for the public good. Mandar explained that Mably had believed the passions that favoured despotism to be common in modern times, but those associated with liberty to be rare. The implication of these quotations was that the moderns should strive to return to the ideals and practices of the ancients, replacing a concern for arts, riches and luxury with one for government, the patrie and the public good. It was this suggestion that lay at the heart of the epigraph chosen by Mandar to head his translation. The lines that Mandar quoted were taken from Rousseau's work on the government of Poland: 'One must seize the occasion of the present troubles to raise souls to the pitch of ancient souls.'[57]

As the presence of this epigraph would suggest, Mandar was heavily influenced by Rousseau. One of his key aims was to demonstrate the similarities between the ideas of Nedham and those of Rousseau. In the third part of the work Mandar followed Nedham in demonstrating that patriarchy had not been the source of legitimate authority since the time of Nimrod; and in arguing, by contrast, that political government founded on the free choice of the people had always existed and still survived in his own time. At this point

---

55 ' "Différentes des républiques modernes, où l'on ne parle que d'arts, de commerce, des richesses, les anciennes républiques parloient, avant toutes choses, de gouvernement, de législation, de patrie, ce mot si touchant, si expressif, si cher pour quiconque a un coeur; et la liberté, ce mot presque oublié ailleurs. Athènes et Rome, en le gravant dans tous les coeurs, le faisoient retentir de toutes parts; il présidoit aux festins de même qu'aux combats, aux jeux aussi bien qu'aux affaires. Dans les places publiques, il assembloit et ravissoit la multitude; dans les maisons privées, il faisoit les délices; et, comme la principale richesse de chaque famille, on l'y entendoit plus souvent que celui même de père, de fils et d'époux; l'enfant le bégayoit au berceau; le vieillard le prononçoit avec chaleur au lit même de la mort; c'étoit, pour ainsi dire, le cri de l'état; après le nom des dieux, il n'est étoit pas de plus connu ni de plus révéré." M. CERUTTI': ibid. i. 31n.
56 Ibid. i. 65.
57 'Il faut saisir la circonstance de l'évènement present, pour monter les ames au ton des ames antiques': ibid. i, title page.

Mandar suddenly introduced a substantial addition to Nedham's text. Nedham had simply stated the following before going on to provide scriptural proof for his argument: 'So that to prevent all objections of this nature, when we speak here of government, we mean only the political, which is by consent or compact; whose original we shall prove to be in the people.'[58] Mandar included a much longer passage before he turned to the government of the Israelites:

> And to set aside all the objections; by political government, we understand the sum of the forces resulting from the uniting of all wills. Now from this aggregation is formed this permanent power, by which each individual obeys only the law that he has imposed [and] enjoys, in a limited manner and without fear, all the rights which deviate neither from justice nor from public liberty. The result is therefore that all the forces and all the wills, find themselves thus reunited, contributing at the same time towards a single centre – that which assures and increases the perfect security and happiness of all.

> But it is evident that, without the agreement of the will of each of the members that compose this association, the government offers only a frightful chaos of forces and of opposed interests. And it is undeniable that the mode by which all things concur with this order and this activity, which gives to authority its vigour and all its energy, and under which the agreement of citizens is indispensable to consent and act together, depends essentially on the people, and that all who constitute the sovereign power belong to the people, which is the source of it.[59]

It is not difficult to see the Rousseauian echoes in this passage and any doubts are removed by the fact that the two quotations that Mandar inserted as footnotes into the passage come from Rousseau's *Social contract*, and are concerned precisely with political union and the social pact. Mandar thereby succeeded in making Nedham appear more of a precursor to Rousseau than he actually was. Similarly, the purpose of Mandar's inclusion of an extract from Rousseau's *Social contract* as an appendix to the second volume of his

---

[58] Nedham, *The excellencie of a free state*, 86.
[59] 'Et pour écarter toutes les objections; par gouvernement politique, nous entendons la somme des forces résultantes de la réunion de toutes les volontés. Or de cette agrégation est formé ce pouvoir permanent, par lequel chaque individu n'obéissant qu'à la loi qu'il s'est imposée, jouit, d'une manière illimitée et sans crainte, de tous les droits qui ne dévient ni de la justice, ni de la liberté publique. Il résulte donc que toutes les forces et toutes les volontés, se trouvant ainsi réunies, concourent à la fois vers un seul et même centre; ce qui assure et multiplie la parfaite sécurité et la félicité de tous. / Or il est évident que, sans l'accord de la volonté de chacun des membres qui composent cette association, le gouvernement n'offre qu'un affreux chaos de forces et d'intérêts opposés; et il est incontestable que le mode par lequel toutes choses concourent avec cet ordre et cette activité qui donnent à l'autorité sa vigueur et toute son énergie, et sous lequel l'accord des citoyens est indispensable pour consentir et agir ensemble, dépend essentiellement du peuple, et que tout ce qui constitue la souveraine puissance appartient au peuple, qui en est la source': Mandar, *De la Souveraineté*, ii. 5–9.

translation was said to be to demonstrate that the division of legislative and executive power found in that work, and for which Rousseau was often praised, was in fact prefigured in Nedham's text. Thus, Mandar insisted that if Rousseau was to be praised for this 'discovery' then Nedham should also be given some of the credit. Following this rather controversial suggestion, Mandar pre-empted the views of those inclined to criticise him for drawing parallels between Nedham and Rousseau, insisting that 'It is therefore particularly to these two great men that we are indebted for this knowledge, with the aid of whom the friends of liberty will ever succeed in opposing all the tricks, and thwarting all the schemes of the agents of tyranny.'[60]

Despite his respect for Rousseau, there appears to have been one key point on which Mandar felt the Englishman to be superior. This was perhaps the most important message that he wanted to transmit from Nedham to his French contemporaries. As we have seen, Rousseau – despite having favoured popular government – was not convinced that it could be implemented in the large nations of the modern world. Mandar, like his fellow Cordeliers, was unwilling to adopt the Brissotin solution of representative government. Just like other members of the Cordeliers Club, Mandar was explicit about his favouring of 'democratic' government. In a long footnote, which he added towards the end of the third part of Nedham's text, Mandar explicitly addressed those readers who remained convinced that monarchy is the best form of government. Having demonstrated the negative features of both monarchy and aristocracy, Mandar described his own preferred form of government as follows: 'I propose a democracy; its dignity is equal to that of the good people governed by it.'[61] In Nedham's republicanism Mandar found a concept that accorded with his own views and those of his fellow Cordeliers Club members, as well as a model that could help to turn theoretical beliefs into practical realities.

In his work Nedham had developed the idea of rotation. Elections, both to the legislative body and to executive offices, would be held frequently and those who had just held office would not be eligible for re-election. By this means participation would be made possible for a large number of citizens, even in a large state, and corruption would be limited by ensuring that citizens would have to live under the laws that they made: 'The observation then arising from hence, is this, that the only way for a people to preserve themselves in the enjoyment of their freedom, and to avoid those fatal inconveniences of faction and tyranny, is, to maintain a due and orderly succession of power and persons.'[62] The way in which Mandar incorporated Rousseau's

---

60 'C'est donc particulièrement à ces deux grands hommes que nous sommes redevables de ces lumières, à l'aide desquelles les amis de la liberté parviendront toujours à s'opposer à toutes les ruses, et à déjouer toutes les entreprises des agens de la tyrannie': ibid. ii. 187.
61 'Je propose une démocratie; sa dignité est égale à celle du bon peuple qu'elle gouverne': ibid. ii. 23n.
62 Nedham, The excellencie of a free state, 7–8.

concerns into the text suggests that he saw Nedham's proposal of frequent rotation within popular national assemblies as a way of overcoming the problem of the large size of modern states as highlighted by Rousseau:

> FIFTH REASON. Liberty consists in entrusting power to the successive representatives of the people alone*; because this succession is an obstacle to the ambition of individuals, to all the temptations of personal interest.[63]

* One of the great inconveniences of large states, which most renders liberty difficult to conserve, is that the legislative power can only appear there and can only act, by deputation. This has its disadvantages and its advantages, but the disadvantages win out. The legislature as a body is impossible to corrupt, but easy to deceive. The representatives are difficult to deceive, but easily corrupted – and it rarely happens that they aren't. You have under your eyes the example of the English parliament; and by the free veto, that of your own nation. One can throw light on that which deludes, but how can one keep that which is sold? Without being instructed in the affairs of Poland, I would bet all the world, that there is much knowledge in the diet and many virtues in the members of the diet. J. J. ROUSSEAU, *Gouvernement de Pologne*. [Un des plus grands inconvéniens des grands états, celui de tous qui y rend la liberté le plus difficile à conserver, est que la puissance législative ne peut s'y montrer elle-même, et ne peut agir que par députation. Cela a son mal et son bien; mais le mal l'emporte. Le législateur en corps est impossible à corrompre, mais facile à tromper. Les représentans sont difficilement trompés, mais aisement corrompus, et il arrive rarement qu'ils ne le soient pas. Vous avez sous les yeux l'exemple du parlement d'Angleterre; et par le *liberum veto*, celui de votre propre nation. Or on peut éclairer celui qui s'abuse; mais comment retenir celui qui se vend? Sans être instruit des affaires de Pologne, je parierois tout au monde, qu'il y a plus de lumières dans la diète, et plus de vertus dans les diétines.]

Mandar's democratisation of Nedham's *The excellencie of a free state*

In general, Mandar's translation followed Nedham's original; there are just a few points where he changed Nedham's meaning substantially or omitted part of the text. For the most part these changes are of little more than stylistic relevance. For example, in the original, Nedham had likened liberty or freedom to a virgin whom everyone wishes to violate: 'The truth of it is, the interest of freedom is a virgin that every one seeks to deflour; and like a virgin, it must be kept from any other form, or else (so great is the lust of mankind after dominion) there follows a rape upon the first opportunity.'[64] Though Mandar cut this passage from his translation, he did elsewhere express a similar sentiment without mentioning the violation of virgins. One must assume, therefore, that his omission of it was simply due to his concern not to upset eighteenth-century French sensibilities. On the question of

---

[63] 'CINQUIÈME RAISON. La liberté consiste à ne confier le pouvoir qu'aux représentans successifs du peuple*, parce que cette succession est un obstacle à l'ambition des particuliers, à toutes les tentations de l'intérêt personnel': Mandar, *De la Souveraineté*, i. 44–5.

[64] Nedham, *The excellencie of a free state*, 18–19.

religion, where one might have expected Mandar to have made changes, he remained surprisingly loyal to Nedham's original. Mandar did, however, add a disclaimer in which he explained that although he had translated all Nedham's criticisms of Catholicism and the pope, these referred to abuses committed in the name of religion and should not be seen as an attack on the Christian religion itself.[65]

While Mandar did not alter the religious content of Nedham's text, he did subtly change other aspects of it. Mandar not only drew on the, relatively democratic, republicanism of Nedham, but he also altered Nedham's original to make it appear even more democratic.[66] In the English version, Nedham's thirteenth argument in favour of the regular succession of popular assemblies opened as follows:

> The thirteenth reason, to prove the excellency of a free-state above any other form, is, because in free-states there are fewer opportunities of oppression and tyranny, than in the other forms. And this appears, in that it is most part, to preserve, *not an equality, (which were irrational and odious) but an equability of condition among all the members*; so that no particular man or men shall be permitted to grow over-great in power; nor any rank of men be allowed above the ordinary standard, to assume unto themselves the state and title of nobility.[67]

Mandar, in his translation, placed no such limit on equality:

> Free states offer fewer opportunities to oppress and tyrannise the people than all other forms of government. In a free state, *the first aim is to establish the greatest equality among all the citizens*, in order to prevent one or many individuals from acquiring too great a power, and [so] that whoever exercises power cannot usurp it, and that no authority [can] destroy this harmony so necessary *to the maintenance and conservation of a perfect equality, without which liberty is only a name*.[68]

Similarly, in the fourth part of the work Nedham had insisted that the people must not 'suffer particular persons to grandise, or greaten themselves more than ordinary'.[69] In his translation, Mandar made his own significant addition to Nedham's point claiming that the people must oppose 'any citizen

---

65 Mandar, *De la Souveraineté*, ii. 40.
66 For an argument about more democratic versions of classical republicanism during the English Revolution see Glover, 'The Putney debates'.
67 Nedham, *The excellencie of a free state*, 38–9, my italics.
68 'Les états libre offrent moins d'occasions d'opprimer et de tyranniser le peuple, que toutes les autres formes de gouvernement. Dans un état libre, *le premier objet est de mettre la plus grande égalité entre tous les citoyens*, afin d'empêcher qu'un ou plusieurs individus ne puissent acquérir un trop grand pouvoir, et que qui soit ne puisse usurper des droits et une autorité qui détruiroient cette harmonie si nécessaire *au maintien et à la conservation d'une parfaite égalité, sans laquelle la liberté n'est qu'un nom*': Mandar, *De la Souveraineté*, i. 98, my italics.
69 Nedham, *The excellencie of a free state*, 106.

raised up with pride, so that he cannot acquire more credit, nor appear with a splendor *that insults the equality of citizens*'.[70]

Mandar's sense of 'the people' who were to participate in politics also appears to have extended beyond that of his English mentor. Nedham's original included the following passage:

> Let this serve to manifest, that a government by a free election and consent of the people, settled in a due and orderly succession of their supreme assemblies, is more consonant to the light of nature and reason; and consequently, much more excellent than any hereditary standing power whatsoever. *To take off all mis-constructions; when we mention the people, observe all along, that we do not mean the confused promiscuous body of the people, nor any part of the people who have forfeited their rights by delinquency, neutrality, or apostasy, &c. in relation to the divided state of any nation; for they are not to be reckoned within the lists of the people.*[71]

Mandar cut this entire passage from his translation, thereby suggesting that he entertained no such restrictions on who was to be included among 'the people'.

Reactions to Mandar's translation of Nedham

Mandar's translation of Nedham did not prompt an immediate popular response, raising the possibility that it should be dismissed as the product of the fleeting obsession of a slightly eccentric revolutionary.[72] There is, however, evidence to suggest that a broader interest in Mandar's translation was aroused a year after its publication and that Mandar's own interest in English republicanism was far from fleeting.

In the midst of the sudden popularity of republican ideas, following the king's flight to Varennes, reviews of Mandar's translation of Nedham appeared in two important revolutionary newspapers. The first review, in the fourth issue of Momoro's *Journal du Club des Cordeliers* in July 1791,[73] picked up on and endorsed several of Mandar's comments and ideas regarding Nedham's text. For example, the parallel with Rousseau's ideas was emphasised. The reviewer commented: 'This work, the most eloquent and the deepest of all those that have appeared since the social contract – &

---

[70] 'à ce qu'aucun citoyen ne s'élève avec fierté, qu'il ne puisse acquérir plus de crédit, et ne paroisse avec un éclat *qui insulte à l'égalité des citoyens*': Mandar, *De la Souveraineté*, ii. 61, my italics.

[71] Nedham, *The excellencie of a free state*, 38, my italics.

[72] The work was reviewed in January 1791 by Louise Robert for *Mercure national*. Robert herself praised the work highly, describing it as being 'vraiment dignes des états républicains' [truly worthy of republican states], but she admitted that it had not been well reviewed in the press: *Mercure national*, iii. 135.

[73] Momoro, *Journal du club*, 31–4.

superior to it in quotations – was composed under the protectorate of Cromwell', and he referred to the claim that Nedham's work 'treats admirably the effects of that which the *Genevan* developed the causes'.[74] Similarly, the reviewer echoed Mandar's belief that the work was of particular relevance in revolutionary France because of its discussion of the means by which liberty had been maintained and lost throughout history. Interestingly, the reviewer also described the work as 'worthy of the happy centuries of Athens and ancient Rome', thus reinforcing both the perception of the work as part of a classical republican tradition, and the predilection of members of the Cordeliers Club for that tradition.[75] Mandar's preface, appendices and notes were singled out for particular praise. The positive nature of the review, and the fact that the reviewer was willing to recognise Mandar as a member of the club, reinforces the sense that the ideas expressed in the work were both accepted and deemed important by the Cordeliers in 1791.

The second review appeared in the issue of *Le Moniteur* dated 8 August 1791.[76] *Le Moniteur* was a daily newspaper that had been established in Paris by Charles Joseph Panckoucke in 1789. It enjoyed a wide circulation and in addition to reviews of recently published books it reproduced official documents and reported on National Assembly business and on domestic and foreign politics. The anonymous review of Mandar's translation was favourable, and again echoed Mandar himself in stressing the relevance of the work, and the ideas behind it, to eighteenth-century France. Its relevance was linked to Nedham's focus on liberty and the sovereignty of the people, and his provision of arguments designed to counter the objections of the 'partisans of tyranny'. Connections were drawn between Nedham's views and ideas as expressed in the work, and those of later and more familiar thinkers, not least Rousseau. It was suggested that, contrary to popular opinion, Rousseau had not invented the idea of the inalienable sovereignty of the people, but had simply reduced to a convenient system that which he had seen in practice in many republican states. The wide circulation enjoyed by *Le Moniteur* may have meant that knowledge of Mandar's translation, and therefore of Nedham's original text, reached a larger audience than would otherwise have been expected.

---

[74] 'Cet ouvrage, le plus éloquent et le plus profond de tous ceux qui ont paru jusqu'ici avant le contract social, et qui lui est supérieur en citations, a été composé sous le protectorat de Cromwell . . . traitoit admirablement des effets dont le *Génevois* a développé les causes': ibid. 32–3.

[75] 'digne des siècles heureux d'Athènes et de l'ancienne Rome': ibid. 33.

[76] *Moniteur universel*, iv. 335.

Des Insurrections

Mandar's translation of Nedham's work does not appear to have sated his interest in English republican ideas or his use of those ideas to support and justify the democratic republicanism of the Cordeliers. In 1793 Mandar published a book with the Cercle Social publishing house which was entitled *Des Insurrections: ouvrage philosophique et politique sur les rapports des insurrections avec la prospérité des empires*.[77] This was perhaps Mandar's best-known work and he certainly considered it to be important: 'I regard my work on INSURRECTIONS as my political profession of faith.'[78] In it Mandar referred to and advocated the ideas not just of Nedham but also of other seventeenth-century English republicans including Harrington, Milton and Sidney.

Although not published until 1793, Mandar had apparently written *Des Insurrections* much earlier and he acknowledged that he had long hesitated over whether or not to publish it. The 'Avertissement de l'éditeur' states that the decision to publish was taken following the *journée* of 10 August 1792 (which Mandar had supported) and the September massacres that followed (which Mandar claimed could have been prevented had *Des Insurrections* already appeared). The work was refused by at least one Parisian bookseller before the Cercle Social agreed to take it on.[79] As with *De la Souveraineté du peuple*, it consisted of more than just the text itself. The 'Avertissement de l'éditeur' is followed by Mandar's own preface in which he provided his reasons for writing and publishing the work. Then comes a preliminary discourse, of over a hundred pages, which Mandar dedicated to the future French race. In it he defined his understanding of insurrection and demonstrated the connection between insurrection and liberty. *Des Insurrections* itself is followed by a number of Mandar's other short works and letters, including *Essai sur la sorte d'eloquence la plus propre à servir utilement la cause de LA LIBERTÉ dans un gouvernement POPULAIRE, auquel on a joint quelques exemples, etc.*, *GENIE des siècles*, and a revised version of his *Observations sur les commerce et l'esclavage des nègres* which had originally appeared in his translation of Nedham.[80]

The purpose behind *Des Insurrections* was to consider whether insurrections could ever be justified and how, and by what means, an insurrection

---

[77] T. Mandar, *Des Insurrections: ouvrage philosophique et politique sur les rapports des insurrections avec la prospérité des empires*, Paris 1793.

[78] 'Je regarde mon ouvrage sur les INSURRECTIONS comme ma profession de foi politique': ibid. 579.

[79] As well as publishing the work, the Cercle Social included extracts from it in their *Bulletin des amis de la verité* in January 1793: T. Mandar, 'Des mouvemens populaires en général', *Bulletin des amis de la verité, publie par les directeurs de l'imprimerie du Cercle Social*, Paris 1793 [l'an II], i, no. xx, 3, and 'Moyens proposés pour prevenir les insurrections, les émeutes, etc.', i, no. xxiii, 3; no. xxiv, 2–3. The work was also advertised in i, no. xxvi, 1.

[80] An edition of *Génie des siècles* also appeared in 1795.

should be carried out. Mandar began by defining 'insurrection' as the right given to man by nature of rising up against all that opposes his happiness and degrades his morality.[81] He distinguished it from a revolt – which, he claimed, was not justified under a free government – and from sedition – which was never acceptable. Insurrection was justified under the appropriate circumstances, Mandar insisted, because it was aimed at improving men, the *patrie* and the universe; and he claimed that the art of making insurrections should be taught to the children of a free state: 'I want our children to learn the art of making, *when necessary*, a general insurrection. It is an art that should be added to the science of governments.'[82] Having established its value in theory, Mandar went on to consider and provide examples of how an insurrection could be avoided, when it would be necessary and how it should best be carried out.

There are many similarities between *Des Insurrections* and Mandar's translation of Nedham. Mandar's continued support for the policies of the Cordeliers Club and its members is made explicit.[83] He also quoted passages from works by Louis de la Vicomterie de Saint Samson. On the subject of the crimes of kings, Mandar referred his readers to La Vicomterie's *Des Crimes des rois de France*: 'it suffices, I say, that the reader devotes himself to the [kind of] reflections that are born of themselves, and the book of la Vicomterie be read and thought about'.[84] In *Génie des siècles*, which was one of the works appended to *Des Insurrections*, Mandar condemned tyranny and quoted the following passage from La Vicomterie's *République sans impôt*:

'A single man, a wise man, can stop the march of tyrants, can make them grow pale, can save his country. Armed with the force of reason, everywhere he calls them, he challenges them, he attacks them, reveals their crimes, opposes their weakness and their barbarous sophisms.'[85]

The themes of liberty and the establishment and maintenance of a free state were as central to *Des Insurrections* as they had been to Mandar's earlier work. Mandar condemned monarchical government:

It appears evident to me that the royal form of government incurs all the vices, and increases a hundredfold for the people, all the inconveniences which

---

81 Mandar, *Des Insurrections*, 149.
82 'Je veux que nos enfans apprennent l'art de faire, *à heure donnée*, une insurrection générale; c'est un art qu'il est nécessaire d'ajouter à la science des gouvernemens': ibid. 345.
83 Ibid. 290.
84 'il suffit, dis-je, que le lecteur se livre aux réflexions qui naissent d'elles-mêmes, et le livre *de la Vicomterie* aura été lu et médité: ibid. 337.
85 ' "Un seul homme, un sage peut arrêter la marche des tyrans, peut les faire pâlir, peut sauver sa patrie. Armé de la force de la raison, par-tout il les appelle, il les défie, il les attaque, dévoile leurs forfaits, oppose à leur lâcheté et à leurs barbares sophismes" ': ibid. 556n.

result from the ineptitude, the stupidity of some kings; or, even when the kings are great men, it modifies the human race at the will of these great men.[86]

In place of monarchy he advocated the rule of law and regular and successive popular assemblies:

> All authority which deviates from that of the law, cannot be legitimate and sacred: there cannot be for the citizens either happiness or peace in a state where the public thing is at the mercy of a single person . . .

> The only means that the people have of maintaining themselves in a state of liberty, and of preventing the fatal consequences of faction and tyranny, are therefore of supporting the power by the successive and regular choice of its representatives; such is the rule that a wise republic must prescribe to keep itself free for a long time.[87]

And, in line with his Cordeliers contemporaries, Mandar insisted that all laws should be ratified by the people:

> I have a need, my friend, that the love of order and of laws has succeeded in conquering for liberty all our fellow citizens.

> I understand by the laws those which have been consented to by the people.[88]

Mandar's concern throughout the work was his native country and particularly the events of the recent Revolution. As in *De la Souveraineté* he presented the French Revolution as having ushered in an era of liberty: 'The fourteenth of July, I salute you! you are forever the epoch of the liberty of my country.'[89] He also made it clear that he saw the issue of 'insurrections' as being of direct relevance to revolutionary France: 'What days! those of 14 July, 5 and 6 October 1789, 21 June 1791, and 10 August 1792!'[90] The circumstances and events of seventeenth-century England were never far from Mandar's mind, however, and he evidently still believed that the French

---

[86] 'Or, il me paroît évident que la forme de gouvernement royale contracte tous les vices, et centuple pour les peuples, tous les inconvéniens qui résultent de l'ineptie, de la stupidité de quelques rois; ou, alors que les rois sont de grands hommes, elle modifie le genre humaine au gré de ces grands hommes': ibid. 325–6.
[87] 'Toute autorité qui dévie de celle de la loi, ne peut être légitime et sacrée: il ne peut y avoir pour des citoyens, ni bonheur, ni paix dans un état où la chose publique est à la merci d'un seul. . . . Le seul moyen qu'ait un peuple de se maintenir dans un état de liberté, et d'éviter les fatales conséquences de la faction et de la tyrannie, est donc d'entretenir le pouvoir par le choix successif et régulier de ses représentans: telle est la règle qu'une république sage doit se prescrire se conserver long-tems libre': ibid. 217, 222–3.
[88] 'J'ai besoin, mon ami, que l'amour de l'ordre et des loix ait achevé de conquérir à la liberté tous nos concitoyens. / J'entends par les loix, celles qui auront été consenties par le peuple': ibid. 550.
[89] 'Quatorze juillet, je te salue! sois à jamais l'époque de la liberté de ma patrie': ibid. 202.
[90] 'Quelles journées! celles du 14 juillet, 5 et 6 octobre 1789, 21 juin 1791, et 10 août 1792!': ibid. 307.

revolutionaries could learn much from the seventeenth-century English republicans:

> It was during the reign of Charles II [sic] that one saw these great writers appear whose genius forged the sceptre of the people out of the debris of . . . crowns. Nedham published this immortal work that earned him a reputation as a profound political thinker, if one considers the time in which he wrote. [Then there was] Algernon Sidney who sealed with his blood the cause of the liberty of the people: his book about monarchy brought him the immortal honour of having been the first to die in the name of the rights of the people. Harrington, so little known among the French, consoled the world with his works when Milton gave up political arguments for [poetry].[91]

Mandar himself drew a connection between *Des Insurrections* and his earlier translation of Nedham's work in his preface to the former:

> I refer the reader to the profound arguments of Sidney and of J. J. Rousseau; I refer him to J. Locke, and invite him to meditate on the work of Marchamont Nedham.*[92]

* This author, whose work I have published under this title: DE LA SOUVERAINETÉ DU PEUPLE, ET DE L'EXCELLENCE D'UN ÉTAT LIBRE, has treated, in a most proud and most manly manner, the question of the permanence of power in the hands of a single person; it is particularly in the second volume of this work that the reader will see, in all their austerity and in their ancient majesty, what laws suit free states; what dangers threaten liberty, while tyranny seeks to recover its power; and the rules of politics that must be followed. Nedham *knows kings*. [Cet auteur, dont j'ai publié l'ouvrage sous ce titre: DE LA SOUVERAINETÉ DU PEUPLE, ET DE L'EXCELLENCE D'UN ÉTAT LIBRE, a traité, de la manière la plus fière et la plus mâle, la question de la permanence du pouvoir dans les mains d'un seul; c'est particulièrement dans le second volume de cet ouvrage, que le lecteur verra, dans toute leur austérité et dans leur majesté antique, quelles loix conviennent aux états libres; quels dangers menacent la liberté, alors que la tyrannie parvient à recouvrer sa puissance, et les règles de politiques qu'il importe de suivre; NEEDHAM *savoit les rois*.]

The connection was further made in the advertisement for *Des Insurrections*, which appeared in the *Bulletins des amis de la verité*: 'Théophile Mandar is

---

[91] 'Ce fut sous le règne de Charles II [sic] que l'on vit paroître ces grands écrivains dont le génie forgea le sceptre des peuples, des débris de toutes les couronnes. Néedham publia cet ouvrage immortel qui le plaça si haut parmi les politiques, si on considère en quel tems il écrivoit: on vit Algernon Sydney, sceller de son sang la cause de la liberté des peuples: son livre DE LA MONARCHIE lui procura cet immortel honneur d'avoir été le premier à qui la manifestation des droits du peuple a coûté la vie. Harrington, trop peu connu parmi nos Français, consola l'univers par ses ouvrages de la perte de Milton, qui se délassoit des querelles politiques, par des chants divins': ibid. 211n.

[92] 'Je renvoie le lecteur aux profonds raisonnemens de Sidney et de J. J. Rousseau; je le renvoie à J. Locke, et je l'invite à méditer l'ouvrage de Marchamont Néedham': ibid. 299.

favourably known in political literature, through the translation of an English work, which has for its title *de la souveraineté du peuple*.'[93]

Of the seventeenth-century English republicans it was Sidney who received the most attention from Mandar in *Des Insurrections*: he used Sidney to underline the folly of monarchical government:

> Descend, Sidney, descend from the high Olympus, where Brutus and Cato are envious of your immortal renown. Oh Sidney! you of the laborious watch, you of the wise works that have traced for us with much eloquence the infinite evils which are born and which perpetuate themselves under the step of despotism. Oh you, whose name has been dreaded by tyrants, [whose] life [was] so beautiful, [whose] death so heroic, hurry to my aid, divine genius, heir of Plato, of Solon, and of all the virtue of the Romans. Speak here in the cause of the people, and your life, and your works; that your death will without cease be present in the minds of my fellow citizens: that they fix the tyrant, that they contemplate his victim . . .

> August head, head of Sidney, the tyrant has not ended your glory with your life . . .

> Sidney has revealed the turpitude of the courts, he has proclaimed the crimes of kings; he has, ingenious wise man [that he was], traced a line of twists and turns between the tyrant and liberty; he arms the citizens with the arms of reason, he announces to them the kings, and the evils with which they have beaten the human race, he uncovers royalty.[94]

[93] 'Théophile Mandar est avantageusement connu dans la littérature politique, par la traduction d'un ouvrage anglois, qui a pour titre de *la souveraineté du peuple*': *Bulletin des amis de la verité*, i, no. xxvi, 1.

[94] 'Descends, Sidney, descends du haut Olympe, où Brutus et Caton portent envie à ton immortelle renommée. O Sidney! toi, dont les veilles laborieuses, toi, dont les savans ouvrages nous ont tracé avec tant d'éloquence les maux infinis qui naissent et qui se perpétuent sous les pas du despotisme; ô toi, dont le nom a été l'effroi des tyrans, la vie si belle, la mort si héroïque, accours à mon aide, divin génie, héritier des Platon, des Solon, et de toute la vertu romaine. Fais parler ici dans la cause des peuples, et ta vie, et tes ouvrages; que ta mort soit sans cesse présent à l'ésprit de mes concitoyens: qu'ils fixent le tyran, qu'ils contemplent sa victime. . . . Tête auguste, tête de Sidney, le tyran n'a pas terminé ta gloire avec ta vie . . . Sidney avoit révélé la turpitude des cours, il avoit proclamé les crimes des rois; il avoit, ingénieur savant, tracé une ligne de circonvallation entre le tyran et la liberté; il arma les citoyens des armes de la raison, il leur annonça les rois, et les maux dont ils ont frappé le genre humaine; il révéla la royaute': Mandar, *Des Insurrections*, 233–6. Sidney was probably the best known seventeenth-century English republican in eighteenth-century France. His works had been translated into French in 1702 and reprinted in 1755. It was, however, as a symbol of a revolutionary martyr that Sidney was best known by the French: Parker, *The cult of antiquity*, and P. Karsten, *Patriot-heroes in England and America*, Wisconsin 1978, which refers specifically to Sidney's reputation in France in ch vi, n. 2. On the changing fortunes of Sidney's reputation in England see Worden, 'The commonwealth kidney', and *Roundhead reputations*, chs v, vi, vii. In 1789 there appeared an anonymous pamphlet entitled *Lettre de felicitation de Milord Sidney*. In that work Sidney spoke to the French to remind them of the importance of liberty and to emphasise to them the superiority of the assembled nations over all other types of ruler. Interestingly, given Mandar's practice, Rousseau, Mably and Hélvetius are described in the pamphlet as 'Sidney's friends'.

Moreover, Mandar was not content with simply referring to Sidney and praising him as a martyr to liberty. He quoted from Sidney's works too. Indeed, the last six chapters of *Des Insurrections* were extracted from Sidney's *Discourses concerning government*.[95] These were all designed to illustrate and support the points that Mandar had been making throughout the text: that insurrection can be justified and of benefit to the nation, and that liberty is essential for happiness and success. Mandar then invited his readers to medi-tate upon these passages and to draw republican conclusions from them:

> the sublime maxims on which this publicist has based the rights of citizens, their duties, and the advantages that they can enjoy under a free form of gov-ernment I invite them to persuade themselves of this principle; that kings RISK all against the people; that it is crucial to the happiness of the people to oppose oneself with consistency against all who could favour, in whatever manner, the return of royalty.

> Now the royal statues have fallen, and the busts of *Sidney*, of *Nedham*, of *Beccaria*, of *Montesquieu*, of *Fénelon*, of *J. Locke*, of *J. J. Rousseau* (and yours *Harrington*), replace these royal effigies, the stormy shadow of which insults the generations.[96]

Des Insurrections demonstrates Mandar's continued interest in issues and ideas first raised in his translation of Nedham. Moreover, it reinforces the fact that Mandar was interested not just in Nedham, but in a tradition of seven-teenth-century English republican writing that also included Sidney, Harrington and Milton.

Mandar was not the only Cordelier to turn to seventeenth-century English republican writers to further the cause of establishing a classical, democratic, republic in late eighteenth-century France. Just as Nedham's works have been

---

95 A. Sidney, *Discourses concerning government*, ed. T. G. West, Indianapolis 1996: the general revolt of a nation cannot be called a rebellion, ch. iii.36; tumults and wars are not the greatest evils that befall nations, ch. ii.26; a general presumption that kings will govern well, is not a sufficient security to the people, ch. iii.15; there is no disorder or prejudice in changing the name or number of magistrates, whilst the root and principle of the power continues entire, ch. ii.13; Samuel did not describe to the Israelites the glory of a free monarchy: but the evils the people should suffer, that he might divert them from desiring a king, ch. iii.3; the glory, virtue and power of the Romans began and ended with their liberty, ch. ii.12.
96 'les maximes sublimes sur lesquelles ce publiciste a basé les droits des citoyens, leurs devoirs, et les avantages dont ils peuvent jouir sous un mode de gouvernement libre; je les invite à se persuader de ce principe: que les rois OSENT tout contre les peuples; et qu'il importe essentiellement au bonheur du peuple de s'opposer avec constance à tout ce qui pourroit favoriser, de quelque manière que ce puisse être, le retour de la royauté. / Maintenant les statues des rois soit tombées, et les bustes des *Sydney*, des *Néedham*, des *Beccaria*, des *Montesquieu*, des *Fénelon*, des *J. Locke*, des *J. J. Rousseau* (et le tien, *Harrington*), remplaceront ces effigies royales, dont l'ombre orgueilleuse insultoit aux générations': Mandar, *Insurrections*, 435–6.

more profitably understood when placed alongside those of Milton, Harrington, Ludlow, Neville and Sidney, so Mandar's translation of Nedham's text makes more sense when considered together with works by other members of the Cordeliers Club.

3

Jean Jacques Rutledge's Le Creuset: A Harringtonian Text

What moral and political spectacle the late seventeenth century offers in France (said J. Rutledge (*), in his éloge de Montesquieu) to the small number of people capable of not being seduced by the flashiness of false grandeur and by the swelling of these advantages of ostentation – the distinctive feature of which is to disguise to nations, and above all to vain nations, their real emptiness beneath deceptive appearances?[1]

* 'Rutledge, whatever your enemies say, you are a great man!' T. MANDAR. ['Rutledge, quoiqu'en disent tes ennemis, tu es un grand-homme!' T. MANDAR.]

These words were covered by murmurs and applause. M. DE RUTLEDGE, whose eloquence can be compared to the tranquil flow of a deep river and who transmits all his sentiments to those who hear him, spoke for a long time. He preceded me on the platform, but if he was listened to with pleasure, my speech was anticipated with the greatest impatience.[2]

As these quotations from *Des Insurrections* demonstrate Théophile Mandar clearly knew of Jean Jacques Rutledge and his works. The two men probably became acquainted at the Cordeliers Club during the early 1790s. As well as being members of the club, Mandar and Rutledge also shared an interest in seventeenth-century English republican ideas. Just as Mandar had translated Marchamont Nedham's republican text, so Rutledge drew on the works and ideas of James Harrington.

---

[1] 'Quel spectacle morale et politique la fin du dix-septième siècle offroit-elle en France (dit J. Rutledge (*), dans son éloge de Montesquieu) au petit nombre de mortels capables de ne pas être éblouis par le clinquant des fausses grandeurs, et par l'enflure de ces avantages d'ostentation, dont le propre est de déguisser aux nations, et sur-tout aux nations vaines, leur néant réel sous des apparences décevantes: Mandar, *Des Insurrections*, 113.

[2] 'Ces paroles furent couvertes de murmures et d'applaudissemens, M. DE RUTLEDGE, dont l'éloquence peut être comparée au cours tranquille d'un fleuve profond, et qui imprime tous ses sentimens à ceux qui l'entendent, avoit depuis long-tems la parole: il me préda à la tribune. Mais si on l'écouta avec plaisir, on attendoit mon discours dans la plus grande impatience': ibid. 470–1n.

James Harrington

James Harrington was born in 1611, at Upton in Northamptonshire. Almost no personal papers or manuscripts have survived and little is known of his early life.[3] There is no clear evidence that he played any part in the first civil war (1642–6), but in 1647 he was employed by Parliament as gentleman of the bedchamber to Charles I, who was being held captive by the parliamentary forces at Holdenby House. Harrington moved with the king to several other locations and was only separated from him shortly before the regicide.

Harrington's major work, *The commonwealth of Oceana*, was published in 1656 (it was recorded in the Stationer's Company Register on 19 September 1656 and was in print by early November).[4] The background against which it was written was the Cromwellian Protectorate. Although it was dedicated to Oliver Cromwell, as Lord Protector, it is clear that Harrington's aim was to criticise, and to offer a better alternative to, the commonwealth under which he lived. Indeed, Blair Worden has gone so far as to call the dedication an anti-dedication.[5]

The work is divided into several parts. Following a short introduction are two preliminary discourses in which Harrington set out the theoretical basis of his ideas. In the first he focused on the principles of government according to the ancients or 'ancient prudence'. In the second he dealt with the principles of government since the fall of the Roman empire, which he called 'modern prudence'. He then went on to explore the practical application of these theories in 'The council of legislators' and 'The model of the commonwealth of Oceana' (the main body of the work) where he sought to demonstrate how ancient prudence could be revived in the modern world and how a classical republic could be established in seventeenth-century England. The work concludes with 'The corollary' in which Harrington set out the implications of the form of government he had proposed. His application of classical republican ideas to seventeenth-century England was grounded on his belief that political power follows the balance of property. Thus he emphasised the

[3] On Harrington's life see J. Aubrey, *Brief lives*, ed. R. Barber, Woodbridge 1982, 127–30; A. Wood, *Athenae oxoniensis: an exact history of all the writers and bishops who have had their education in the University of Oxford*, ed. P. Bliss, London 1817, iii. 1115–26; J. Toland, 'The Life of James Harrington', in *The Oceana of James Harrington, and his other works . . . with an exact account of his life prefix'd, by John Toland*, London 1700. The latter has recently been reprinted in L. Borot (ed.), *The Oceana of James Harrington and the notion of a commonwealth* (Collection Astraea 6), Montpellier 1998, 23–77. The best recent account appears in the introduction to *The political works of James Harrington*, ed. J. G. A. Pocock, Cambridge 1977, 1–152.
[4] On the text and the circumstances of its publication see *Political works of James Harrington*, 1–152; B. Worden, 'James Harrington and *The commonwealth of Oceana*, 1656', and 'Harrington's *Oceana*: origins and aftermath, 1651–1660', in Wootton, *Republicanism, liberty, and commercial society*, 82–110, 111–38.
[5] Worden, 'Harrington's *Oceana*', 124.

importance of the ownership of land. As J. G. A. Pocock explained in his introduction to Harrington's political works, 'to the Machiavellian hypothesis that arms are the foundation of citizenship, Harrington adds the hypothesis that land is the foundation of arms'.[6]

Oceana prompted much criticism and most of Harrington's subsequent works were concerned with defending and restating the ideas set out in that text. These included direct replies to particular critics, such as *Pian piano or intercourse between H. Ferne, Dr in divinity and J. Harrington esq. upon the occasion of the Doctor's censure of the commonwealth of OCEANA* and *Politicaster or a comical discourse in answer unto Mr Wren's Book intituled monarchy asserted against Mr Harrington's OCEANA*, and works such as *Aphorisms political* and *A system of politics* in which the ideas expressed in *Oceana* were restated in aphoristic form. Harrington was probably working on *A system of politics* at the time of the restoration of the monarchy in 1660; the manuscript of that work was said to have been seized when Harrington was arrested by the authorities on 28 December 1661. During his time in prison Harrington suffered some kind of physical and mental breakdown. He was released in 1662 and lived in Westminster until his death fifteen years later.

Oceana was republished, together with many of Harrington's other works, by John Toland in 1700, under the title *The* Oceana *of James Harrington and his other works . . . with an exact account of his life prefix'd, by John Toland*. A subsequent edition, which included works left out of Toland's volume, appeared in 1737. It was via these two editions that Harrington and his works became widely known in the English- and French-speaking worlds.[7]

Knowledge of Harrington's works in France arose largely due to reviews of the 1700 and 1737 editions, which appeared in the francophone Huguenot press.[8] An article on Harrington under the heading 'Rutland' (the county in which he had resided) written by the chevalier de Jaucourt (who himself had a Huguenot background) appeared in the *Encyclopédie*.[9] Full French translations of Harrington's works did not appear until 1795.[10] Nevertheless, from the mid-1780s Rutledge was both seeking to introduce Harrington and his ideas to a French audience and urging the French to read Harrington's works for themselves.

---

6 *Political works of James Harrington*, 43.
7 On the influence of Harrington's works and ideas in eighteenth-century Britain and America see Russell Smith, *Harrington and his* Oceana, chs vii, viii, and Pocock, *Machiavellian moment*, chs xiii, xiv, xv.
8 'Harrington's *Oceana* and other works by Toland', in Bernard, *Nouvelles de la république* (sept. 1700), 243–63; '*Oceana* and other works of Harrington by Toland', in Kemp and others, *Bibliothèque britannique* (juill.–sept. 1737), 408–30.
9 Le chevalier de Jaucourt, 'Rutland', *Encyclopédie, ou dictionnaire raisonnée des sciences, arts et des métiers, par une société des gens de lettres*, Stuggart 1967, xiv. 446–7.
10 Harrington, *Oeuvres politiques*, and *Aphorismes politiques*.

Jean Jacques Rutledge[11]

Jean Jacques (James) Rutledge was born in Dunkirk on 5 August 1742.[12] His mother was French and a native of Dunkirk but his paternal relatives were Irish. Consequently, Jean Jacques grew up to be bilingual and possessed a deep knowledge of, and respect for, French and English literature, culture and politics. His father, Walter Rutledge, worked as a ship owner in Dunkirk. It was as a result of his involvement with the Jacobite cause that Jean Jacques gained the title of baronet and for a time, prior to the Revolution, he styled himself 'le chevalier Rutledge'. Following in the family tradition, Jean Jacques himself joined a Franco-Irish cavalry regiment in 1760 and fought with them in the Seven Years War. When the war ended, and the regiment was disbanded, Rutledge travelled to Italy where he was impressed by the Venetian system of government. He subsequently returned to Lille where he married a ship owner's daughter. Both Rutledge's own family, and that of his wife, suffered chronic financial problems. It was for this reason that Rutledge moved to Paris in 1775 and attempted to make a career for himself as a journalist, novelist and playwright.

Rutledge's first major work *Thamar: tragédie* had already appeared in 1769. He followed this with several translations of English works including *Le Retour du philosophe*, a translation of Oliver Goldsmith's *Deserted village* and – in 1776 – a French version of a work attributed to John Andrews (1736–1809) *An account of the character and manners of the French; with occasional observations on the English* (1770).[13] In many ways this work set the tone for his later writings, with its comparison of the English and the French. Rutledge believed that both nations could learn much from the literature and politics of the other, and throughout the rest of his life he sought to bring about an Anglo-French *rapprochement*:

---

[11] The name is spelt in a variety of ways. These include Rutlidge, Rutlige and, most commonly, Rutledge. The latter spelling is adopted here. Pseudonyms used by Rutledge include Rutofle de Lode, K. S. Wexb., Docteur Stearne and the initials M. R. C. B. (Monsieur Rutledge Chevalier Baronet) and M. L. C. J. R. G. A. (Monsieur le Chevalier James Rutledge, Gentilhomme Anglais). There is a French biography of Rutledge: R. Las Vergnas, *Chevalier Rutlidge 'gentilhomme anglais', 1742–1794*, Paris 1932. See also J. G. Alger, *Englishmen in the French Revolution*, London 1889, 19–21, and 'Rutledge, James or John James', in *Dictionary of national biography*, ed. L. Stephen and S. Lee, London 1908–9 (repr. of 1895–1900 edn), l. 518–9; P. Peyronnet, 'J. J. Rutlidge', *Revue d'histoire du théâtre* iv (1992), 330–59, and 'Rutlidge', in J. Sgard (ed.), *Dictionnaire des journalistes, 1600–1789*, Oxford 1999, ii. 891–3; and R. Hammersley 'English republicanism and the French Revolution: the case of Jean Jacques Rutlidge', in E. Tuttle (ed.), *Confluences XVII: républic anglais et idée de tolerance*, Paris 2000, 169–83.

[12] Peyronnet includes a photocopy of the baptismal certificate in his article on Rutledge: 'J. J. Rutlidge', 359.

[13] [J. J. Rutledge], *Essai sur le caractère et les moeurs des françois comparées à celles des anglois*, London 1776.

Although, in general, the English and the French are naturally enemies – on account of the form of their governments, the situation of their states and other occasional causes – their political hatred must not blind them to their beautiful reciprocal qualities. One can and, consequently, one must reconcile the political rivalry with an olive branch.[14]

From the beginning Rutledge's interest in comparing and drawing together the French and the English was both literary and political. In 1776 he participated in the 'Shakespeare controversy', praising the works of the bard against his French critics.[15] More practically, during the 1770s he was involved in an Anglo-French dispute centred on Dunkirk. Through this Rutledge met Anne Robert Jacques Turgot, the politician and *économiste*, whose 'Mémoire au roi sur les municipalités' he claimed to have influenced.[16] Rutledge's *Essais politiques*, which was published in Switzerland in 1777, was also concerned with comparing the French and the English. As well as spending some time in Switzerland, Rutledge made several trips to London during the 1770s, and came to be particularly impressed by English periodicals such as *The Tatler* and *The Spectator* – which had been established by Joseph Addison and Richard Steele in the early eighteenth-century. While still in Switzerland, Rutledge began to produce his own French version of these English-style periodicals, which he entitled *Le Babillard* (the Tatler). It began to appear in 1778 after Rutledge had returned to Paris. Rutledge's writing career was temporarily interrupted by his arrest and imprisonment in 1782 for allegedly being an alien and a suspect of the state, and for corresponding with enemies of the state.[17] He returned to the Tatler genre in May 1784 with *Calypso, ou les babillards*, explicitly described as a continuation of *Le Babillard*, which had ceased to appear in April 1779.[18]

---

[14] 'Quoiqu'en général les Anglois et les François soient naturellement ennemis par la forme de leur Gouvernement, la situation de leurs Etats et d'autres causes occasionnelles, leur haine politique ne doit pas les aveugler sur leurs belles qualités réciproques. On peut & par conséquent on doit concilier la rivalité publique avec la concorde particuliere': ibid. 142.
[15] This controversy was provoked by Le Tourneur's translations of Shakespeare's works, which were criticised by Voltaire. See Las Vergnas, *Le Chevalier Rutlidge*, ch. vii, and Peyronnet, 'J. J. Rutlidge', 342–3.
[16] For Rutledge's claim see J. J. Rutledge, *Mémoire au roi pour le clier Rutledge*, Bnet, Paris 1790, 9. There is no evidence of this alleged influence in the work itself: Las Vergnas, *Le Chevalier Rutlidge*, 64.
[17] Las Vergnas, *Le Chevalier Rutlidge*, 173–4.
[18] [J. J. Rutledge], *Calypso, ou les babillards, par une société de gens du monde et de gens de lettres*, Paris 1785, i. 3.

Rutledge's pre-revolutionary interest in Harrington

Rutledge had already come to know and be interested in the works of Harrington before the outbreak of the Revolution, and he wrote about him in *Calypso*.[19] The periodical claimed to be written by 'a society of men of the world and men of letters' ('une société de gens du monde et de gens de lettres') and there were supposedly seven collaborators. In reality, Rutledge probably worked alone.[20] The scope of the periodical very much reflected Rutledge's own interests, which ranged from theatre to politics; and, once again, Anglo-French relations were central. Moreover, extracts from *Le Babillard* and *Essais politiques* were copied into the text. In April 1785 Rutledge devoted two entire issues to Harrington, his life and works.[21]

Rutledge stated his reason for focusing on Harrington at the beginning of the first article. He explained that a correspondent had written to one of the associates of *Calypso* seeking a copy of Harrington's work, after it had been cited in an earlier issue.[22] In that issue, in the midst of an article on Mably's *Observations sur le gouvernement et les loix des États-Unis d'Amérique*, Rutledge had claimed that both Mably and Montesquieu had read and been strongly influenced by Harrington's works, and he had urged his readers to read Harrington (in the original) for themselves. The value of the works of this little known political theorist lay, in Rutledge's view, in his advice on how one could establish stable and successful democratic government:

> M. Mably is well placed to feel strongly, and to recognise, that the genius of the unfortunate Harrington was solidly founded with an intrepid hand, and offers the base on which all Philosophical Legislators, from whatever government, can solidly set down and raise the Edifice of the most equal and the most durable democratic constitution.[23]

In response Rutledge acknowledged that Harrington's works were rare – especially in Paris – and so instead he offered to tell his readers all that he knew about the Englishman.

The focus, in the first issue, was Harrington's character and life. Rutledge referred explicitly to the accounts of Harrington's life by John Toland and Anthony Wood, and his version is heavily dependent on theirs. Rutledge was particularly keen to describe, and stress the importance of, Harrington's travels in Europe. Perhaps projecting the inspiration behind his own trips

---

[19] On *Calypso* see the article by P. Peyronnet in J. Sgard, *Dictionnaire des journaux, 1600–1789*, Paris–Oxford 1991, 195.
[20] Ibid.
[21] [Rutledge], *Calypso*, iii. 313–60.
[22] Ibid. iii. 217–25.
[23] 'M. Mably est fait pour la bien sentir, & pour reconnoître que le génie de l'infortuné Harrington a bâti d'une main intrépide, & offert la base, sur laquelle tout Législateur Philosophe, de quelque Gouvernement que ce soit, peut solidement poser & élever l'Edifice de la constitution démocratique la plus égale & la plus durable': ibid. iii. 221.

onto his subject, he claimed that Harrington had decided to visit Europe in order to observe 'men and their manners'.[24] In Rutledge's view, Harrington's European tour had profoundly influenced his thought and left its mark on his future writings. Rutledge had no doubt that in Holland, the first stop on his trip, Harrington would have been amazed by the speed at which power and prosperity had emerged once that nation had gained its liberty. Moreover, Rutledge suggested that it was probably this experience that led Harrington to meditate on subjects such as the art of legislators and the fundamental principles and necessary effects of diverse constitutions.[25] Rutledge also mentioned Harrington's stay in France, and suggested that as well as learning the French language Harrington had spent his time gathering notes on French manners and politics. In Italy, Rutledge noted, it was Venice that had impressed Harrington, just as it had impressed the young Rutledge during his visit. Rutledge claimed that Harrington 'preferred Venice out of all the places he visited, to the extent that he had not ceased subsequently to give preference to the original and purely democratic constitution of this republic over all those of the universe',[26] and he urged all those who could to read Harrington's ideas on Venice for themselves. It was also whilst in Italy, according to Rutledge, that Harrington became familiar with the works of Donato Giannotti and Machiavelli, 'the masters of all those who wish to make a study of the great art of governing people'.[27] Having described Harrington's European tour in some detail, Rutledge then briefly discussed his life from his return to England until the publication of *Oceana* in 1656.

In the second issue of *Calypso* that was devoted to Harrington, Rutledge turned his attention towards *Oceana* itself. He began by describing the structure of the work. He referred to the two preliminary discourses, the section entitled 'The council of legislators', 'The model of the commonwealth of Oceana' and 'The corollary'. Despite acknowledging that it was the main body of the work, Rutledge did not seem interested in 'The model of the commonwealth of Oceana'. This was presumably partly because, as Rutledge himself noted, it was not merely an imaginary republic but was firmly modelled on England. Rather, Rutledge's interest lay in the preliminaries of the work and, in particular, Harrington's account of the causes of the English civil war and the establishment of the English republic. Harrington had shown, Rutledge claimed, that the civil war had arisen in England not because of the actions or faults of those involved but rather due to long-term changes. In particular, he emphasised the role played by the shift in the

24 'les hommes & leurs moeurs': ibid. iii. 315.
25 Ibid. iii. 316.
26 'préféra le séjour de Venise à tout autre, ainsi qu'il n'a point cessé après, de donner la preference, à la constitution originelle & purement démocratique de cette République sur toutes celles de l'univers': ibid. iii. 319.
27 'les maîtres de tous ceux qui veulent se faire une étude du grand art de gouverner les Peuples': ibid. iii. 320.

balance of property (ownership of land) in England towards the commons since the reign of Henry VII. Rutledge praised the hypothesis that empire follows the balance of property and insisted that the discovery could justly be attributed to Harrington.[28] Rutledge then went on to detail some of the key features of Harrington's two preliminary discourses. In the first, which focused on ancient prudence, Rutledge highlighted, among other things, the distinction between direct and foreign empire, the agrarian law, equality, elections and the rotation of office. He hailed Harrington as the first writer to have considered these important matters in any detail. In relation to the second discourse, the focus of which was modern prudence, Rutledge again referred to Harrington's account of the causes of the English civil war and the origins of the English republic: 'or rather of the anarchy to which this name was prostituted under Cromwell'.[29] Finally, he described the chapter of Harrington's book entitled 'The council of legislators'. He seemed impressed by Harrington's idea of looking back at the theory and practice of ancient and modern legislators and examining popular governments in history as a basis on which to develop an ideal model of government. Having described *Oceana* itself, Rutledge also considered the attempts made to put Harrington's ideas into practice. He referred to the Rota Club and to Harrington's friend and fellow republican Henry Neville, who had sought to introduce a Harringtonian form of government in seventeenth-century England.[30] Rutledge's two-part discussion of Harrington ended with a detailed account of Harrington's life following the restoration of the monarchy in 1660, which included a translation of the interrogation of Harrington by Lord Lauderdale, the Chevalier Carteret and Edward Walker as it had appeared in Toland's edition of Harrington's works.

A year later, in 1786, Rutledge published another work, entitled *Éloge de Montesquieu*, in which he referred back to the April issues of *Calypso* and in which he again stressed the importance of Harrington's ideas. The *Éloge* was a somewhat late response to an essay competition sponsored by the Academy of Bordeaux. While many elegies to Montesquieu had been produced, both in response to this competition and otherwise, Rutledge's version was certainly unique. Its originality lay in the parallel that Rutledge drew between Montesquieu and Harrington.

Rutledge described Montesquieu as a man of genius, on the grounds that he had created 'la politique de nouveau' at a time when the politics of philosophers had faded from memory and had been replaced by the systematic atrocities of tyranny.[31] He suggested that in rejecting prejudice in favour of reason Montesquieu was influenced by Holland and England, which were the most advanced and civilised nations of his time. Rutledge then turned explic-

---

[28] Ibid. iii. 329.
[29] 'ou plutôt de l'anarchie à laquelle ce nom fut prostitué sous Cromwel': ibid. iii. 341.
[30] On the Rota Club see Russell Smith, *Harrington and his* Oceana, 101–9.
[31] [J. J. Rutledge], *Éloge de Montesquieu*, London 1786, 4.

itly to Harrington, noting that he – like Montesquieu – had aimed at crushing despotism and had brought politics to a nation that had previously known only poetry and literature.[32] Not only did Rutledge draw out similarities between the ideas of these two political writers, but he went so far as to suggest, despite Montesquieu's brief and rather scathing treatment of Harrington in *The spirit of the laws*, that Montesquieu greatly admired Harrington and that the works of the Frenchman represented the perfect development of the ideas of his English predecessor.[33] Moreover, Rutledge implied that both writers were republicans at heart, despite, particularly in the case of Montesquieu, being limited and restrained by the context in which they were writing. Rutledge did, however, acknowledge one important difference between their ideas. Montesquieu had spoken of there being three simple forms of government (republics, monarchies and despotisms), on which all mixed systems were based. By contrast, Harrington had identified just two distinct forms: that in which the nation is ruled by a master and that in which the nation rules itself. However, Rutledge insisted that this difference was more due to circumstances than ideas. Harrington had demonstrated that monarchical government, as it was commonly defined

> Is only a matter of reason, an imposing chimera, which seeks to abuse the people and of which the hearts and minds of good Princes persuade themselves, so to speak, out of habit and without realising the reality, while their perfidious agents each day make manifest the imposture.[34]

While Rutledge acknowledged that Montesquieu never spoke in this language, he insisted that he had upheld the same ideas.

Thus it is evident that, as early as the mid-1780s, Rutledge knew of Harrington and his works and believed them worthy of consideration by the French. Following the outbreak of Revolution, Rutledge's works on Harrington were read and were presented as having contemporary relevance. In 1789 the *abbé* François Jean Philibert Aubert de Vitry published a work entitled *Jean Jacques Rousseau à l'assemblée nationale* in which he referred to Rutledge and, in particular, to his works on Harrington.[35] Aubert de Vitry claimed that Rutledge had been working, for over twenty years, on a book that was to be based on the ideas of Harrington, and he insisted:

32 Ibid. 19.
33 Montesquieu's references to Harrington appear in Montesquieu, *The spirit of the laws*, 166, 618.
34 'n'est qu'un être de raison, une chimere imposante qui sert à abuser les peuples, & dont les coeurs & les esprits des bons Princes se persuadent eux-mêmes, pour ainsi dire par habitude & sans s'en appercevoir, la réalité, tandis que leur agens perfides, chaque jour, en manifestent l'imposture: [Rutledge], *Éloge de Montesquieu*, 21.
35 On Aubert de Vitry and his work see Barny, *L'Éclatement révolutionnaire du Rousseauisme*, 9–27; Sonenscher, 'The nation's debt', 296–8.

It will surely not be long in appearing, since we are at last sufficiently mature to read it, since we are happily disposed to profit from the ideas [and] the *sublime plan* of the friend of the unfortunate Charles I, who will always be regarded, by those who know him, as one of the most virtuous political writers because he always lived his life according to his principles.[36]

Aubert de Vitry went on to advise his readers to read several of Rutledge's existing works including *Calypso* and *Éloge de Montesquieu*.

The 'boulanger affair'

Towards the end of the 1780s Rutledge began to shift the focus of his attentions from literature to politics and from writing to action. His last novel *Alphonsine ou les dangers du grand monde* appeared in 1789.[37] In the same year he was drawn into the 'boulanger affair', which involved him in a bitter argument with Jacques Necker, resulted in his imprisonment and ultimately led him into association with the Cordeliers.

In February 1789, in the context of a provisioning crisis in Paris, Rutledge wrote a *Mémoire* on behalf of the city's bakers.[38] The bakers of Paris were facing a fine because they had allegedly tried to raise the price of the bread they produced. Their situation was brought to Rutledge's attention by one of their number, Sulpice Garin. He met Rutledge in early 1789 and expressed his own anger and that of his colleagues at 'a few individuals' who had been monopolising the grain trade within the city for some time. In particular he complained of two brothers Eloi-Louis and Dominique-César Leleu who ran the *moulins de Corbeil* near Paris.[39] Knowing that Rutledge himself had an interest in the provisioning issue, and that he was experienced at writing for the public, Garin put a proposal to Rutledge: that he take on the defence of

---

[36] 'Il ne tardera sûrement pas à paroître, puisqu'enfin nous sommes mûrs pour le lire, puisque nous sommes heureusement disposés pour mettre à profit les idées, le *plan sublime* de l'ami de l'infortuné Charles Ier, qui sera toujours regardé, par ceux qui le connoîtront, comme un des plus vertueux écrivains politiques, parce qu'il fut toujours confirmer sa vie à ses principes': [F. J. P. Aubert de Vitry], *Jean Jacques Rousseau à l'assemblée nationale*, Paris 1789, 232.

[37] A further novel, *Mémoires de Julie de* *, may have been by Rutledge. It appeared in 1790.

[38] [J. J. Rutledge], *Mémoire pour la communauté des maîtres boulangers de la ville et faubourgs de Paris*, Paris 1789. The unpublished material on this affair can be found in AN, Dossier Y10504. See also Las Vergnas, *Le Chevalier Rutlidge*, 183–95, and S. L. Kaplan, *The bakers of Paris and the bread question, 1700–1775*, Durham, NC 1996, 13, 425, 558.

[39] The mills at Corbeil had been used for provisioning the capital for some time. In 1765 a contract was drawn up between the government and the then owner of the mills which stated that the latter would buy grain and mill it as necessary to be released for making bread in times of shortage. In return, the owner of the mills would receive 2% on all grain purchases. The position was apparently exploited by the mill owners from the outset: Jarrett, *The begetters of revolution*, 100.

the community of master bakers against the monopolisers.[40] Rutledge accepted. In his *Mémoire* Rutledge explained that the bakers had been forced into their current practices to avoid personal ruin. The real blame, he argued, lay with the Leleu company, which had been placing a high price on basic foodstuffs and had also sought to limit sales and deliveries to further their own interests. In conclusion Rutledge insisted 'that this company alone could be, as indeed it is, the true and sole monopoliser and monopolist'.[41] Rutledge urged the bakers to sign a register requesting government assistance.

Rutledge followed up this *Mémoire* with a second, which appeared in the summer and was read to the *bureau des subsistances* of the National Assembly.[42] It had a bigger impact than the first *Mémoire* and Rutledge gained the support of the bureau. He also received a letter from Necker welcoming his demands on behalf of the bakers and asking for his assistance in drawing up legislation on the matter of provisioning the capital that could be offered to the National Assembly.[43]

In response to Rutledge's accusations, the Leleu brothers produced two pamphlets of their own: *Compte rendu au public par les sieurs Eloi-Louis & Dominique-César Leleu*, and *Obsérvations des sieurs Eloy-Louis and Dominique-César Leleu*.[44] In the former they set out the aims of the *moulins et magasins de Corbeil*. These included maintaining abundance in the markets of Paris, sustaining the price of wheat at a good rate and breaking the power of monopolisers and speculators. They also provided details of their administration of the establishment over the previous fourteen years. In particular they sought to demonstrate, against the accusations of Rutledge, that they had not only fulfilled the tasks required of them, as set out in their treaty with the king of 1774, but that they had done so in a spirit of patriotism and in the interests of the public rather than for their own private gain. In *Obsérvations* they responded directly to Rutledge's *Second Mémoire*, systematically rebutting the various 'errors' of that text, including the alleged existence of a 'compagnie de Corbeil' and the suggestion that they had been exporting grain to make a profit while Paris faced a shortage.

The Leleu brothers had friends in high places. In an extract from the

---

40 Rutledge had been concerned about the distribution of bread since 1779: Peyronnet, 'J. J. Rutledge', 334.

41 'que cette Compagnie seule peut être, comme elle est en effet, la véritable & unique accapareuse & monopoleuse': [Rutledge], *Mémoire pour les boulangers*, 12.

42 Idem, *Second Mémoire pour les maîtres boulangers: lu au bureau des subsistances de l'assemblée nationale par le chevalier Rutledge*, Paris 1789.

43 This work was published in 1790 under the title *Projet d'une législation des subsistances, composée pour M. Necker*, Paris 1790.

44 E. L. Leleu and D. C. Leleu, *Compte rendu au public par les sieurs Eloi-Louis & Dominique-César Leleu, négocians; sur l'établissement des moulins de Corbeil*, Paris 1789, and *Obsérvations des sieurs Eloy-Louis and Dominique-César Leleu, frères, négocians: sur un écrit intitulé: 'Second Mémoire pour les maîtres boulangers: lu au bureau des subsistances de l'assemblée nationale'*, Paris 1789.

Registres du conseil d'état du roi, which the Leleu brothers appended to their *Compte rendu*, the king is said to have sided with the brothers against Rutledge, whose first *Mémoire* he condemned as injurious, calumnious and defamatory. Appended to the *Observations* was a letter from Necker to the Leleu brothers, dated 26 September 1789 (precisely the time when Necker was asking Rutledge for his help), in which he voiced his awareness that they had been subject to attacks and promised that justice would be done.

Perhaps aware of Necker's treachery, Rutledge saw that he was in danger. He did not write anything more on the issue, but the cause was not abandoned. Rutledge's role in attacking the Leleu brothers was taken over by another future member of the Cordeliers Club, Camille Desmoulins. In his *Réplique aux deux mémoires des sieurs Leleu* Desmoulins referred explicitly to Rutledge and presented himself as Rutledge's successor:

> It is the chevalier de Rutlidge, who has written the pamphlet accusing the Leleu brothers for the community of bakers . . . He allows us to take care of his reputation; and without saying any more about the motive behind his very respectful silence, we will continue to prove that he is not a slanderer.[45]

Continuing Rutledge's cause in responding to the *Observations* of the Leleu brothers, Desmoulins set out the 'falsehoods' contained in it. In particular he insisted that, contrary to their claims, they had exported grain from Corbeil, and that in this and other actions they had been acting purely in their own self-interest.

Despite Rutledge's attempt to distance himself from the 'boulanger affair' in the autumn of 1789, he was arrested on the orders of Necker on 2 November. Following his release from prison in January 1790, he produced a whole series of works attacking the director-general of finances.[46] At the same time he approached the Cordeliers District to ask for their support and protection.[47] Although his request was rejected, Rutledge did become associated with various leading figures within the district and, when the club was

[45] 'C'est le chevalier de Rutlidge, qui a écrit pour la communauté des boulangers, le mémoire accusateur des freres Leleu. . . . Il nous permettra de prendre soin de sa réputation; & sans approfondir le motif de son silence trop respectueux, nous allons continuer de prouver qu'il n'étoit point calomniateur': C. Desmoulins, *Réplique aux deux mémoires des sieurs Leleu*, Paris 1789, 12–13.
[46] [J. J. Rutledge], *Vie privée et ministérielle de M. Necker, directeur général des finances, par un citoyen*, Geneva 1790; *Dénonciation sommaire faite au comité des recherches de l'assemblée nationale contre M. Necker, ses complices, fauteurs et adherents*, Paris 1790; and *Procès fait au chevalier Rutledge, baronet, avec les pièces justificatives, et sa correspondence avec M. Necker*, Paris 1790; Rutofle de Lode [J. J. Rutledge], *L'Astuce dévoilé* [sic]: *ou origine des maux de la France perdue, par les manoeuvres du ministre Necker, avec des notes et anecdotes sur son administration*, n.p. 1790; J. J. Rutledge, *Requète du sieur de Rutlidge aux comités des rapports et des recherches, de mandant qu'on pris des mesures pour mettre obstacle à la suite présumable de M. Necker*, 8 Sept. 1790, AN, DXXIXbis 12, no. 130. It was also in 1790 that Rutledge finally published his *Mémoire au roi*, which he had written in 1787.
[47] *Moniteur universel*, iii. 200.

established later that year, he became an influential, though controversial, member.[48] He acted as club secretary for a time and his newspaper *Le Creuset*, which appeared during 1791, has been described as a Cordeliers organ.

Le Creuset

On 3 January 1791 Rutledge began publishing *Le Creuset*. Although all issues of the paper appeared during 1791, this was not the date printed on the title page. Instead, Rutledge adopted the phrase 'l'an deuxieme de la liberté'. This form of reference to 1789 was eventually adopted by the National Assembly, but only in January 1792, a year after Rutledge's newspaper had appeared.[49] The Cordeliers had been referring to 1789 as the year of liberty for some time. Rutledge published *Le Creuset* from his own publishing house (the *imprimerie du Creuset*) at no. 219 rue Saint Martin. It was available from there and from various other offices across the city, including from Rutledge's friend and fellow Cordelier Jean Honoré Dunouy at the Café du Place-Royale, rue des Egoûts.[50]

The full title of the newspaper was *Le Creuset: ouvrage politique et critique*. The meaning of 'le creuset' is almost identical to the English word 'crucible', a melting pot, and by extension a test or trial. Rutledge explained in the first issue that his intention was to provide an impartial and independent analysis of events, day-by-day as they occurred. The newspaper was originally to appear twice weekly (although as the year progressed its appearance became rather erratic). It could be purchased by month, by quarter, or by year (Rutledge evidently did not foresee when he embarked on the project that the newspaper would run for only six months, the last issue appearing on 30 June 1791), and Rutledge appears to have regarded it as a national organ. The price was the same for customers from outside Paris as for those in the city, and postage was included. At several points he explicitly addressed his readers in the provinces.[51] In particular, Rutledge appears to have been keen to inform these provincial readers of events in the capital and of the debates conducted in the National Assembly and in the Jacobin and Cordeliers Clubs. The polemical stance of *Le Creuset* was typical of the Cordeliers Club at the time. The main targets of Rutledge's attack were Bailly (the mayor of

---

48 For an account of Rutledge's rejection by the district see Bougeart, *Les Cordeliers*, 198–9. Rutledge appears on Robertson's list of club members: 'The society of the Cordeliers', 279.

49 Interestingly, the practice had also been employed in England during the 1650s when 1648–9 was referred to as 'the first year of freedom': S. Kelsey, *Inventing a republic: the political culture of the English commonwealth, 1649–1653*, Manchester 1997, 101; Norbrook, *Writing the English republic*, 5.

50 Dunouy is mentioned in this capacity from the third issue (10 Jan. 1791): J. J. Rutledge, *Le Creuset: ouvrage politique et critique*, Paris 1791, i. 64.

51 See, for example, ibid. ii. 128, 142, 165.

Paris), the marquis de Lafayette (commander of the Parisian national guard) and the comte de Mirabeau. While the ostensible purpose of *Le Creuset* may have been to provide an analysis of everyday events for patriots across the country, its underlying aim was to put the case for the establishment of democratic government in France. In order both to justify his case, and to show how a democracy could be put into practice in France, Rutledge appealed to the ideas of Harrington.

Rutledge did not acknowledge in *Le Creuset* that he was drawing on Harrington's works.[52] Yet there can be no doubt, for anyone familiar with Harrington's ideas, that he was the major source behind much of the political theory in *Le Creuset*. In the first issue Rutledge adopted Harrington's axiom that political power follows the balance of property. At the beginning of the second issue Rutledge explained that he was going to tell a story which came from the work of 'a great friend of liberty and of social justice, who is no longer known'.[53] There followed Harrington's story from *Oceana* of the two girls dividing a cake: the girls realise that the only way for them to divide the cake they have been given to share fairly, is for one of them to cut it in two and for the other to choose which half she wants. Harrington had applied this analogy to politics, to emphasise the importance of separating discussion of policy from decision-making, and Rutledge picked up on it for the same purpose. Finally, beginning in the fifth issue of *Le Creuset*, without admitting that the ideas were not his own, Rutledge embarked on a translation of the first six chapters of Harrington's *A system of politics*. In addition to drawing on the works and ideas of Harrington himself, Rutledge also demonstrated a keen interest in the sources that had been central to Harrington's own thought, in particular the works of Machiavelli and the model of the republic of Venice.

That Rutledge chose to draw on Harrington in order to promote democracy is not entirely surprising. While Harrington favoured a mixed over a purely democratic government, and while he accepted the aristocratic idea of superiority of merit being linked to wealth and birth, there were various aspects of his thought that were overtly democratic. These included the more equal distribution of land that would follow from the imposition of an agrarian law, low property qualifications for citizenship and an emphasis on local politics – all of which would provide the opportunity for a large proportion of the population to participate in the government. Rutledge's preference, at least at this stage, for *A system of politics*, over the better-known *Oceana*, was probably due to the differences in structure between the two works. Where *Oceana* was designed as a constitutional model for mid

---

[52] Harrington's name is mentioned ibid. ii. 13, where he is presented as a legislator alongside Lycurgus and Solon. However, no reference is made here to the use of his ideas in earlier issues of the journal.

[53] 'un grand ami de la liberté et de la justice sociale, que vous ne connoissez pas encore': ibid. i. 25.

seventeenth-century England, *A system of politics* was written in the form of political aphorisms, which made it much easier for particular points to be picked up and applied to other circumstances.

Land

In the first issue of *Le Creuset* Rutledge addressed the question of the causes of the recent revolution in France: 'What have been the radical and permanent causes, and what are the accessory and accidental causes, which have provoked, and which have effectively necessitated, the revolution?'.[54] Rather than simply launching into a reply, he explained that he believed it necessary to return to basic principles in order that his audience should fully comprehend his argument. He thus began by explaining that all reciprocal relations of command and obedience share a single foundation. That foundation is the ability to procure subsistence. One individual will only obey another out of need, and therefore an individual will only be able to command others successfully if he or she possesses the materials of their natural or moral needs, control of which depends upon the possession of land:

> But this is the first of these two orders of needs, which form the primitive connection that determines all political subordination: authority and subjection proceed therefore from *subsistence*.

> The earth, which produces subsistence, is at the same time the root and the base of authority. The earth supports the cause and the force of all authority. The modes of dividing the earth between the constituent parties . . . become, by a material consequence, the productive causes of the division of power between constituent members.[55]

While Rutledge did not reveal the Harringtonian origins of this theory in *Le Creuset*, he had done so in his earlier journal *Calypso*:

> That *authority*, or coercive power, always follows the . . . balance of national property, whether in a single, a small number, or a multitude of hands; is a

[54] 'Quelles ont été les causes radicales et permanentes, et quelles sont les causes accessoires et accidentelles, qui ont du provoquer, et qui ont effectivement nécessité la révolution?', ibid. i. 10.
[55] 'Mais ce sont ceux du premier de ces deux ordres de besoins, qui forment le lien primitif qui détermine toute subordination politique: empire et sujétion procedent donc de *subsistance*. / La terre qui produit la subsistance, est en meme-temps la racine et la bâse de l'empire. La terre étant l'appui de la cause et de la force de tout empire: les modes du partage de la terre entre les parties constituantes de tout empire, deviennent, par une conséquence matérielle, les causes productrices de la répartition de la puissance entre les membres constituans, et dans l'ensemble de chaque empire': ibid. i. 11–12.

truth that is fundamental and relevant to Politics. The discovery of it can be justly attributed to the celebrated Harrington.[56]

On the basis of this principle Rutledge suggested, again following Harrington, that the establishment of different forms of government – monarchy, aristocracy and democracy – was dependent on the ownership of the means of subsistence within the state. The economic underpinning of democracy was described by him thus:

> Finally, if for the two preceding hypotheses [those that described the economic foundations of monarchy and aristocracy] one substitutes that of the inhabitants of a region, numbering many millions, among whom all, or at least the majority, are each in possession of some portion of its productive surface – above all with the condition that there can never be between their respective properties a preponderant inequality . . . the two necessities, *material* and *moral*, establish in this last region democracy.[57]

Having established his Harringtonian principles, Rutledge went on to apply those principles to French history, just as Harrington had applied them to the history of England.

In *Oceana*, Harrington had argued that the first step towards civil war in England had been the actions of Panurgus (Henry VII) who, in seeking to abate the power of the nobility and strengthen that of the monarchy, had allowed land, and consequently power, to fall into the hands of the people. This move, combined with that accomplished by Panurgus' successor Coraunus (Henry VIII), which brought a similar shift of ecclesiastical power into popular hands, meant that by the end of the sixteenth century the balance of power in England had shifted. Landed power was now dominated not by the nobility, as was natural in a 'tempered monarchy', but by the people. Thus, Harrington presented the English civil war of the mid-seventeenth century as an inevitable attempt to bring political power into line with the new balance of landed property.

In Rutledge's parallel (though less detailed) account of French history Cardinal Richelieu took on the role of Harrington's Panurgus:

> Crushed over the centuries by the nobles, on the part of whom oppression was more direct and as a result more strongly felt, the people imagined justice to be

---

[56] 'Que l'*Empire*, ou puissance coactive, suive toujours le sort de la balance de la propriété Nationale, soit dans une seule, un petit nombre, ou une multitude de mains; c'est une vérité fondamentale & sensible de la Politique, dont la découverte nous paroît justement attribuée au célèbre Harrington': [Rutledge], *Calypso*, iii. 29.

[57] 'Enfin, si aux deux hypoteses précédentes on substitue celle des habitans d'une région, au nombre de plusieurs millions, parmi lesquels tous, au dumoins la plupart, soient chacun en possession de quelque portion de sa surface productive, sur-tout avec la condition qu'il ne puisse jamais y avoir entre leurs propriétés respectives, une inégalité prépondérante; par un effet non moins naturel de toutes les causes productrices du genre et des modifications

on the side of the Monarch. The unfortunates! they believed, as all impoverished people do, the phantom of their hopes mistaking a deceitful consistency for a comforting reality! The despotic agent of the suzerain [Richelieu] sought to profit from this illusion, not in favour of those who had been duped, but against the small number of great vassals whom the predecessors of the Prince had left him to destroy.[58]

On this basis Rutledge concluded that, since Richelieu's time, economic conditions in France had been right for democratic government. Its failure to be implemented, so he claimed, was due to the actions of the ministers of Louis XV and Louis XVI.

On the basis of the connection that he had drawn between the possession of land and the wielding of political power, Harrington had realised that it was not sufficient simply to establish a popular government on the appropriate balance of property. To maintain stability, one also needed to ensure that the balance would not subsequently shift, thereby rendering the government unstable again. Harrington's solution to the problem was to pass an agrarian law, designed to maintain the balance of property appropriate to the form of government. Following his discussion of the connection between the balance of property and the form of government in the first issue of Le Creuset, Rutledge went on to argue for the benefits of an agrarian law.

While a form of agrarian law was advocated by some other writers in late eighteenth-century France, Rutledge's definition and description reveal the influence of Harrington's views on his ideas.[59] Indeed, he drew a clear distinction between this and other proposals of a similar kind:

This . . . doctrine will very probably offend some readers who are quick to alarm themselves at words, rather than seeking to penetrate things. The term agrarian law will awaken in their thoughts, the idea of an exact or almost equal division between all the members of a political society of the productive land or of representative fortunes.[60]

du gouvernement civil parmi les hommes, les deux nécessités, matérielle et morale, établiront dans cette derniere région la démocratie': idem, Le Creuset, i. 13.
58 'Ecrasés depuis des siecles, par les Nobles, de la part de qui l'oppression étoit plus directe, et plus aperçue par conséquent, les peuples se figurerent la justice aux côtés du Monarque. Les infortunés! Ils prenoient, comme tous les misérables, le fantôme à qui leur espoir donnoit une consistance trompeuse, pour une consolante réalité! L'agent despotique du suzerain [Richelieu] sut mettre à profit cette illusion, non pour ceux qui en étoient dupes, mais contre le petit nombre des grand vassaux, que les prédécesseurs du Prince lui avoit laissé à détruire': ibid. i. 17–18.
59 On the theory and practice of an agrarian law in revolutionary France see R. B. Rose, 'The "red scare" of the 1790s: the French Revolution and the "agrarian law"', P&P ciii (1984), 113–30, and P. M. Jones, 'The "agrarian law": schemes for land redistribution during the French Revolution', P&P cxxxiii (1991), 93–133.
60 'Cet échantillon de doctrine blessera très vraisemblablement quelques lecteurs plus prompts à s'allarmer des mots, qu'attentifs à se pénétrer des choses: celui de loi agraire réveillera dans leur pensée, l'idée d'un partage exactement ou à peu près égal, entre tous les

Given this attitude, Rutledge found himself compelled to explain more precisely his own understanding of an agrarian law:

> The only [kind of] agrarian law that is practicable and that can be envisaged as socially effective, will be that which limits itself to prohibiting inequalities in property so large that the citizen who invests in it, or the small number of those who seize hold of it, can make the laws for all the others.[61]

Rutledge linked the idea of an agrarian law to that of a constitution, and thus laid the basis for his attempt to persuade the National Assembly to institute an agrarian law. He welcomed their redistribution of clerical property, which had taken place in November 1789; and he justified this redistribution as the foundation of a new agrarian law:

> We have established as a principle elsewhere, that the lack of an agrarian law leads to the *absence and deprivation of any constitution.*
>
> Have legislators ever had such a beautiful chance, to pose with discernment and with the assurance of a crown of immortal glory, the bases of a truly profitable *agrarian law*, on the debris of tyrannic feudalism [and] clericalism?[62]

For Rutledge the agrarian law provided a welcome alternative to the economic proposals of other revolutionaries and, in particular, to the *assignat* scheme of Clavière. That scheme, which was designed to solve the financial crisis in which the French nation found itself, was born of Clavière's belief that republican government needed to be made compatible with commercial society.[63] Clavière's *assignat* scheme was adopted by the National Assembly and *assignats* were recognised as currency from April 1790.

Rutledge explicitly opposed Clavière's *assignat* system and he criticised various aspects of it in *Le Creuset*.[64] In particular, he expressed concern that under Clavière's system the public treasury still remained in the hands of the

---

membres d'une société politique, de la surface productive ou des fortunes représentatives': Rutledge, *Le Creuset*, i. 14.

[61] 'La seule loi agraire, qui soit praticable et qui puisse être envisagée comme efficacement sociale, ne sera jamais que celle qui se bornera a proscrire dans les propriétés, les inégalités assez grandes pour que le citoyen qui en seroit investi, ou le petit nombre de ceux qui s'en seroient emparés, pussent faire la loi à tous les autres': ibid. i. 14–15.

[62] 'Point de loi agraire, avons-nous mis en principe ailleurs, *absence et privation de toute constitution.* / Jamais législateurs eurent-ils plus beau jeu, pour poser avec discernement et avec l'assurance d'une couronne de gloire immortelle, les bases d'une *loi agraire*, réellement salutaire, sur les débris de la tyrannique féodalité cléricale?': ibid. i. 147.

[63] See Sonenscher, 'Republicanism', 282–8. On the financial crisis and the role it played in determining events see also Sonenscher, 'The nation's debt', 64–103, 267–325; Ramaswamy, 'Reconstituting the "liberty of the ancients" '.

[64] Rutledge, *Le Creuset*, i. 158–9, 186–7, 402–5, 490; ii. 110. See also [J. J. Rutledge], *Rappel des assignats à leur véritable origine: où démonstration d'un plagiat dangereux du premier ministre et comité des finances*, Paris 1790.

executive.[65] He was also worried about the implications of a system of paper money, not least because the value of the *assignats* would fluctuate and might be discredited as the number of them circulating multiplied.[66] For this reason he presented the *assignat* system as simply the revival of the sort of policy, associated with the name of John Law, that had been discredited earlier in the century: 'To monopolise money, to substitute for it in circulation a paper which discredits itself as it multiplies, is nothing but to revive the practices of Law.'[67] In particular, Rutledge was concerned about the threat the *assignat* scheme posed to a fair distribution of land. Addressing the National Assembly, Rutledge complained:

> you have been inconsistent in making *assignats* which are forced and without order! You have failed to establish laws according to which the citizens could possess, and beyond which none of them could invade, a portion of the common *agricultural* land necessary or harmful to another.[68]

According to Jean François de La Harpe, Rutledge was ridiculed in the Jacobin Club for having spoken of an agrarian law in their midst.[69] It was probably for this reason that Rutledge turned to the alternative system of a land bank.[70]

Rutledge had first explored the idea of a land bank in his *Essais politiques* of 1777.[71] In that work he advocated both economic and political reform. The establishment of a land bank was to be accompanied by a more popular form of government – based on merit rather than property. By these means, he insisted, inequality could be reduced and the French economy brought up to

65 Idem, *Le Creuset*, i. 159.
66 Ibid. i. 158, 187.
67 'Accaparer l'argent, y substituer dans la circulation un papier qui se discrédite à mesure qu'il se multiplie, n'est autre chose que, rappeler l'opération de Law': ibid. i. 186–7. Later in *Le Creuset* (i. 402) Rutledge described the invention of forced *assignats* as a nasty idea borrowed from Necker and again drew a parallel with John Law: 'genius not less but incomparably more disastrous than that of the Scot Law' ('génie non moins incomparablement plus funeste que celui de l'Ecossois Law'). For an account of Law's life and works see A. Murphy, *John Law: economic theorist and policy maker*, Oxford 1997.
68 'vous avez eu l'inconséquence de faire des assignats forcés & sans ordre! Vous avez omis d'établir les loix suivant lesquelles les citoyens pourroient posséder, & au-delà desquelles aucun d'entre-eux ne pourroit envahir une portion, nécessaire ou nuisable à autrui, du domaine, *agraire* commun': Rutledge, *Le Creuset*, i. 490.
69 Aulard, *The French Revolution*, i. 228.
70 Though Rutledge was critical of Law in *Le Creuset*, Law himself had advocated the idea of a land bank in the early eighteenth century, prior to his time as director-general of French finances: *John Law's 'Essay on a land bank'*, ed. A. Murphy, Dublin 1994. Even Law was not the first to advocate a land bank. Similar schemes had been proposed in England during the 1690s: D. Rubini, 'Politics and the battle for the banks, 1688–1697', *EHR* lxxxv (1970), 693–714. There is, however, no evidence that Rutledge knew of the earlier land bank proposals.
71 M. R. C. B. [J. J. Rutledge], *Essais politiques sur l'état actuel de quelques puissances*, London [Geneva] 1777. On this subject I am indebted to Michael Sonenscher.

the standard of the English: 'it will cause the subdivision, it will multiply and enrich with more redivision, the agricultural class and, as an indirect consequence, those who are accessories to it – that is to say the whole body politic of which it is the supporter and the nanny'.[72]

Following the outbreak of the French Revolution, Rutledge saw an opportunity for the implementation of his ideas for political and economic reform. On the economic side he supported the proposal for a land bank drawn up by Jacques Ferrières.[73]

Jacques Annibal Ferrières, the author of *Plan d'un nouveau genre de banque nationale et territoriale*, was a merchant (*négociant*) by trade who had moved from Lyon to Paris at the beginning of the Revolution. Following his arrival in the capital, he presented his plan for a territorial bank to the National Assembly for consideration. It was said to be the fruit of eighteen years of study and preparation. The project was explicitly designed as a solution to the financial problems faced by France at that time. Ferrières's proposal was firmly grounded in land. It thus presented an alternative to speculative proposals and to the *assignat* solution that had been adopted by the National Assembly. Basing his ideas on a system that already existed in Lyon, Ferrières proposed the creation of a treasury (*caisse*) in every department of the nation, with a general treasury in Paris. Any landowner (whether a collective body or an individual) would be able to mortgage his property at one of these treasuries in exchange for a written contract. The contract could then either be kept by the landowner, for reimbursement at a future date, or be exchanged, circulating throughout France and even abroad like any other negotiable good. A sign (letter or number) known only to the borrower and administrators would guarantee the property. The interest, to be set at 4 per cent, would be divided between the administration of the system (1.5 per cent) and the national treasury (2.5 per cent), the latter being used to pay off the national debt. By being based on land rather than paper or fiction, Ferrières claimed, the system would guarantee the value of the contracts and they would not therefore be subject to the usual fluctuations.

On 27 March 1790 the plan was presented to the National Assembly by one of its number Jérôme Pétion. A lively discussion ensued and it was eventually decreed that the committees of finance and of agriculture and commerce should each name six members to examine the plan; its author should be available to these commissioners to answer questions; and the plan

---

[72] 'elle en causera la subdivision; elle multipliera & enrichira, avec plus de répartition, la classe agricole, & par contre-coup, celles qui lui sont accessoires, c'est-à-dire tout le corps politique dont elle est le soutien et la nourrice': ibid. 125.

[73] J. A. Ferrières, *Plan d'un nouveau genre de banque nationale et territoriale*, Paris 1789. For Rutledge's references to the territorial bank plan of Ferrières in *Le Creuset* see i. 318–20, 403; ii. 456. Rutledge also discussed the plan in *Rappel des assignats*. In the latter he referred to an earlier work of his entitled *Démonstration rigoureuse de la base du plan de la banque territoriale de M. de Ferrières*. Unfortunately I have been unable to locate a copy of this work.

should be published and distributed.[74] In *Rappel des assignats* Rutledge was critical of most of the members of the commission and described their report as 'arbitrary and dubious'.[75] The same year he published another work, *Sommaire d'une discussion importante*, in which he addressed the opposition that had been voiced against Ferrières's plan and against his own defence of it.[76] Rutledge began by criticising Pétion for not trying hard enough to get Ferrières's proposals accepted. Indeed Pétion, Rutledge noted, had been converted to Clavière's *assignat* system. Rutledge then went on to deal explicitly with the objections of three opponents of Ferrières's system.

Following the unfavourable report little more was heard of Ferrières's plan until the summer of 1791, when Rutledge was one of the commissioners named by the Cordeliers Club to examine it.[77] In the meeting of 30 June the commissioners offered their report, in which they praised the plan in extravagant terms. For Rutledge, at least, Ferrières's territorial bank offered the ideal solution to the recent financial troubles. More important, it provided an alternative to the unpopular measure of an agrarian law that would, none the less, reduce inequality in land ownership and secure the balance of property – thus making it possible to bring Harringtonian ideas into play in eighteenth-century France.

Democracy

If the agrarian law/land bank provided the central plank of Rutlidge's economic proposals, it was democratic government that was at the heart of his political system. Central to Rutlidge's conception of democracy was his belief in the equality of all citizens and their right to participate in both the military and the political functions of the state. On these grounds he, like his fellow Cordeliers, criticised the National Assembly's adoption of the distinction between active and passive citizens.[78]

The military aspect of citizenship was at the forefront of debates during the spring of 1791, as the National Assembly discussed the composition and organisation of the national guard, an issue that the Cordeliers Club generally, and Rutledge in particular, engaged with fully. On 22 March Rutledge included in *Le Creuset* a copy of a Cordeliers motion opposing the exclusion of passive citizens from the national guard. He went on in issues 29 and 30 of

---

74 A report of the ensuing discussion can be found in *Moniteur universel*, iii. 719–20.

75 'arbitraire et louche': [Rutledge], *Rappel des assignats*, 6.

76 Idem, *Sommaire d'une discussion importante (relative au plan de banque territoriale du modeste M. de Ferrières)*, [Paris] 1790.

77 For a discussion of the report of the commissioners selected by the Cordeliers Club to examine M. Ferrières's plan see Momoro, *Journal du club*, 27–8.

78 Active citizens were to enjoy both civil and political rights whereas passive citizens (including all women and children as well as poorer men) were only to be granted civil rights.

Le Creuset, which appeared in mid-April, to address the discussions of the *comité militaire* on this subject. He began by criticising the members of the committee and by suggesting that they read and took note of what he had to say.[79] He then proceeded by citing principles drawn from Machiavelli's *Arte de la guerra* (one of the sources on which Harrington himself had drawn). Rutledge used Machiavelli's ideas to propose that a militia composed of all citizens should form the basis of military defence in a popular state.

Despite the decision of the *comité militaire* of 28 April 1791 to exclude passive citizens from the national guard, the Cordeliers continued to call for the establishment of a full citizen army. That idea was voiced in a speech given by Réné Girardin to the Cordeliers Club on 29 May 1791: 'Our army is not just one hundred, two hundred, or three hundred thousand men; it is the whole nation capable of bearing arms, and making of its exercises the spectacle and the recreation of its fêtes.' Following the speech, the same point was endorsed by the club as a whole: 'consequently, among a free people, the public force must be nothing but the whole nation armed, for the defence of its territory and its liberty'.[80] Moreover, Rutledge was named as one of four Cordeliers commissioners who were to present Girardin's speech, and the club's opinions on it, to the president of the National Assembly; and it was Rutledge who was responsible, through his *imprimerie du Creuset*, for publishing the speech. A month later, in the Cordeliers Club, Rutledge responded to the appeal of a passive citizen who had been refused the right to participate in the auxiliary army because of his status:

> Certainly, those who refuse to admit among the numbers of the defenders of the *patrie*, a citizen who comes to offer himself in a moment when the *patrie* is in danger, commits a double crime: the first against the *patrie*, which has been robbed of a defender; the second against the citizen, who has been deprived of the right to oppose himself to the enemy who attacks his country.[81]

Rutledge not only upheld the right of passive citizens to participate in the military affairs of the state, he also insisted on their right to political participation.

Rutledge was evidently aware of the contemporary view, based on the

---

[79] Rutledge, *Le Creuset*, ii. 41.

[80] 'Notre armée, ce n'est pas cent, deux cens, trois cens mille hommes; c'est toute la nation capable de porter les armes, et faisant de ses exercices le spectacle et la récréation de ses fêtes. . . . il faut par conséquent que chez un peuple libre, la force publique ne soit autre que celle de toute la nation armée pour la seule défense de son territoire et de sa liberté': R. Girardin, *Discours sur l'institution de la force publique, par Réné Girardin, commandant de la guard nationale d'Erménonville, and appended Opinion du club des Cordeliers*, Paris [1791], 10, 1.

[81] 'Certainement, celui qui refuse d'admettre au nombre des défenseurs de la patrie, un citoyen qui vient s'offrir dans un moment où elle est en danger, commet un double crime; l'un envers la patrie, à laquelle il enlève un défenseur; l'autre, envers le citoyen, qu'il prive du droit de s'opposer à l'ennemi qui attaque son pays': quoted in Momoro, *Journal du club*, 13–14.

opinions of Montesquieu and Rousseau, that popular participation in politics would be impossible in the large nations of the modern world.[82] He addressed the reasons given by them and drew on Harringtonian ideas to provide solutions, showing how democratic government could, and should, be established in late eighteenth-century France.

Harrington had himself acknowledged the difficulty of building a democracy in a large state. In A *system of politics* he explained:

> 22. The ultimate result in the whole body of the people, if the commonwealth be of any considerable extent, is altogether impracticable; and if the ultimate result be but in a part of the people, the rest are not in liberty, nor is the government democracy.[83]

In his translation of Harrington's text Rutledge echoed this idea, bringing it up to date with a reference to Montesquieu:

> XIX The exercise of supreme executive power, residing in the body of the nation, has often, at first glance, appeared impractical. This is what made Montesquieu, and many others before him, believe democratic forms and institutions to be irreconcilable with a large population and a vast area.
>
> One can easily admit with these writers, that if the supreme deliberative power belongs only to a part of a large people, the rest cease in effect to be free; and consequently the government will not truly be democratic.[84]

However, Rutledge was unwilling simply to accept this pessimistic view. Instead, he proposed the Harringtonian alternative solution as set out in the subsequent aphorism:

> 23. As a whole army cannot charge at one and the same time, yet is so ordered that every one in his turn comes up to give the charge of the whole army; so, though the whole people cannot give the result at one and the same, yet may they be so ordered that every one in his turn may come up to give the result of the whole people.[85]

Rutledge's translation read:

> XX In truth, it is not possible for an immense army to charge at the enemy at once; but it is easy to imagine that this immense army can be organised in such

---

82 For the views of Montesquieu and Rousseau on this issue see chapter 1 above.

83 *Political works of James Harrington*, 842.

84 'XIX. L'exercice du pouvoir exécutif suprême, résidant dans le corps de la nation, souvent, au premier apperçu, a paru impraticable. C'est ce qui a décidé Montesquieu, & beaucoup d'autres avant lui, à croire l'institution des formes démocratiques inconciliable avec une grande population & une vaste étendue. / On conviendroit facilement avec ces publicistes, que si le pouvoir délibératif suprême n'appartenoit qu'à une partie d'un grand peuple, le reste de ce même peuple cesseroit en effet d'etre libre; & par conséquent le gouvernement n'y seroit point réellement démocratique': Rutledge, Le Creuset, i. 293.

85 *Political works of James Harrington*, 842.

a way that each of its divisions, that each of its soldiers, present themselves in turn – whether to attack or to defend.

Similarly, although it is impractical for the whole of a large people, living in a large area, to take part in the exercise of supreme deliberative power all at once, it is however very possible to make all their divisions and each of the individuals participate, by equal and regular turns, and to establish an order of rotation such that general and common legislation can never be enacted unless it has been consecrated by the people as a whole.[86]

Thus, just like Mandar, Rutledge saw the adoption of the practice of rotation as the means by which to solve the problem of instituting a democratic government in a large state.

Rutledge was also concerned, in *Le Creuset*, to tackle the other problem facing modern republics that had been highlighted by Montesquieu and Rousseau. They had both emphasised the need for civic virtue in the population in order for this kind of government to function successfully, yet it was generally agreed that the people of the modern world did not possess the same degree of civic virtue as their ancient predecessors.

Closely following Harrington's discussion of the opposition between reason and the passions, in the 'preliminaries' to *Oceana*, Rutledge argued in the fourth issue of *Le Creuset* that virtue was simply reason in action and that it was essential that government be conducted in accordance with reason. Just as an individual who is guided by reason rather than the passions will be wise, virtuous and at peace within himself, he explained, so a government that is guided by reason, rather than by the passions and interests of its members, will be one in which true authority rules to the benefit and happiness of all.[87] Rutledge also acknowledged that the achievement of this goal was hindered in France by its monarchical past:

Unquestionably, it is of course infinitely easier to bring savages and rustic humans to a state of civilisation, than to lead to it men whose right and natural sense has been obscured by prejudices and whose habits are sullied with the varnish of a brilliant corruption and the polish of principles.[88]

---

[86] 'XX. A la vérité, il n'est point possible qu'une immense armée charge l'ennemi tout à la fois; mais il est aisé de concevoir que cette immense armée peut être disposée de maniere que chacune de ses divisions, que chacun de ses soldats se présente à son tour, soit pour attaquer soit pour défendre. / Pareillement, quoiqu'il soit impraticable que tout un grand peuple, habitué sur de vastes espaces, puisse à la fois prendre part à l'exercice du pouvoir délibératif suprême, il est cependant très possible d'y faire participer, par tours égaux & réguliers, toutes ses divisions &, chacun des individus; & d'établir un ordre de rotation tel, que la législation générale & commune ne puisse jamais émaner, ni se trouver consacrée que par le peuple entier': Rutledge, *Le Creuset*, i. 293–4.

[87] Ibid. i. 65. See also *Political works of James Harrington*, 170.

[88] 'Sans contredit, il est plus aisé infiniment d'amener de sauvages et agrestes humains à un état de civilisation bien entendu, que d'y ramener des hommes en qui le sens droit et naturel se trouve obscurci par des préjugés et dont les habitudes sont entachées du vernis d'une corruption brillante et polie de principes': Rutledge, *Le Creuset*, i. 42.

For many revolutionaries, not least the Brissotins, the main solution to the problem of how to generate civic virtue was education. Many works were produced, and much time spent debating, how the education system should be organised so as to produce virtuous republican citizens. Rutledge certainly seems to have realised the importance of education and in *Le Creuset* he expressed the view that the dangers of corruption were made far worse by the ignorance of the masses.[89] He saw his own activity as a journalist as crucial to the task of educating the ordinary people. Newspapers like *Le Creuset*, he believed, were the ideal vehicles through which to educate the masses, particularly on the subject of politics.

This pedagogical aim is evident throughout *Le Creuset*. In the first issue Rutledge emphasised that he intended to present an independent analysis of the situation and that in order for his readers to make sense of that analysis, and to judge the events for themselves, he would begin by answering some preliminary questions designed to elicit the basic principles behind the contemporary situation and behind politics in general. In the fifth issue of the journal, Rutledge again stressed the importance of education. Here he inserted the first of several chapters from Harrington's *A system of politics*, which he had translated into French. Rutledge suggested that in educating his readers in these basic (Harringtonian) principles he would allow them to see the opposition between some of the recent decrees of their representatives and the features of wise and fair government. Moreover, he saw it as a means of securing citizens against future abuses by their representatives in the National Assembly:

> Reader! I beseech you to sustain your attention. That which I present to you certainly has a metaphysical aspect which is a little off-putting, but think about it and follow me, and I dare to assure you – however little instructed you are in these matters [that are] so important for the happiness of your sort, you will have never read with constancy and with a desire for common happiness the summary of all political doctrines in which I have resolved to initiate you – that none of the representatives to whom you have given your votes will dare any longer to form the project of abusing your confidence and your powers.[90]

Yet, as this quotation suggests, the purpose of education for Rutledge was to remove ignorance – and thus to prevent the representatives from being able to dupe the masses. It was not a means of inculcating civic virtue.

---

[89] Ibid. i. 82.

[90] 'Lecteur! je vous supplie de vouloir bien soutenir votre attention. Ce que je vous présente, a certainement un aspect métaphisique un peu rebutant; mais méditez et suivez moi; et j'ose vous assurer, que quelque peu instruit que vous soyez dans des matieres si importantes pour le bonheur de votre espece, vous n'aurez point lu avec constance et désir de la félicité commune, l'abregé de toute la doctrine politique dans laquelle j'ai resolu de vous initier; qu'aucun des représentans à qui il vous arrivera de donner votre suffrage, n'osera plus former le projet d'abuser de votre confiance ni de vos pouvoirs': ibid. i. 87–8.

As Jonathan Scott has pointed out, Harrington was unusual among seventeenth-century English republicans in denying the possibility (and therefore the necessity) of popular civic virtue.[91] Accepting Hobbes's scepticism about human nature, Harrington had not believed it possible for people to behave completely virtuously without any reference to their self-interest.[92] Thus, instead of simply aiming at the suppression of self-interest, Harrington had sought means of harnessing the self-interest of individuals to the public interest. He therefore adopted a variety of constitutional mechanisms that were designed to make people behave in a virtuous way while they simply pursued their own interests. In particular, Harrington turned to those constitutional mechanisms enshrined in the Venetian system of government.

Harrington had praised the Venetian constitution in *Oceana* and had argued that, in spite of its contemporary reputation as an aristocratic state, the original orders of this republic in relation to its original citizens were the most democratic and popular that had ever existed.[93] Rutledge concurred with this.[94] He claimed that, in relation to the descendants of its original citizens, the constitution of Venice offered the best political model in either ancient or modern experience.[95] Moreover the title which headed Rutledge's discussion of the constitution of Venice in the twenty-first issue of *Le Creuset* was: 'Of Venice and of its truly *democratic* forms.'[96] Venice was in fact the only modern state described by Rutledge as democratic, and he presented it as being modelled on the ancient constitutions of Athens and Sparta: 'By the general survey that we have given of the constitution of Venice, it has been very clear that the government of this republic was modelled on those of Athens and Sparta.'[97] It was for this reason that Rutledge offered his readers a detailed description of the constituent elements of the Venetian constitution, of the relations between those elements and of the functioning of this democratic state.

---

[91] J. Scott, 'Classical republicanism in seventeenth-century England and the Netherlands', in Van Gelderen and Skinner, *Republicanism*, i. 61–81, and 'The rapture of motion: James Harrington's republicanism', in N. Philipson and Q. Skinner (eds), *Political discourse in early modern Britain*, Cambridge 1993, 139–63.

[92] On Harrington's relationship to Hobbes see A. Fukuda, *Sovereignty and the sword: Harrington, Hobbes and mixed government in the English civil war*, Oxford 1997.

[93] *Political works of James Harrington*, 168.

[94] David Wootton has suggested that Harrington was essentially the last writer to uphold the 'myth of Venice' and that after Harrington views of Venice became much more negative, effectively constituting an anti-myth. Rutledge, in speaking favourably of Venice, seems to ignore the conventional views of his own day and to revive those of Harrington: D. Wootton, 'Ulysses bound? Venice and the idea of liberty from Howell to Hume', in Wootton, *Republicanism, liberty, and commercial society*, 341–67.

[95] Rutledge, *Le Creuset*, i. 416–17.

[96] 'De Venise; et de ses formes vraiment *démocratiques*': ibid. i. 416.

[97] 'Par l'apperçu que nous avons donné de la constitution de Vénise, il a été assez sensible que le gouvernement de cette république s'est modelé sur ceux d'Atthénes & de Lacédémone': ibid. i. 441.

The Venetians had introduced practices designed to ensure the subjugation of the passions by reason in the practice of popular government. In relation to the passing of laws the Venetians made use of the principle of separating discussion of legislation from decision-making. Rutledge had already stated the Harringtonian version of this principle at the beginning of the second issue of his newspaper. Harrington, as has been shown, advocated the principle through the story of the two girls dividing a cake. Rutledge followed Harrington in applying this story to political practice: 'To return to the analogy, *cutting the cake* is *debating, proposing, or leading*. Choosing between *the parts*, is *adopting, resolving, giving a verdict*.'[98] Rutledge referred to this analogy in order to demonstrate that this basic principle of democratic or popular politics was the first to have been forgotten by the French following their Revolution. In his translation of the fifth chapter of Harrington's *A system of politics* in issue fifteen, and in his discussion of the Venetian constitution in issues twenty-one, twenty-two and twenty-three, Rutledge presented this principle as good democratic practice. A small body of citizens, the senate, would debate issues and put forward proposals so that the whole citizen body – the grand council in the case of Venice – could simply vote for or against the proposals without any need for discussion on their part. Such a system, Rutledge believed, would allow for the best of both worlds: all citizens would be provided with the opportunity to participate in government – which was crucial to a democratic state – but because they were not all permitted to discuss political issues, the system would avoid the danger of anarchy associated with popular debate. At the same time, a more manageable few would participate in political debate but would be restrained from simply pursuing their own personal interests by the knowledge that their proposals would be submitted to the masses for ratification.

The principle of separating discussion from decision-making was held by Harrington to solve the problem of subjugating the passions to reason in the practice of legislation, but this was not the only task that was to be carried out by the people within a democratic state. They were also required to choose the officials who were to carry out the executive and judicial functions of the state. Here too there were fears of corruption – of the human passions triumphing over reason. But again there was a solution:

> But the only certain means of preventing among men the crimes and the faults that are the result of a partiality arising from their passions, is to bring into political institutions the combination of relations, such that there is always a veritable lack of moral and material power.

> It is Venice where this secret exists; and where it is daily put into practice.[99]

---

98 'Pour revenir à l'apologue, *couper le gâteau* veut dire *débatre, proposer, conduire*. Choisir entre *les parts*, veut dire, *adopter, résoudre, statuer*': ibid. i. 28.

99 'Mais le moyen certain & unique de prévenir parmi les hommes les délits & les fautes qui deviennent les conséquences d'une partialité dont leur passions sont la source, c'est

The solution was the Venetian ballot. Harrington had employed the Venetian ballot in *Oceana*. Rutledge believed the idea to be so crucial, and so relevant to the French nation at this time, that he offered his readers a detailed description of the ballot, complete with an annotated plan of the room in which it was carried out.[100]

The ballot worked by dividing the process of election into two. Electors would be chosen from among the popular assembly by lot. These electors would then nominate candidates for the various available positions, and those candidates would be accepted or rejected by the popular assembly as a whole. By dividing the process into lot and election and by making the election itself secret (votes being cast by placing coloured balls into a ballot box) this system, Rutledge claimed, avoided the problems of corruption and bribery that plagued the alternatives.

Rutledge also thought it necessary for the French to reorganise the central executive powers of the state. He dealt with this problem specifically in issues nine to twelve of *Le Creuset*, which were headed 'Louis, roi des français, au creuset'.[101] Here Rutledge put forward his belief that in order for ministerial corruption to be destroyed for good, it would be necessary for Louis XVI to remove all his existing ministers and to reduce ministerial powers considerably.[102] As an alternative to the existing system he offered his own 'projet de discours pour S. M.' (dated June 1790) in which he proposed the creation of a privy council and an *aulique* council, the latter being divided into councils of religion, administration, military affairs and justice. This system too was modelled on Harrington's ideas as laid out in *Oceana* and *A system of politics*.

It was not only the political system that needed to be brought into line with democracy. Religion too had to be made subject to its demands. As Rousseau had noted, in his discussion of religion at the end of the *Social contract*, the pagan religions of the ancient world had been ideally suited to providing support for popular government, but Christianity was far less suited to that task.[103] As a solution to the problem Rousseau had expounded his idea of a civil religion. Following Rousseau's ideas, the National Assembly had, on 12 July 1790, adopted the civil constitution of the clergy – its conception of post-revolutionary religious organisation. This act was designed to bring the religious order into line with the civil. The Church would be structured along the same lines as the state. It too would be based on constitutional sover-

---

d'apporter, dans les institutions politiques, des combinaisons de rapports, tels, qu'ils soient toujours placés dans une véritable impuissance morale & matérielle d'en écouter les suggestions, leur intention fut-elle même de ne point y résister. / C'est à Venise que ce secrete existe; & qu'il est journellement mis en pratique': ibid. i. 442–3.

[100] Rutledge's annotated plan was taken directly from Toland's 1700 edition of Harrington's *Political works*. See plates 2, 3 at pp. 111, 113 below.

[101] Rutledge, *Le Creuset*, i. 161–234.

[102] As this would suggest, Rutledge did not share the rabid anti-monarchism of some of the other Cordeliers. None the less he did always insist upon democratic government.

[103] Rousseau, *The social contract*, 142–52.

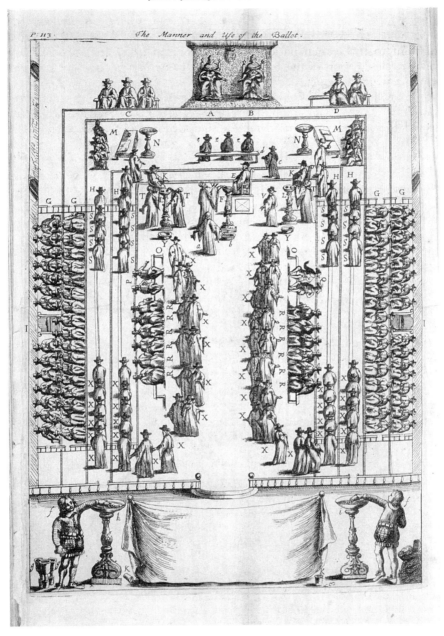

Plate 2. 'The manner and life of the ballot', from J. Toland, *The Oceana of James Harrington, and his other works . . . with an exact account of his life prefix'd by John Toland,* London 1700 [BL, 521.M27].
Reproduced by permission of the British Library.

eignty – deriving its legitimacy from popular election and, consequently, all links with the papacy would be severed. Not surprisingly, this act provoked opposition, which was particularly strong in the winter of 1790 to 1791 when the National Assembly sought to put the act into practice by insisting that all ecclesiastical public officials swear an oath to the civil constitution.

Le Creuset appeared in the midst of the National Assembly's attempt to implement this act, and at a time when counter-revolutionaries were seeking to use the piety and faith of the ordinary people to turn them against the Revolution. Thus it is not surprising that fairly early in his newspaper Rutledge interrupted his preliminary discussions to address the urgent question of religion from a democratic perspective. Responding, so he claimed, to an inquiry from a reader on the role of the clergy, Rutledge set out to answer the question: 'Is it the spirit of religion, or is it only the greed of Churchmen, that is contradicted by the decree that obliges them to preach the civic sermon?'[104] He then translated the two chapters of Harrington's *A system of politics* that he believed to be relevant to this issue, chapter iv, 'Of the form of government', and chapter vi 'Of form in the religious part'.

Rutledge used chapter iv of *A system of politics* to set out the necessity of religion in a state such as France. In that chapter Harrington had argued:

19. The body of a people, not led by the reason of the government, is not a people, but a herd; *not led by the religion of the government, is at an inquiet and an uncomfortable loss in itself*; not disciplined by the conduct of the government, is not an army for defence of itself, but a rout; not directed by the laws of the government, has not any rule of right; and without recourse to the justice or judicatories of the government, has no remedy of wrongs.[105]

Rutledge's translation read:

16. Deprived of the torch of the reason of its government, a nation ceases to be a *nation*: it is then only a confused multitude, a stupid herd.

A nation which is not held back by the principles of religion, is a crowd of beings without modesty and without morality; deprived of order and of discipline, it is from that moment on deprived of preservation and of defence; deprived of a fixed and hierarchic judicial order, it no longer counts within its heart either on the reparation of wrongs, or on the righting of injuries.[106]

104 'Est-ce l'esprit de la religion, ou n'est-ce que la cupidité des *Eglisiers*, qui se sent contredire, par le décret qui les oblige a prêter le serment civique?': Rutledge, *Le Creuset*, i. 105.

105 *Political works of James Harrington*, 838, my italics.

106 '16. Privée du flambeau de la raison de son gouvernement, une nation cesse d'être une *nation*: elle n'est plus qu'une multitude confuse, un troupeau stupide. / *Une nation qui n'est point retenue par des principes de religion, est une cohue d'êtres sans pudeur et sans morale*; privée d'ordre et de discipline, elle est dès-lors privée de préservation et de défense; privée d'un ordre judiciaire fixe et hierarchique, il ne faut plus compter dans son sein ni sur réparation des torts, ni sur redressement des injures': Rutledge, *Le Creuset*, i. 108, my italics.

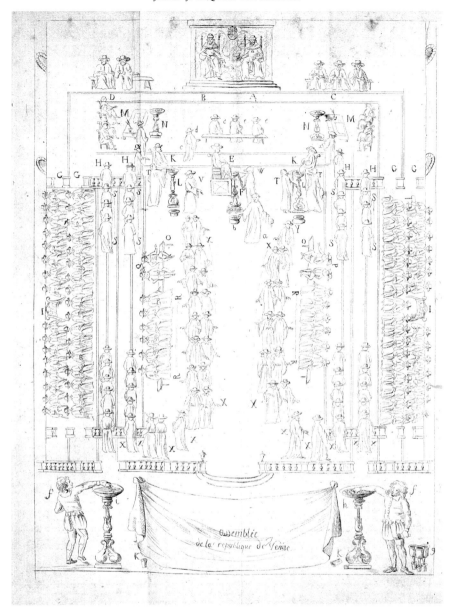

Plate 3. 'Assemblée de la république de Venise', from Jean Jacques Rutledge, *Le Creuset: ouvrage politique et critique*, Paris 1791 [BL, F. 770.1]. Reproduced by permission of the British Library.

Having established the necessity of religion, Rutledge turned to the question of its organisation. Here he drew on chapter vi of *A system of politics*. Translating Harrington, he argued that in a democracy it was essential to guarantee liberty of conscience, since it and civil liberty are inextricably bound together. It was also essential to the maintenance of democratic government, he insisted, that the clergy be salaried rather than landed and that they be elected by the votes of the people. These principles in themselves, Rutledge suggested, revealed the answer to the question on the civil constitution of the clergy: '*It is not in the least the spirit of religion; it is, by contrast, the singular passions of its ministers that are contradicted by the necessity of preaching the civic sermon.*'[107] Rutledge then went on to show that in fact the civil constitution of the primitive Church had been democratic, and he therefore argued that all the National Assembly was doing in introducing the civil constitution of the clergy was returning to the system of the primitive Church prior to the corruption of Roman Catholicism:

> The sermon concerning the civil constitution of the clergy, can be legitimately preached; even *in Christian terms*. This sermon must be offered. All refractory priests [those who rejected the civil constitution and refused to take the oath] will only prove a truth that is already known; that the spirit of Peter, of Paul, of Matthew, these good *citizens* of the primitive *spiritual republic*, has nothing in common with that which animates the *princes* of the modern religious *aristocracy*.[108]

In *Oceana* Harrington had explained that according to ancient prudence the principles of government were two-fold: internal, or the goods of the mind, and external, or the goods of fortune: 'To the goods of mind answers authority; to the goods of fortune, power or empire.'[109] The ultimate aim of a legislator, according to Harrington, was to bring the two into line with each other, so that the government would be supported by the powers of both authority and empire: 'These [the principles of authority] the legislator that can unite in his government with those of fortune, cometh nearest unto the work of God, whose government consisteth of heaven and earth.'[110]

Rutledge's combination of an economic policy based on land (and exercised through either an agrarian law or a land bank) and a political policy centred on a democratic form of government – in which the people would participate in both the military and the political functions of the state – was

---

[107] '*Ce n'est nullement l'esprit de la religion; ce sont tout au contraire, les seules passions de ses ministres, qui se trouvent contredites par la nécessité de prêter le serment civique*': ibid. i. 121.
[108] 'Le serment concernant la constitution civile du clergé, pouvoit être légitimement prêté; *chrétiennement* même, ce serment doit être offert. Tout refractaire ne prouvera qu'une vérité déja connue; c'est que l'esprit de Pierre, de Paul, de Mathias, ces bons *citoyens* de la primitive *république spirituelle*, n'a rien de commun avec celui qui anime les *princes* de la moderne *aristocratie* religieuse': ibid. i. 135.
[109] *Political works of James Harrington*, 163.
[110] Ibid. 169.

his means of uniting the principles of empire with those of authority. More-over, in drawing on Harrington's works, Rutledge found solutions to the problems associated with instituting democratic republican government in the modern world. Like Mandar he adopted the practice of rotation in order to overcome the large size of modern states. In addition, he endorsed the constitutional mechanisms used by Harrington in order to obviate the need for civic virtue among the population.

In many respects Rutledge's use of Harrington in *Le Creuset* corresponds to Harrington's approach in the 'Preliminaries' of *Oceana*. Principles are laid down and justified, and it is left to the reader to derive a constitutional model from them. The next chapter will discuss a work presented to the National Convention in September 1792 by Rutledge's friend and fellow Cordelier, Théodore Le Sueur. That work can be seen as complementary to *Le Creuset*, which had concentrated on the Harrington of the 'Preliminaries', in that it presented the Harrington of the 'Model of the commonwealth of Oceana' to the French public.

4

Théodore Le Sueur and the Model Constitution of 1792

The proclamation of the first French republic 'One and Indivisible' on 25 September 1792 raised two key issues: what should be done with the former king and what form the new constitution should take. The fate of the king was perhaps the more prominent, being debated over the subsequent months and bitterly dividing the revolutionaries. But the question of the constitution was not forgotten. The National Convention had been elected as a constitution-building body, and during late 1792 and early 1793 a number of draft constitutions were presented to it for consideration. One of these was *Idées sur l'espèce de gouvernement populaire qui pourrait convenir à un pays de l'étendue et de la population presumée de la France*, which was presented to Jérôme Pétion (deputy to the Convention and former mayor of Paris) in the autumn of 1792.[1]

Pétion received eighty-four copies of the pamphlet and was instructed that one copy should be presented to the Convention and the rest distributed to the departments of the nation. A copy of the work appears in the *Archives parlementaires* for 17 April 1793, alongside the other constitutions that had been presented to the Convention for consideration.[2] Along with most of the rest of these, it attracted little attention. It was, however, rediscovered in the twentieth century by the Scandinavian scholar S. B. Liljegren, who came across it whilst carrying out research at the British Museum into the posthumous influence of James Harrington. He described it as a 'very curious document', not least because it bore a close resemblance to Harrington's *The commonwealth of Oceana*.[3] Liljegren published the text, prefacing it with a long introduction in which he discussed the influence of the ideas of Harrington in eighteenth-century France, and particularly during the Revolution. In the last section of his introduction he offered a comparison between *Oceana* and this French draft constitution of 1792. However, despite undertaking further research at the British Museum and in Paris, Liljegren was unable to discover very much about the work itself: 'When we try to learn

---

[1] *Idées sur l'espèce de gouvernement populaire qui pourrait convenir à un pays de l'étendue et de la population présumée de la France*, Paris 1792.

[2] *Archives parlementaires*, lxii. 548–61. As the *Archives parlementaires* version is the most accessible, I have used it throughout.

[3] Liljegren, *French draft constitution*, 80.

something about the origin and history of the document in question, we have very little to go on. Of Théodore Lesueur himself who signed the preface to the pamphlet, we know next to nothing.'[4]

This chapter will attempt to make sense of this 'very curious document'. It will be suggested that the key to understanding it lies in setting it within the context of the Cordeliers Club and viewing it in the light of Rutledge's *Le Creuset*.

Théodore Le Sueur and the Cordeliers Club

In his study of the Cordeliers Club, Mathiez noted the appearance at a club meeting in March 1791 of 'a certain Le Sueur'.[5] Le Sueur's purpose in attending on that day was to accuse the comte de Mirabeau of being behind the department of Paris's decision to sell the *moulins de Corbeil*, which provided grain for the capital, to a private company.[6]

The issue had initially been brought to the attention of the general council of the commune of Paris in a report given by M. Filleul, an administrator from the *département des subsistances*, on 11 January 1791.[7] In that report he announced that a request had been made to purchase some land within the establishment of Corbeil. Filleul and his department were against the sale because of the potential effect on the mills and warehouses (*moulins et magasins*) in the vicinity. The debates in the general council of the commune on this subject continued over several months. Filleul made regular reports reiterating the point that attempts were being made to sell off parts of the establishment of Corbeil and requesting support in opposing the sales. In February 1791 two commissioners were sent with Filleul to Corbeil to examine the establishment and to report on its utility to Paris.[8] Filleul subsequently suggested that the establishment be bought in its entirety by the municipality on the grounds that it was indispensable to the provisioning of the capital.[9] Filleul's proposals were rejected by the directory of the department of Paris. This was ostensibly on the grounds that, under the regime of liberty that had been introduced concerns about provisioning the capital had disappeared; but some alleged that it was due to the intervention of Mirabeau on behalf of the Leleu brothers, the former managers of the mills and warehouses of Corbeil.[10] It was at this point that Le Sueur made his intervention at the Cordeliers Club, claiming that Mirabeau, greedy for personal riches to

---

4 Ibid. 80.
5 Mathiez, *Le Club des Cordeliers*, 26.
6 My account of the '*moulins de Corbeil* affair' is based on *Actes de la commune*, 2nd ser., ii, iii; *Société des Jacobins*, ii. 313–14; and Rutledge, *Le Creuset*, ii. 80.
7 *Actes de la commune*, 2nd ser., ii. 106–7.
8 Ibid. ii. 568, 572.
9 Ibid. ii. 692.
10 Ibid. iii. 332–7, 474.

fund his ostentatious lifestyle, had been paid by some monopolists (the Leleu brothers) to act in their favour.

The *moulins de Corbeil* and the Leleu brothers had been at the centre of the 'boulanger affair', which had been the focus of Rutledge's concerns during 1789. Given this, and his belief in the Harringtonian axiom that control over the means of subsistence was crucial to the holding and maintenance of political power, it is not surprising that Rutledge became involved. On 11 April he headed a deputation of Cordeliers to the Jacobin Club where he made an announcement that the *moulins de Corbeil* were on the verge of being alienated.[11] He explained that he had already appealed to the *comité d'alienation* and to the directory of the department of Paris to try to get them to suspend the decision – but without success. Rutledge warned that this was simply another attempt by the Leleu brothers to bring about the starvation of the population of Paris. The Jacobin response was largely unfavourable, but through the intervention of Robespierre it was agreed that the issue be examined and five commissioners were appointed for the purpose.[12]

While the '*moulins de Corbeil* affair' may well have marked Le Sueur's first association with the Cordeliers Club, it was neither his first nor his last involvement with Rutledge. In late 1789 and early 1790, Rutledge had written a series of letters to Jean Paul Marat's newspaper *L'Ami du peuple*, in which he attempted to justify his actions during the 'boulanger affair'. In one of these, dated 3 January 1790, Rutledge explained: 'The same day, the 12th if I am not mistaken, the statement of M. Le Sueur took place [along with that of] his wife and their friend M. de Lessart. [Le Sueur is] an individual well acquainted with many of my relations with the minister.'[13] Moreover, the publisher's notice at the end of Réné Girardin's *Discours sur la nécessité de la ratification de la loi* of July 1791 was signed by 'Le Sueur, éditeur du Creuset' on behalf of the 'author' of *Le Creuset* – Rutledge.

Following his speech concerning the *moulins de Corbeil* Le Sueur appears to have maintained contact with the Cordeliers Club and its members. In October 1791 the name Théodore Le Sueur appeared alongside those of Boucher Saint-Sauveur, Saudis, Mayeux and Virchaux (all of whom were members of the club) on a petition to the Legislative Assembly headed *Adresse aux parisiens*.[14] These signatories were not themselves the authors of the *Adresse* but it was they who had supported the idea of turning it into a

---

11 Ibid. iii. 337–8; *Société des Jacobins*, ii. 312–13.

12 In particular Prieur and Kersaint rejected Rutledge's claims and insisted that the *moulins de Corbeil* could be alienated without the new owners coming to dominate the provisioning of Paris: *Actes de la commune*, 2nd ser., iii. 337–8; *Société des Jacobins*, ii. 312–13.

13 'Le même jour 12, si je ne me trompe, eut lieu la déposition de M. Le Sueur, particulier bien instruit de plusieurs de mes rapports avec le ministre, son épouse et leur ami M. de Lessart': Marat, *L'Ami du peuple*, no. lxxxvi, 6.

14 *Adresse aux parisiens*, Paris 1791, repr. in *Actes de la commune*, 2nd ser., vii. 689–96. Le Sueur's name also appears on Robertson's list of club members: 'The society of the Cordeliers', 278.

petition to be presented to the Legislative Assembly. The *Adresse aux parisiens* has been deemed important by Sigsmund Lacroix for its content and, in particular, its reflection of the arguments developed by Parisian radicals in their hostility towards the municipality during October and November 1791.[15] Though it was not specifically presented as a Cordeliers petition, the tone and content of the *Adresse* was typical of the club. Liberty and the *Declaration des droits* were presented as the great benefits of the Revolution and as the essential foundations of any just regime. Concern was expressed, however, that despite the crucial role of its citizens in bringing about the Revolution, Paris remained in chains owing to the violations of rights and general corruption of those in power in the municipality – most notably M. Bailly. The *Adresse* went on to suggest that the only solution to these problems would be for the current municipality to be subdivided into six separate municipalities. This solution would reduce the concentration of vast amounts of power in the hands of a very small number of men and would instead place power in the hands of the people, to whom it rightfully belonged:

> The legislative body must assure public happiness by [enacting] general laws. But it is up to individual societies, in short to the commons, to stipulate for themselves the laws by which they wish to be ruled. The inhabitants of a city, contributing all their common expenditure to this same city, must regard themselves as co-owners of the goods that it possesses, and they are justified in complaining when the inhabitants of other cities wish to make rules regarding their particular interests, which those inhabitants have no knowledge of.[16]

Not only were the signatories to the *Adresse aux parisiens* members of the Cordeliers Club, but they were all closely connected to Rutledge. Earlier in the month, all the signatories except Le Sueur had signed another petition on the subject of the national guard, this time alongside Rutledge himself.[17] Moreover several of the signatories to the *Adresse aux parisiens* would, in the following month, take Rutledge's side in the schism that divided the Cordeliers Club.

---

15 *Actes de la commune*, 2nd ser., viii. 284–5.
16 'Le Corps législatif devait assurer la félicité publique par des lois générales. Mais c'est aux sociétés particulières, aux communes enfin, à se prescrire les lois par lesquelles elles veulent être régies: les habitants d'une cité, contribuant tous aux dépenses communes de cette même cité, doivent se regarder co-propriétaires des biens qu'elle possède, et ils sont fondés à se plaindre lorsque des habitants d'autres cités veulent régler leurs intérêts particuliers qu'ils ne connaissent point': ibid. vii. 690.
17 Ibid. vii. 47–56.

The Cordeliers schism[18]

On 25 November 1791 a deputation from the Cordeliers Club appeared at a meeting of the Jacobins and announced that they had expelled one 'James Rutledge' from their care. The reason for this was said to be his outrageous talk against the Jacobins and his distribution of seditious works. The cause of the trouble was the project for a territorial bank produced by the Lyonnois merchant Jacques Ferrières.[19] Both Rutledge and Virchaux (one of the signatories to the *Adresse aux parisiens*) had been among the commissioners from the Cordeliers Club responsible for examining Ferrières's project. Their report was very favourable, but it expressed concern that the proposal was not being given a fair hearing in the nation as a whole. In an attempt to remedy the problem, the authors suggested that the report, together with a covering letter, be sent to all the departments of the nation to gain their views on the project.[20] Following the presentation of the report, a heated discussion broke out in the Cordeliers Club. While Rutledge did not participate in the debate himself, he did produce his *Sommaire d'une discussion importante* on the subject.[21] As a result he was accused of attempting to denigrate key patriots – in particular Brissot, Clavière and Pétion – and it was for this reason that the Cordeliers took the decision to dismiss him from their midst. Antoine Boucher Saint-Sauveur, who was Rutledge's friend and also the president of the club at this time, tried to allow Rutledge a fair hearing. However, he soon realised the futility of his efforts and retired from the meeting; a motion against Rutledge was subsequently passed. Following the announcement in the Jacobin Club on 25 November 1791, M. Buirette de Verrières (who was also a member of the Cordeliers Club and who had himself written a report in which he had explicitly opposed Ferrières's territorial bank) criticised Rutledge and his supporters and suggested that a group of commissioners from the Jacobin Club should join with those from the Cordeliers Club to take the news of the problem to M. Prévost de Beaumont.

---

[18] My account of the schism is drawn from several sources: J. H. Dunouy, *Vérités incontestables*, n.p. 1794 [BN, Lb41 923]; A. S. Boucher Saint-Sauveur, *Déclaration du citoyen Boucher Saint-Sauveur (au sujet d'un dénonciation faite contre Rutledge)*, Paris 1793 [BN, Lb41 903]; *Société des Jacobins*, iii. 262–70; *Actes de la commune*, 2nd ser., iv. appendix; G. Isambart, *La Vie à Paris pendant une année de la Révolution*, Paris 1896, 151; F. Braesch, *Papiers de Chaumette*, Paris 1908; Bourdin, *Les Sociétés populaires*. See also Robertson, 'The society of the Cordeliers', 56–7, and De Cock, *Les Cordeliers*, 78–9.

[19] In frimaire an III (Nov.–Dec. 1794) the Jacobins reproached Ferrières for having 'brought trouble and division to the Cordeliers Club' ('mis le trouble et la division dans les clubs des Cordeliers'): quoted in Bourdin, *Les Sociétés populaires*, 344. For more detail on Ferrières's plan for a territorial bank see chapter 3 above.

[20] *Rapport des commissaires nommés par la société des amis des droits de l'homme et du citoyen, pour l'examen du plan de banque territoriale de M. de Ferrières*, repr. in Mathiez, *Le Club des Cordeliers*, 70–8. For a brief analysis see Momoro, *Journal du club*, 27–31.

[21] Rutledge, *Sommaire d'une discussion importante*.

Rutledge, however, was not willing to forego responding to the accusations. On 29 November he appeared at a Jacobin meeting to protest against the earlier Cordeliers deputation and their announcement. He asked that Boucher Saint-Sauveur be allowed to speak on his behalf. The Jacobins were apparently unwilling to hear the plea. As a result, Rutledge left the Cordeliers Club taking a small group of about twenty members with him. No full list of this group has survived. However, it certainly included Chaumette, Dunouy (who had been one of the distributors for *Le Creuset*), Boucher Saint-Sauveur and Virchaux.[22] It is also probable that it included Mayeux (another of the signatories to the *Adresse aux parisiens*) since it was from his publishing house – Mayer [Mayeux] & Compagnie – that various works associated with this group appeared – including the *Adresse aux parisiens* itself and *Idées sur l'espèce de gouvernement populaire*. The location of this publishing house was given as no. 219, rue Saint-Martin, the same address as the *imprimerie du Creuset* from where Rutledge's newspaper, and the speeches by Réné Girardin, had been published.[23]

On 2 December 1791 delegations from both Cordeliers Clubs appeared at a meeting of the Jacobins. The deputation from the new club complained bitterly at the conduct of their old colleagues in relation to Rutledge, insisting that an injustice had been done. The Jacobin president responded simply by expressing his concern over the current discord and its effect on the public good. He urged reconciliation and reunion between the two sides, but appeared to be unwilling to involve the Jacobins in the dispute. With no sign of reconciliation, the two clubs continued to meet separately, each under the title of the 'Société des amis des droits de l'homme et du citoyen'.

Among the papers of Pierre Gaspard (Anaxagoras) Chaumette, one of the dissidents, there is a circular written on behalf of the new '*Société des amis des droits de l'homme et du citoyen* séante Section des Lombards, No. 8, rue de la Vieille-Monnaie', which provides some sense of the philosophy and aims of the new club.[24] The circular stressed the need for the various popular societies

22 Interestingly, given Rutledge's views, Chaumette appears to have been a supporter of the agrarian law. De Cock refers to a reference in the *Journal français*, of Monday 25 February 1793, on the subject: 'Last Saturday, at a meeting of the Cordeliers Club, Robespierre sharply rebuked Chaumet on the agrarian law, which he called a law of murder and of blood. He demanded that Chaumet be reprimanded and regarded as a slanderer for having professed the principles of anarchy.' ('Samedi dernier, à la séance du club des cordeliers, Robespierre a tancé vertement Chaumet sur la loi agraire qu'il a appellé une loi de meurtre et de sang. Il a demandé que Chaumet fût blâmé et regardé comme un calomniateur, pour avoir professé des principes d'anarchie.'): *Journal français*, ci, quoted in De Cock, *Les Cordeliers*, 85n.

23 It was not long after this that Girardin himself was removed from the list of members of the Cordeliers Club. While this was allegedly on account of his connection with the Feuillants, one wonders whether he too was involved in the Cordeliers schism: *Société des Jacobins*, iii. 312.

24 A. Chaumette, 'Circulaire de la société populaire de la section des Lombards', reproduced in Braesch, *Papiers de Chaumette*, 176–7.

to work together to secure liberty and to defeat the enemies of the nation. Despite the schism, the sentiments expressed in the text were typical of the Cordeliers. The declaration of rights was described as the gospel (*evangile*) of the club and as the basis of all liberty and justice. The description of the objectives of the new club also had a Cordeliers ring to it:

> To defend the oppressed . . . to search the depths of the dungeons [and] pull out the innocent; to stamp the mark of disgrace on the foreheads of violators of the law; to march, even in front of spears and bayonets, everywhere where liberty is attacked; to nurture in [human] souls the hatred of tyranny and the love of the *patrie*. There you have it, brothers and friends, these are our principles.[25]

The new club was also gripped by the same intrigues and in-fighting that had characterised the old. In his 'Notes autobiographiques', under January 1792, Chaumette wrote:

> I established a new club, in the rue de la Vieille-Monnaie; soon the schemers came along, citizens were lost as a result of being made to take part in personal quarrels. Two men established a kind of dominion. I abandoned this club and these two ambitious men unrelentingly worked to turn against me the fools over whom they reigned.[26]

There is no direct evidence that Le Sueur moved with Rutledge to the new club on the rue de la Vieille-Monnaie. However, we can be sure of Le Sueur's continuing association, and even friendship, with Rutledge himself. In October 1793 Rutledge was arrested by the authorities following a denunciation by Philippe François Nazaire Fabre d'Eglantine.[27] Two statements protesting against Rutledge's arrest and defending his character were sent to the *comité des recherches*. One was signed by Boucher Saint-Sauveur, and dated 23 Brumaire (13 November) 1793; the other, dated 31 October 1793,

25 'Défendre les opprimés envers et contre tout, sonder la profondeur des cachots pour en arracher l'innocence; imprimer le cachet de l'opprobre sur le front des violateurs de la loi, marcher, fût-ce à travers des dards, des baïonnettes, partout où la liberté serait attaquée, nourrir dans leur ame la haine des tyrans et l'amour de la Patrie. Voilà, frères et amis, voilà nos titres': ibid. 177.
26 'Je fonde un nouveau club, rue de la Vieille-Monnaie; bientôt les intrigants s'y introduisent, on y égare les citoyens en les faisant prendre part dans des querelles personnelles; il s'y établit une espèce de domination de la part de deux hommes. J'abandonne ce club et ces deux ambitieux acharnent contre moi les sots sur lesquels ils règnent': A. Chaumette, 'Notes autobiographiques de Chaumette', in Braesch, *Papiers de Chaumette*, 134. There has been some confusion over Chaumette's claim that he founded the new club in January 1792. While Chaumette was one of the original members, the club was almost certainly founded by Rutledge, probably at the end of 1791.
27 According to R. R. Palmer, Fabre d'Eglantine denounced Rutledge as part of a vast foreign conspiracy: *The year of the Terror: twelve who ruled France, 1793–1794*, 3rd edn, Oxford 1989, 113–14. See also Peyronnet, 'J. J. Rutlidge', 338–41.

was signed by Théodore Le Sueur. Le Sueur objected to the grounds on which Rutledge's arrest was based and expressed concern that he was being badly treated in prison.[28]

Idées sur l'espèce de gouvernement populaire

The preface to Idées sur l'espèce de gouvernement populaire was signed by 'Théodore Le Sueur citoyen de la Section de Réunion', and was dated 25 September 1792 . . . l'an IV de la liberté et le 1er de l'égalité'. Coincidentally this was also the day on which the first French republic was officially proclaimed.

While Le Sueur was the author of the preface, he made it clear that he was not the author of the work as a whole. Following his opening expression of the desire for a constitution that would secure forever the reign of liberty, Le Sueur went on to say something of the origins of this particular draft constitution. It was, he explained, the fruit of ten years of thought and observations. The author, wishing to remain anonymous, had asked Le Sueur to present the work to the Convention on his behalf: 'He gave to me the fragment that I offer to you on the condition that his name would remain unknown. I will keep my word to him.'[29] At the request of the true author, very little information was provided to guide readers towards his identity:

> He who wrote it proclaimed the language of liberty in an epoch when such an idiom was hardly known in France. He pursued it without rest and unmasked intrigue everywhere that he found it – without distinction or exception. He was for a long time the plaything of fortune, the object of slanders and of persecutions of all kinds. He is still exposed to merciless and oblique acts of the envy that follows men of his character to the grave.[30]

Given the resemblance of this description to Rutledge's life, together with the close association that existed between these two men, and the long history of Rutledge's interest in Harrington, he would seem a strong candidate for being the author of the text. However, this can be no more than spec-

---

28 Boucher Saint-Sauveur, Déclaration du citoyen Boucher Saint-Sauveur. This was another of the pamphlets published by Mayer et compagnie. For Le Sueur's statement see AN, F7 4775/8, dossier 2.

29 'Il m'a abandonné le fragment que je vous offre sous la condition que son nom resterait ignoré: je lui tiendrai parole': Archives parlementaires, lxii. 548–9.

30 'Celui qui l'a composé tint le langage de la liberté à une époque où son idiom était à peine connu en France. Il poursuivit sans relâche et démasqua l'intrigue partout où il la trouva, sans acception ni exception de personnes. Il fut longtemps le jouet de la fortune, l'objet des calomnies et des persécutions de tous genres. Il est encore en butte aux traits impitoyables et obliques de l'envie qui poursuit jusque dans la tombe les hommes de son caractère': ibid. lxii. 548

ulation and we should take heed of Le Sueur's own assertion in his preface: 'But what does the name of the author matter, judge the work.'[31]

The full title, *Idées sur l'espèce de gouvernement populaire qui pourrait convenir à un pays de l'étendue et de la population présumée de la France*, offers a good guide as to the main concerns of the work. Just like Robert's *Républicanisme adapté à la France* and Rutledge's *Le Creuset*, the work was concerned with refuting the pessimistic views of Montesquieu, Rousseau and many revolutionaries by demonstrating how a democratic republic could be built in late eighteenth-century France. Moreover, as in Rutledge's *Le Creuset*, the ideas and practices put forward by Harrington are central to the argument.

Although Harrington is not mentioned anywhere in *Idées sur l'espèce de gouvernement populaire*, there are resemblances to *Oceana*, which, as Liljegren noted, are too strong and too close to be accidental. For example, the author opens, as Harrington had, with an order to divide the territory of the nation into electoral units and to organise its citizens according to their place of habitation, age and wealth. There then follow several sections which discuss central Harringtonian ideas, in particular, the agrarian law and Venetian voting practices (Harrington's 'ballot of Venice').

In the section of *Idées sur l'espèce de gouvernement populaire* devoted to the agrarian law the author laid down limits on the amount of land that could be inherited and the amount that could be transferred by dowry, with the intention of avoiding the concentration of too much land in too few hands. Unlike Harrington's *Oceana*, the work also included measures designed to address the succession of land to orphans under the age of eighteen. Besides this, the only real difference between the two accounts is the fact that, where Harrington's model insisted on the division of estates over £5,000, *Idées sur l'espèce de gouvernement populaire* proposed no such limit, simply insisting that estates be divided more or less equally regardless of their size. Harrington's emphasis on the importance of land is also reflected throughout the rest of the work. If anything, *Idées sur l'espèce de gouvernement populaire* contains even more references than *Oceana* to the importance of land as the key basis for subsistence, and therefore as the ideal foundation for a popular state. For example, the work insisted that the division of the land was to be carried out on the basis of its current capacity and productive density – 'in their direct relation to the subsistence of men, and that of animals'.[32]

Harrington's explanation of the ballot of Venice and its application within *Oceana* appeared in the fourteenth order of his constitutional model and in the ensuing discussion.[33] In *Idées sur l'espèce de gouvernement populaire* the account of the ballot of Venice is even more extensive, amounting to an

---

[31] 'Mais qu'importe le nom de l'auteur, jugez de l'ouvrage': ibid. lxii. 549.

[32] 'dans leur rapport direct à la subsistance des hommes, et à celle des animaux': ibid.

[33] *Political works of James Harrington*, 241–7.

introduction and four separate chapters.[34] The author separated out the three elements of this ballot (lot, election and limited duration of office), describing each in detail and setting out the reasoning behind them. Ultimately the aim of this system, it was explained, was to remove the corrupt effects of partiality in the allocation and transfer of public roles caused by the influence of individual passions. In addition, the applicability of such a system, even within large states and among large numbers of people, was demonstrated. Other Harringtonian devices mentioned in the text include an indirect system of election via a series of provincial assemblies, the separation of discussion of legislation from decision-making and a system of national councils.[35]

Liljegren himself provided a detailed account of the Harringtonian features of the model constitution and offered a comparison of it with Harrington's original. He did not make the point, however, that the author of *Idées sur l'espèce de gouvernement populaire* did not simply follow Harrington's model slavishly, but rather manipulated and adapted it in particular ways.

The democratisation of Harrington's *Oceana*

As was suggested in chapter 1, members of the Cordeliers Club developed their notion of democratic republicanism (involving elements of both delegate and semi-direct democracy) in opposition to the form of modern representative government that was being advocated by other revolutionaries. The ways in which ideas taken from Harrington's *Oceana* were manipulated and adapted in *Idées sur l'espèce de gouvernement populaire* reflects this, with the democratic elements of Harrington's system being reinforced and expanded and additional democratic features being introduced.

In recent years some attention has been paid to the differences between ancient democracy and the form of modern representative government that emerged in the seventeenth and eighteenth centuries.[36] One key difference that has been emphasised is that in ancient democracies political offices were filled by lot, whereas in modern representative governments lot is almost unknown (the one exception being jury service) and election is used to select political representatives.[37] In Athens what was crucial was not so much that many powers were held in the hands of the people as a whole, but rather that powers lay in the hands of magistrates who had gained their positions by a

---

34 *Archives parlementaires*, lxii. 558–61.

35 As in Le Creuset, the choice of councils is more reminiscent of A *system of politics* than of *Oceana*.

36 This section is indebted to B. Manin, *The principles of representative government*, Cambridge 1997 (originally published in French as *Principes du gouvernement représentatif*, Paris 1995). See also Fontana, *Invention of the modern republic*, and P. A. Rahe, *Republics ancient and modern: classical republicanism and the American Revolution*, Chapel Hill 1992.

37 On the issue of lot and election see Manin, *Principles of representative government*, 42–93.

process of lot. This use of lot was coupled with the principle of rotation of office. Together, these mechanisms would ensure that every citizen had an opportunity to hold some kind of political office at some point during his life.

Harrington made use of both lot and rotation in *Oceana*. Following the Venetian model, however, the employment of lot within his system was limited, being used simply to select the committees appointed to nominate and consider candidates for office, but not to select the magistrates themselves.

Given Harrington's attitude, it is interesting that the author of *Idées sur l'espèce de gouvernement populaire* was explicit about his use of lot, and actually highlighted and explained its role in his discussion of the Venetian ballot. Moreover, he did not simply endorse the small element of lot to be found in Harrington's original, but rather expanded the role played by it within the constitution.

Following Harrington, the author of *Idées sur l'espèce de gouvernement populaire* advocated the use of lot to designate the electors who would then nominate candidates for the various vacant magisterial positions. But, in addition, lot was also to be used to determine deputies at the lowest level – that of the district:

> Art. 3 Assembled in this manner, the thousand citizens of the order of virility, making up a *local* district, select, from among themselves, *by means of lot* not election, *one* citizen in *ten*.

> And the citizens selected in this manner will be qualified as deputies or as *pecuniary representatives*, and will fulfill, during the course of the year following their selection, all relevant functions.[38]

It was from among these deputies that all public officials and higher-level representatives were to be selected. Moreover, the president and censors of the district were also to be taken from among this body, again by a process of lot.

The use of election, rather than lot, in modern representative governments was, in part, designed to ensure that those elected into power would be superior in some way to those who had elected them.[39] In addition, despite appeals to the notion of free elections, various additional mechanisms were often introduced to ensure that this was the case. Though this was often couched in the language of rule by the most virtuous, or by a natural aristocracy, virtue was believed by many at the time to be reflected in wealth. Thus

---

[38] 'Art. 3. Assemblés de cette manière, les mille citoyens de l'ordre de virilité, composant un district *local*, éliront, entre eux *par la voie du sort*, et non par la voie des suffrages, *un* citoyen sur *dix*. / Et les citoyens élus de cette manière seront qualifiés de députés ou de *représentants pécuniaires*, et rempliront, durant le cours de l'année de leur élection, toutes les fonctions relatives': *Archives parlementaires*, lxii. 550–1.

[39] Manin labels this 'the principle of distinction'; he discusses it in detail in *Principles of representative government*, 94–131.

Harrington began by dividing his citizens into those owning over £100 *per annum* in goods and land and those owning less. At this point Harrington's division was ostensibly to divide the citizens into the cavalry and the infantry; the wealth distinction was thus justified on the grounds that those in the cavalry would require the money to provide themselves with a horse and other relevant equipment. Later in *Oceana*, however, it becomes clear that Harrington also intended to use this division to ensure that at the highest level of government it was the wealthier who would be dominant. The election of the national representatives was to be carried out at a regional level.[40] In each region two knights and three deputies would be elected from among members of the cavalry and four deputies from the infantry. The knights would come together to form the senate and the deputies the prerogative tribe. Thus the wealthier (cavalry) would completely control the senate (and therefore also the councils of the commonwealth – members of which were to be elected from among the senate) and in addition would enjoy a sizeable minority within the prerogative tribe. Moreover, it would be the wealthy who would control political debate since only members of the senate would be allowed to debate political issues, the prerogative tribe being simply a silent assembly of resolution.

Like Harrington, the author of *Idées sur l'espèce de gouvernement populaire* also proposed the division of the population on the basis of wealth. Here the threshold was set at 1,500 livres annual revenue from land (sufficient to keep three individuals) or a net industrial revenue of 3,000 livres (sufficient for six individuals). Citizens earning less than this figure were to be placed in the class of the first order of proprietors or 'minus possidentes', those worth more fell into a second order or 'plus possidentes'. In contrast with Harrington's model, however, this division was not used to determine cavalry and infantry members, who instead were simply chosen from among the men aged between eighteen and thirty. Moreover, where the distinction of wealth was brought into play, it was used to weight power not in favour of the wealthy (the *plus possidentes*) but in favour of those who were less well off (the *minus possidentes*). The grand national legislative council was to be composed of three-quarters *minus possidentes* to one-quarter *plus possidentes*. The grand national executive council was to be made up solely of *minus possidentes*. Thus the author of the later work reversed Harrington's bias, giving greater political power at a central level to the less well off. Moreover, the way in which the national bodies were organised is also significant. Unlike Harrington, the author of *Idées sur l'espèce de gouvernement populaire* did not propose a bicameral legislature, but instead a unicameral system. This meant that there was nowhere for a natural aristocracy to reside.

Another key indicator of democracy is the nature and degree of political participation by the citizen body. In this respect too *Idées sur l'espèce de*

---

[40] *Political works of James Harrington*, 226–7.

gouvernement populaire reflects an extension of democracy from Harrington's original model. It expanded the number of people directly involved in political tasks and increased the number of political tasks in which the people could participate.

In line with *Oceana*, the French work embodied the practice of separating discussion of policy from decision-making. There was, however, a difference in the way in which it was implemented. In Harrington's *Oceana* it was the senate that discussed the issues and presented them in statement form to the prerogative tribe which, by means of a simple yes/no vote, accepted or rejected the proposal as set out by the senate.[41] Thus the whole of the political decision-making process was carried out at the national level. This was not the case in *Idées sur l'espèce de gouvernement populaire*. There it was a national body (the legislative council) that debated the issues and put forward proposals, but those proposals would then be accepted or rejected, not by another national body, but by the people gathered in their various primary assemblies:

> Art. 3. Final *Ratification* or *sanction* of the law, *first proposed*, then *discussed* and finally *presented* by the great national legislative council, belongs exclusively to the nation represented legally: 1. in its *centuries civiques*; 2. in its *tribus politiques*; 3. in its *assemblées de cercles*, where this sanction must be expressed on the presentation of the laws discussed, by *yes* for the *affirmative*, and by *no*, for the negative.[42]

By placing the responsibility for making decisions in the local assemblies, the author was automatically expanding the number of citizens who would participate directly in the political decision-making process.

Moreover, decision-making was not the only task in which the citizens could be involved. They would also have the power to raise issues and propose potential laws to be placed before the national legislative council for discussion. Even men under thirty, who could not hold political office, were given this right:

> Art. 1. A proposition or proposed discussion of an aspect of *law* must be, and will always be, received, on behalf of any citizens, whether from the order of youth, whether from the order of virility, whether on the part of a voluntary gathering of the citizens, in whatever number; but purely and simply as a proposition of law, with the only obligation, on the part of the legislators, of report-

---

41 Ibid. 133–5.

42 'Art. 3. *Ratification* ou *sanction* définitive de la loi, *proposée d'abord*, ensuite *discutée* et puis *présentée* par le grand Conseil national législatif, appartient exclusivement à la nation représentée légalement: 1. dans ses centuries civiques; 2. dans ses tribus politiques; 3. dans ses assemblées de cercles, où cette sanction doit être exprimée, sur la présentation des lois discutées, par *oui* pour *l'affirmative*, et par *non*, pour la négative': *Archives parlementaires*, lxii. 553.

ing it *to the office* and of presenting it publicly for discussion in the assembly of the great national legislative council.[43]

The only citizens denied the right to propose legislation were those who made up the national executive council, the aim of this being to maintain the separation of legislative and executive functions. This was in contrast to Harrington's model, in which legislative proposals could only be presented to the senate *via* the councils of state.

It was not only the legislative process in the two constitutions that was different. The author of *Idées sur l'espèce de gouvernement populaire* also extended to a wider number of citizens the power of accepting or rejecting magistrates. In Harrington's model, magistrates were to be chosen at each level by the deputies at that level gathered together in their particular assembly. Thus national magistrates would be chosen and ratified solely at a national level. In *Idées sur l'espèce de gouvernement populaire* national magistrates were also to be chosen at a national level but those choices were then to be subject to ratification by the citizens gathered in their local assemblies.[44]

Thus, despite the strong resemblance between Harrington's *Oceana* and *Idées sur l'espèce de gouvernement populaire*, there were also crucial differences between the two works. In altering Harrington's ideas on lot, rotation, property qualifications and the aspects of government in which the ordinary citizens could participate, the author of the French draft constitution engaged in a systematic democratisation of Harrington's original work.

Essai d'une déclaration des droits de l'homme et du citoyen

After being submitted to the National Convention by Le Sueur, copies of *Idées sur l'espèce de gouvernement populaire* were sent to each of the eighty-three departments of the nation in late September 1792. An additional copy was handed to a *comité d'analyse*. The committee was then due to report back to the convention at some future date.

Le Sueur, however, was impatient to further the democratic campaign. In November 1792 he presented a second work to the National Convention, using his announcement of it to remind its members of the earlier work:

---

43 'Art. 1er. Proposition ou mise en question de quelque projet de *loi* que ce puisse être, pourra être faite, et devra en tout temps, être reçue, de la part de tout citoyen, soit de l'ordre de la jeunesse, soit de l'ordre de la virilité, soit de la part de toute réunion volontaire de citoyens, en quelque nombre qu'il leur arrive de la faire; mais purement et simplement comme proposition de loi, avec la seule obligation, de la part des législateurs, d'en faire rapport *sur le bureau*, et de la présenter publiquement à la discussion dans l'assemblée du grand conseil national legislatif': ibid.
44 Ibid. lxii. 554.

Tribute to the national Convention by M. Théodore Le Sueur, to be distrib-uted to the 83 departments, 84 copies of a sketch of a declaration of the Rights of Man and of the Citizen, and reminding them that at the beginning of the session he had addressed to M. Pétion 84 copies of a work entitled; Idées sur l'espèce de gouvernement populaire qui pourroit convenir à un pays tel que la France – 5 November 1792.[45]

Essai d'une déclaration des droits de l'homme et du citoyen and Quelques Pensées sur l'unité du législateur, which was bound in with it, were described as having been written by the same author as Idées sur l'espèce de gouvernement populaire.[46] Moreover, both the Essai and Quelques Pensées certainly reflect the same interests and concerns as the earlier work.

The very form taken by the Essai – of a declaration of rights – suggests a Cordeliers association. Moreover, in Article XXVII of the Essai we find the Cordeliers view that all constitutions that are grounded in the rights of nature are necessarily good. The Cordeliers understanding of and emphasis on liberty was also central to the work, and that liberty was presented as being threatened by the forces of arbitrary authority and corruption. Harringtonian echoes, similar to those employed by Rutledge in Le Creuset, are also in evidence. In Article VIII one finds the same distinction between authority and empire that was drawn in the fourth issue of Le Creuset, and which came originally from Harrington. Similarly the language of reason and passion was employed in Article XXVII – again echoing Rutledge in the same issue of Le Creuset. Furthermore, the importance of land, which had been central to the theories of both Harrington and Rutledge, underlies the entire work. The idea of an agrarian law is hinted at in Article XIV and the discussion of mili-tary defence and armed forces in Article XXII is reminiscent of Harrington's assertion that 'an army is a beast that hath a great belly which must be fed'.[47]

Just like Idées sur l'espèce de gouvernement populaire, the Essai also displays a democratic orientation. This is particularly evident in the emphasis on equality that is apparent from the very beginning. The opening article of the Declaration des droits of 26 August 1789, which had initially been the focus of Cordeliers support, had read:

---

[45] 'Hommage à la Convention nationale par le sieur Théodore Le Sueur, pour être distribués aux 83 départements, de 84 exemplaires d'un Essai d'une déclaration des Droits de l'homme et du Citoyen, et rappelant qu'au début de la session il avait adressé à M. Pétion 84 exemplaires d'un ouvrage intitulé; idées sur le'espèce de gouvernement populaire qui pourir convenir à un pays tel que la France – 5 Novembre 1792': Essai d'une déclaration des droits d l'homme et du citoyen: suivi de quelques pensées sur l'unité du législateur, par l'auteur des Idées sur la constitution populaire etc., Paris l'an I [1792], 1.

[46] The two works were bound together for presentation to the Convention and the pagi-nation is continuous through them both. However, since in terms of content they are effec-tively two separate works, I shall treat them separately in my analysis.

[47] Political works of James Harrington, 165.

I. Men are born and remain free and equal in rights; social distinctions can only be established in the interests of common utility.[48]

By contrast the first article of this declaration focused on equality alone:

FIRST ARTICLE: Men are born equal: parity of intellectual and physical faculties, parity of natural needs; errors, or abuses of strength alone have introduced differences between men, in the various parts of the earth.[49]

Throughout the text, the principle of equality continues to enjoy a predominant role. Significantly, the new emphasis on equality had already been implied on the title page of *Idées sur l'espèce de gouvernement populaire* where, again echoing *Le Creuset*, the work was dated '25 septembre, l'an IV de la liberté' but this time the date was rounded off 'et le Ier de l'égalité'.[50]

Quelques Pensées sur l'unité du législateur

Quelques Pensées sur l'unité du législateur appears to have been written explicitly with the circumstances of autumn 1792 in mind. In particular it can be seen as an attack on the appointment of the National Convention as a constitution-building body. The work opposed the very practice of establishing a constitution by committee and argued instead in favour of the appointment of a single legislator. In this sense its connection to *Idées sur l'espèce de gouvernement populaire* is obvious.

The case that was made in favour of a single legislator in the work echoed Rutledge's rehearsal of the same argument in *Le Creuset*. Literary and musical analogies were employed to demonstrate the superiority of a single over a multiple or conciliar legislator:

FIRST EXAMPLE: Twelve poets, each better than Homer and Virgil, could each write a Poem superior to the Illiad or the the Aeneid, but these twelve Poets, working together, could write neither an Illiad, nor an Aeneid.

SECOND EXAMPLE: Forty musicians more skilful than Gluck, could each compose an overture richer in harmony than that of Iphigenia, but these forty musicians, together, could never compose the overture to Iphigenia.

---

48 'I. Les hommes naissent et demeurent libres et égaux en droits. Les distinctions sociales ne peuvent être fondées que sur l'utilité commune': 'Déclaration des droits de l'homme et du citoyen', *Archives parlementaires*, ix. 236.

49 'ARTICLE PREMIER: Les hommes naissent égaux: parité des facultés intellectuelles et physiques, parité de besoins naturels; les erreurs, ou les abus de la force ont seuls introduit les différences entre les hommes, sur les diverses parties de la terre': *Essai d'un déclaration des droits de l'homme et du citoyen*, 1.

50 *Archives parlementaires*, lxii. 549. From 11 August 1792 the assemblée des commissaires des sections apparently dated its acts 'l'an 4me de la liberté et l'an 1er de l'égalité': Genty, *L'Apprentissage*, 184.

THIRD EXAMPLE: Twelve or forty Legislators more skilful than Moses, could each draw up a Constitution more perfect than that of the Hebrews; but these twelve or forty could never invent together the Mosaic Constitution.[51]

When arguing in favour of the idea of a single legislator in the second issue of *Le Creuset* Rutledge had made use of the same literary analogy:

A political constitution, a work of the mind of man as all works that spring from intelligence, is, in its first elements, simple and singular. It is like a speech or a poem or a painting: the plan of works of each of these different genres can only be imagined by an individual, whatever its perfection, or its execution, it cannot involve the work of several heads or hands. Twelve poets more skilful than Homer or Virgil, have without contradiction been able to produce, each on his own, a poem superior to the Illiad or the Aeneid: but these same twelve poets together would never have been able to compose an Aeneid or an Illiad.[52]

Nor was Rutledge the originator of the analogy. In the fifth chapter of Harrington's *A system of politics* there appeared the following aphorism:

18. A parliament of physicians would never have found out the circulation of the blood, nor could a parliament of poets have written Virgil's *Aeneis*; of this kind therefore in the formation of government is the proceeding of a sole legislator. But if the people, without a legislator, set upon such work by a certain instinct that is in them, they never go further than to choose a council; not considering that the formation of government is well a work of invention as of judgement, and that a council, though in matters laid before them they may excel in judgement, yet invention is as contrary to the nature of a council as it is to musicians in consort, who can play and judge of any air that is laid before them, though to invent a part of music they can never well agree.[53]

---

[51] 'PREMIER EXEMPLE: Douze Poètes, meilleurs tous qu'Homere et Virgile, pourroient faire chacun un Poème supérieur à l'Iliade et à l'Enéide, mais ces douze Poètes, travaillant ensemble, n'eussent fait ni une Iliade, ni une Enéide./ DEUXIÈME EXEMPLE: Quarante musiciens plus habiles que Gluck, auroient fait chacun, une overture plus riche encore en harmonie que celle d'Iphigénie, mais ces quarante musiciens, ensemble, n'eussent jamais fait l'overture d'Iphigénie./TROISIÈME EXEMPLE: Douze ou quarante Législateurs plus habiles que Moyse, auroient pu faire, chacun, une Constitution plus parfaite que celle des Hébreux; mais jamais ces douze ou ces quarante n'eussent inventé, ensemble, la Constitution Mosaïque': *Quelques Pensées sur l'unité du législateur*, 12.

[52] 'Une constitution politique, oeuvre de l'esprit de l'homme, comme toutes celles dont son intelligence peut être la source, dans ses premiers élémens est une oeuvre simple et une. Il en est d'elle comme d'un discours, où d'un poëme ou d'un tableau: le plan de chacun des ouvrages de ces différens genres, ne peut être imaginé que par une persone, quoique leur perfection, ou leur exécution, demande, ou qu'elle puisse admettre le concours d'un certain nombre de têtes ou de mains. Douze Poëtes plus habiles que ne furent Homere ou Virgile, auroient sans contradit pu produire, chacun en particulier, un poëme supérieur à l'Iliade ou l'Enéide: mais ces mêmes douze poëtes réunis n'auroient jamais pu composer une Enéïde ou une Illiade': Rutledge, *Le Creuset*, i. 38.

[53] *Political works of James Harrington*, 842.

The use of the same analogy was not the only echo of Harrington in the work. In addition, the way in which the argument was structured can be seen as a development of the Harringtonian principle of the separation of discussion of legislation from decision-making. Just as the few should discuss legislative proposals and the many accept or reject those proposals, so it should be a single individual who is responsible for drawing up the plan of the government or constitution in the first place:

> A single person must give life to the plan of Government.
>
> It will be to the political body as it is to the individual, the indivisible principle, thinking: *intellectus*.
>
> Many, authorised by all, must compare and judge the whole work and its harmony.
>
> They will be to the body politic, as it is in the individual, the means of seizing the relations of ideas between them: *judicium*.
>
> All alone can consacrate or reject: *voluntas*.[54]

Thus, once again, we find Harringtonian language and ideas being adopted, but also being manipulated and developed, to support the views of members of the Cordeliers Club – and being applied directly to the circumstances and concerns of revolutionary France in the early 1790s.

Whatever the interest of their content, the real purpose of the *Essai d'une déclaration des droits de l'homme et du citoyen* and *Quelques Pensées sur l'unité du législateur* was undoubtedly to remind the members of the Convention of the model constitution that Le Sueur had delivered to them several months earlier. At the end of the second work the reader was informed that the publisher (which was once again Mayer et compagnie, no. 219, rue St. Martin) still had some copies of *Idées sur l'espèce de gouvernement populaire*. The similarities between it and *Essai d'une déclaration des droits de l'homme* and *Quelques pensées sur l'unité du législateur* were stressed and these works were offered together for anyone who wished to purchase them.

Though we cannot be certain who actually wrote *Idées sur l'espèce de gouvernement populaire*, *Essai d'une déclaration des droits de l'homme et du citoyen* and *Quelques Pensées sur l'unité du législateur* we can be fairly sure that

---

54 'Un seul doit donner l'être au plan de Gouvernement. /Il sera au corps politique ce qu'est à l'individu, le principe indivisible, pensant: *intellectus*./Plusieurs, autorisés par tous, doivent comparer et juger de l'harmonie et de l'ensemble de son ouvrage./Ils seront au corps politique, ce qu'est, dans l'individu, la faculté de saisir les rapports des idées entre elles: *judicium*./Tous pourront seuls consacrer ou rejetter: *voluntas*': *Quelques Pensées sur l'unité du législateur*, 16.

Rutledge was involved. Similarities in style and content between his *Le Creuset* and these works are undeniable.[55]

In particular two common concerns can be identified. First, the preoccupation with land and the belief that control of the means of subsistence, which was associated with the ownership of land, should form the basis of popular government. This idea was openly expressed, often in Harringtonian form, in *Le Creuset*, *Idées sur l'espèce de gouvernement populaire* and *Essai d'une déclaration des droits de l'homme et du citoyen*. It was also reflected in the various actions and concerns with which members of Rutledge's coterie were involved, including Rutledge's own participation in the 'boulanger affair' and his subsequent dispute with Necker; the *'moulins de Corbeil* affair', which brought Le Sueur into contact with the Cordeliers Club; and Ferrières's project for a territorial bank, which was the 'apple of discord' which provoked the schism within the Cordeliers Club in November 1791.[56]

The other issue that appears to have been crucial for this group of revolutionaries was democracy. Once again this idea was central to *Le Creuset*, *Idées sur l'espèce de gouvernement populaire* and *Essai d'une déclaration des droits de l'homme et du citoyen*. In *Le Creuset* Rutledge employed Harringtonian ideas to demonstrate that, contrary to the conventional view, a form of democratic government could be implemented in a nation like France. In *Idées sur l'espèce de gouvernement populaire* the argument was taken a step further, with Harringtonian mechanisms and practices being modified to make them even more democratic. This idea was also reflected in the issues and campaigns in which the members of Rutledge's coterie became involved, including their opposition to the distinction between active and passive citizenship and the *Adresse aux parisiens* which argued for the devolution of greater power into the hands of a larger number of citizens.

As was shown at the end of the previous chapter, these two issues – land and democracy – parallel Harrington's notions of 'the goods of fortune' and 'the goods of authority'. Moreover, the ideas and arguments of Harrington were used to promote and support them both. In Harrington these men found a writer who had presented a vision of a popular state which was based on land and agricultural production and which could support a democratic form of government.

Thus we are now in a much better position to understand the model constitution that so intrigued Liljegren. This constitution, though presented

---

[55] On the basis of Aubert de Vitry's comment in his *Jean-Jacques Rousseau à l'assemblée nationale*, that Rutledge had long been preparing a book based on Harrington's ideas, one might conclude that *Idées sur l'espèce de gouvernement populaire*, *Essai d'une declaration des droits de l'homme et du citoyen*, *Quelques pensées sur l'unité du législateur* as well as parts of *Le Creuset* were the fruits of this work, adapted for the revolutionary circumstances. See [Aubert de Vitry], *Jean Jacques Rousseau à l'assemblée nationale*, 232, and ch. 3 above.

[56] It was Boucher Saint-Sauveur who referred to Ferrières's territorial bank as the 'apple of discord' that divided the club in his defence of Rutledge following the latter's arrest: Boucher Saint-Sauveur, *Déclaration du citoyen Boucher Saint-Sauveur*.

to the National Convention by Le Sueur, was very probably written by Rutledge himself. The intention behind it was to engage in a long-standing Cordeliers campaign to put the case for democratic republicanism against the modern form of representative government that was being advocated and developed by many revolutionaries. The specific aim of *Idées sur l'espèce d'un gouvernement populaire*, and of the two works that followed it, was to bring the campaign into line with the situation in autumn 1792. Seeing the document in this light renders it much less 'curious' than Liljegren claimed. In particular, the connections with *Oceana* can now be seen, not simply as the ramblings of a slightly eccentric anglophile, but as part of a concerted project to bring about a return to 'ancient prudence' in the modern world.[57]

---

[57] There is some evidence to suggest that the works presented to the Convention by Le Sueur did not mark the end of this project. Further research into the circumstances surrounding the post-1794 translations of Harrington, which do not fall within the scope of this book, may reveal continuities and connections with the works discussed here. In 1795 the first full translation of Harrington's political works was published by P. F. Henry. In the same year there appeared a second Harringtonian translation, this time of his aphoristic works *Aphorisms political* and *A system of politics*. In both cases there are possible connections to Rutledge's coterie within the Cordeliers Club. One of the booksellers from which *Oeuvres politiques de James Harrington* was available was Leclerc on rue St Martin. *Aphorisms politique* was translated by P. F. Aubin. It is possible that one or both of these references are to Le Clerc de Saint-Aubin who had been a key member of the séction du Théâtre Français and member of the Cordeliers Club. See Desmoulins, *Les Révolutions de France et de Brabant*, vi. 506.

5

Camille Desmoulins and the Old Cordeliers

In December 1793, at the height of the Terror, one of the original members of the Cordeliers District and Club, Camille Desmoulins, began to publish a newspaper in which he launched a savage attack on the increasingly draconian measures of the revolutionary government. That newspaper was entitled *Le Vieux Cordelier* (the old Cordelier).

Despite the fact that only six issues of *Le Vieux Cordelier* were published during Desmoulins's lifetime, with one further issue appearing posthumously, it is one of the best-known newspapers of the revolutionary period.[1] At least ten editions appeared between 1794 and the end of the nineteenth century and it is much cited in books on the revolutionary government and the Terror.[2] The usual context in which *Le Vieux Cordelier* is set is that of the politics of the time and in particular the growing rivalry and hostility, during late 1793 and early 1794, between three distinct political groups: the revolutionary government, the *Hébertists* led by Jacques Réné Hébert – author of the newspaper *Le Père Duchesne* – and the *Indulgents*, under the leadership of Georges Jacques Danton.[3]

The rise of the revolutionary government

Following its establishment in September 1792, the National Convention became divided between the Montagnards (a faction closely associated with the Jacobin Club and especially with Maximilien Robespierre) and the Girondins (a composite group including deputies from the Gironde region of France and figures formerly associated with the Cercle Social such as Jacques Pierre Brissot and the marquis de Condorcet).[4] The two factions (the

---

[1] On the publication of *Le Vieux Cordelier* see P. Pachet, 'La Restitution du texte de Camille Desmoulins: une exigence politique', in C. Desmoulins, *Le Vieux Cordelier*, ed. P. Pachet, Paris 1987, 13–31. *Le Vieux Cordelier* proved popular from the beginning. A government spy apparently reported that it was being read aloud in cafés such as the café de la Montagne, where it was 'universally applauded': Palmer, *Year of the Terror*, 263.
[2] See, for example, C. Haydon and W. Doyle (eds), *Robespierre*, Cambridge 1999, in which *Le Vieux Cordelier* figures in almost every article.
[3] My account of the context in which *Le Vieux Cordelier* was written is based on *Société des Jacobins*, v. 558–608, together with A. Mathiez, 'Pourquoi parut le "Vieux Cordelier"?', and H. Calvet, 'Hébert et Desmoulins devant les Jacobins', both in C. Desmoulins, *Le Vieux Cordelier*, ed. H. Calvet, Paris 1936, 33–40, 172–7.
[4] On the Montagnard–Girondin conflict see M. J. Sydenham, *The Girondins*, London

members of which also engaged in heated debates in the Paris Jacobin Club until the autumn of 1792, when many of the Girondins stopped attending the club) became polarised over the question of what should be done with the former king – Louis XVI – and over the issue of war. Antagonism increased during 1793. In that year both Robespierre and Antoine Saint-Just made speeches directed against the Girondins.[5] With the purging of the Girondins from the National Convention on 2 June 1793, the Montagnards, and especially Robespierre and Saint-Just, increased their control over that body. In seeking to justify their attacks on the Girondins, they developed the idea of revolutionary necessity.

The idea that a revolutionary situation was extraordinary, and that in such a situation the ordinary rules no longer applied, was not new. Rousseau had accepted the need for extreme measures in times of crisis. He spoke of it in a letter to the marquis de Mirabeau and put the idea into more practical terms in his description of the Roman dictatorship in his *Social contract*.[6] As early as July 1789 several deputies, including Robespierre, had used the argument that the revolutionary circumstances justified the people's violence. Later, Robespierre and his Montagnard associates developed this idea into a justification for revolutionary government. An early statement of this was set out in Robespierre's speech, of 3 December 1792, on what to do with Louis XVI. Addressing his fellow citizens he declared: 'you confuse the situation of a people in the midst of revolution, with that of a people whose government is consolidated'.[7] With the official establishment of the revolutionary government, almost a year later, the idea was developed and endlessly invoked and discussed. While the original task of the Convention elected in September 1792 had been to draw up a new constitution, and while a Montagnard

1901; P. Higonnet, 'The social and cultural antecedents of a revolutionary discontinuity: Montagnards and Girondins', *EHR* (1985), 513–44; and M. S. Lewis-Beck, A. Hildreth and A. B. Spitzer, 'Was there a Girondist faction in the National Convention, 1792–1793?', *FHS* xv (1987–8), 519–36, 537–48 (commentaries by M. J. Sydenham, A. Patrick and G. Kates). For more recent interpretations of the Girondins themselves see Kates, *The* Cercle Social, and F. Furet and M. Ozouf (eds), *La Gironde et les Girondins*, Paris 1991

5 M. Robespierre, 'Contre Brissot et les Girondins', 'Sur les Manoeuvres des Girondins' and 'Contre Brissot et les "hommes criminels" ', in *Oeuvres de Maximilien Robespierre*, VI–X: *Discours*, ed. M. Bouloiseau and A. Soboul, Paris 1950–67, ix. 376–413, 449–51, 532–5; A. Saint-Just, 'Rapport sur les trente-deux membres de la Convention détenus en vertu du décret du 2 juin', in *Oeuvres complètes de Saint-Just*, ed. C. Vellay, Paris 1908, ii. 1–31. Significantly, Desmoulins himself also wrote pamphlets against the Brissotins/Girondins: C. Desmoulins, *Jean-Pierre Brissot démasqué*, Paris 1792, and *Histoire des Brissotins: fragment de l'histoire secrète de la Révolution, et des six premiers mois de la république*, Paris 1793.

6 'Rousseau à Victor Riquetti, marquis de Mirabeau', *Correspondence complète de Jean Jacques Rousseau*, ed. R. A. Leigh, Oxford 1979, xxxiii. 238–41; Rousseau, *The social contract*, 138–40.

7 'vous confondez encore la situation d'un peuple en révolution, avec celle d'un peuple dont le gouvernement est affermi': Robespierre, 'Sur le jugement de Louis XVI', *Oeuvres*, ix. 122.

constitution was accepted by the Convention on 24 June 1793, it was never implemented. In the midst of foreign war, civil uprisings in the Vendée and elsewhere and financial crisis – and spurred on by the *sans-culottes* (who had helped to purge the Girondins from the Convention) – it was agreed that the implementation of the constitution be postponed until peace had been established. In its place a special revolutionary government was to operate for the duration of the war. The idea behind this revolutionary government was that in a time of crisis legitimate public authority should be derived, not from the constitution or the law, but from conformity with the Revolution itself.

The apparatus of the revolutionary government evolved gradually during 1793, but it was Saint-Just's speech on 19 vendémiaire an II (10 October 1793) that officially marked its inauguration:

> [The Committee of Public Safety] has therefore resolved to show to you the state of affairs, and to present to you the means that it believes appropriate to the consolidation of the Revolution, to the destruction of federalism, to the relieving of the people and the procuring of abundance for them, to the fortifying of the armies, to the clearing from the state of the conspiracies that infest it.[8]

The speech ended with a series of proposals, the first of which was that 'The provisional government of France is revolutionary until peace.'[9] In his later speech, 'Sur les principes de morale politique' of 17 pluviôse an II (5 February 1794), Robespierre sought to offer his explanation of the purpose behind the revolutionary government: 'But, to establish and to consolidate democracy among us, to arrive at the peaceful reign of constitutional laws: the war of liberty against tyranny must be ended; the storms of the revolution must be successfully crossed – such is the goal of the revolutionary system that you have regulated.'[10]

Even by the time Saint-Just made his speech, Terror had already become the 'order of the day'.[11] This had been announced following a popular *journée*, led by the *sans-culottes*, on 5 September 1793. Terror became the essential

---

[8] 'Il [the committee of public safety] a donc résolu de vous exposer l'état des choses, et de vous présenter les moyens qu'il croit propres, à consolider la Révolution, à abattre le fédéralisme, à soulager le peuple et lui procurer l'abondance, à fortifier les armées, à nettoyer l'Etat des conjurations qui l'infestent': Saint-Just, 'Rapport sur la nécessité de déclarer le gouvernement révolutionnaire jusqu'a la paix', *Oeuvres complètes*, ii. 76.
[9] 'Le gouvernement provisoire de la France est révolutionnaire jusqu'à la paix': ibid. ii. 88.
[10] 'Mais, pour fonder et pour consolider parmi nous la démocratie, pour arriver au règne paisible des lois constitutionnelles, il faut terminer la guerre de la liberté contre la tyrannie, et traverser heureusement les orages de la Révolution: tel est le but du système révolutionnaire que vous avez régularisé': Robespierre, 'Sur les principes de morale politique', *Oeuvres*, x. 353.
[11] On the Terror see Palmer, *Year of the Terror*; P. Gueniffey, *La Politique de la Terreur: essai sur la violence révolutionnaire, 1789–1794*, Paris 2000; C. Weber, *Terror and its discontents: suspect words in revolutionary France*, Minneapolis–London 2003. The latter also deals directly with Desmoulins's *Le Vieux Cordelier* at pp. 115–70.

arm of the revolutionary government. It was imposed from above by the committees of general security and public safety and at the grass-roots level policies were implemented by *representants-en-mission* from Paris and by local revolutionary committees, such as the committees of surveillance which had been established in March 1793. Gradually the word 'Terror' began to appear and be justified in the writings and speeches of Robespierre and Saint Just, who directly associated it with their belief in virtue:

> If the spring of popular government in peace is virtue, the spring of popular government in times of revolution is at the same time *virtue and terror*: virtue, without which terror is disastrous; terror, without which virtue is powerless. Terror is nothing but prompt, severe, and inflexible justice – it is therefore a product of virtue. It is not so much a particular principle as a consequence of the general principle of democracy, applied to the most pressing needs of the *patrie*.[12]

Saint-Just expressed a similar view in his 'Fragments sur les institutions républicaines': 'A republican government has virtue as its principle; or else terror. What do they want who want neither virtue nor terror?'[13]

For Robespierre, Saint-Just and their colleagues, virtue increasingly became *the* political value.[14] This was illustrated by Robespierre's contribution to the discussions surrounding the implementation of national festivals in brumaire an II (October/November 1793). Fabre d'Eglantine, who was responsible for the introduction of the revolutionary calendar, proposed that the *sans-culottides* festivals be named after genius, labour, actions, recompenses and opinion.[15] Addressing the Convention, Robespierre objected to the placing of the festival of genius at the head of the list, insisting that there must be a festival of virtue that should take precedence over all the others.[16]

---

[12] 'Si le ressort du gouvernement populaire dans la paix est la vertu, le ressort du gouvernement populaire en révolution est à la fois *la vertu et la terreur*: la vertu, sans laquelle la terreur est funeste; la terreur, sans laquelle la vertu est impuissante. La terreur n'est autre chose que la justice prompte, sévère, inflexible; elle est donc une émanation de la vertu; elle est moins un principe particulier, qu'une conséquence du principe général de la démocratie, appliqué aux plus pressans besoins de la patrie': Robespierre, 'Sur les principes de morale politique', *Oeuvres*, x. 357.

[13] 'Un gouvernement républicain a la vertu pour principe; sinon, la terreur. Que veulent ceux qui ne veulent ni vertu ni terreur?': Saint-Just, 'Fragments', *Oeuvres complètes*, ii. 506.

[14] On Robespierre's emphasis on virtue see M. Linton, 'Robespierre's political principles', in Haydon and Doyle, *Robespierre*, 37–53, and for the history of the concept of virtue in eighteenth-century France see M. Linton, *The politics of virtue in enlightenment France*, Basingstoke 2001.

[15] The *sans-culottides* festivals were to be held on the last five days (six in leap years) of the revolutionary calendar. They filled the gap between the revolutionary year (360 days) and the lunar year.

[16] Robespierre, 'Pour la consécration du premier jour sans-cullotide à la vertu', *Oeuvres*, x. 158.

Moreover, in his 'Sur les principes de morale politique' Robespierre was explicit about the importance of virtue:

> Now, what is the fundamental principle of democratic or popular government, that is to say, the essential spring which sustains it and which makes it act? It is virtue; I speak of public virtue which made many marvels in Greece and in Rome, and which must produce even more surprising goods in republican France, of this virtue which is nothing but the love of the *patrie* and of its laws.[17]

The similarity of this passage to ideas expressed in Montesquieu's *The spirit of the laws* reflects the fact that Robespierre saw virtue, as had Montesquieu, as the practice of subordinating one's individual interests to the common good.[18]

As Robespierre, Saint-Just and their colleagues increasingly appealed to notions of revolutionary necessity, terror and virtue to justify the actions of the government, their concern for the individual interests, rights and liberties of France's citizens diminished. In some of his earlier writings Robespierre had appeared to argue in favour of the protection of individual rights. In his speech 'Sur les subsistances', which he gave in December 1792, he declared that the first object of society was 'to maintain the inalienable rights of man'.[19] The following spring, Robespierre reaffirmed this idea by drawing up his own 'Déclaration des droits de l'homme et du citoyen'. In the first article he reiterated the point he had made in his earlier speech: 'The goal of all political association is the maintenance of the natural and inalienable rights of man, and the development of all his faculties.'[20] Later articles suggested individual rights would be secured and protected by the law:

> **Article XVIII**: Any law that violates the inalienable rights of man is essentially unjust and tyrannical: it is not a law.

> **Article XIX**: In all free states, the law must above all defend public and individual liberty against abuses of authority by those who govern.[21]

---

[17] 'Or, quel est le principe fondamental du gouvernement démocratique ou populaire, c'est-à-dire, le ressort essentiel qui le soutient et qui le fait mouvoir? C'est la vertu; je parle de la vertu publique qui opéra tant de prodiges dans la Grèce et dans Rome, et qui doit en produire de bien plus étonnans dans la France républicaine; de cette vertu qui n'est autre chose que l'amour de la patrie et de ses lois': idem, 'Sur les principes de morale politique', ibid. x. 353.

[18] See Montesquieu, *The spirit of the laws*, especially author's foreword at pp. xli–xlii, and 22–4.

[19] 'de maintenir les droits imprescriptibles de l'homme': Robespierre, 'Sur les subsistances': *Oeuvres*, ix. 112.

[20] 'Le but de toute association politique est le maintien des droits naturels et imprescriptibles de l'homme, et le développement de toutes ses facultés': idem, 'Déclaration des droits de l'homme et du citoyen', ibid. ix. 464.

[21] '**Article XVIII**: Toute loi qui viole les droits imprescriptibles de l'homme, est essentiellement injuste et tyrannique: elle n'est point une loi. **Article XIX**: Dans tout état

Yet, at the same time as he was advocating the sanctity of individual rights and freedoms, Robespierre was already acknowledging the fact that in certain situations individuals must be prepared to subsume themselves under the general will and to sacrifice their own needs and wants to those of the republic. At the end of his 'Exposition de mes principes', of May 1792, he had declared that 'We defend it not against the general will and against liberty, but against particular interests and against treachery. We only concern ourselves with individuals when their names are inseperably connected to the public good.'[22]

While Robespierre was already asserting the supremacy of the common good over the interests of individuals in early 1792, the idea was certainly given further weight by the outbreak of war in April of that year and the declaration of 'la patrie en danger' on 11 July. Robespierre opened his speech 'Sur les dangers de la patrie' with the following words: 'The moment has arrived to brush aside all personal interests to focus solely on the public interest.'[23] As the circumstances became more extreme, so too did Robespierre's proposals. On 1 April 1793 he declared: 'Forget individuals, we see only the safety of the republic.'[24]

An even more obvious shift can be detected in Saint-Just's works. As Norman Hampson has suggested, between 1791 and 1794 he replaced his earlier emphasis on individual rights with 'the Rousseauist conviction that it was for society to make men what they ought to be'.[25] In his 'Rapport sur les personnes incarcérées', given on behalf of the committees of public safety and general security on 8 ventôse an II (26 February 1794), Saint-Just developed the idea that individual liberty must be sacrificed to the demands of utility and political necessity and that all who were not prepared to sacrifice their own interests to the needs of the republic should be viewed as its enemies:

> [It is] therefore less [a question of] what is important for such and such an individual, than [a question of] what is important for the republic; less [a matter of] ceding to private views, than of making triumphant universal views. . . .

> When a republic, with tyrants for neighbours, is agitated, it must make strong laws; it must take care against the supporters of its enemies, and even against those who are indifferent to it. . . .

---

libre, la loi doit surtout défendre la liberté publique et individuelle contre l'abus de l'autorité de ceux qui gouvernent': ibid. ix. 467.

22 'Nous la défendrons non contre la volonté générale et contre la liberté, mais contre les intérêts particuliers et contre la perfidie. Nous ne nous occuperons des individus, que lorsque leurs noms seront inséparablement liés à la cause publique': idem, 'Exposition de mes principes', ibid. iv. 15.

23 'Le moment est arrivé d'écarter tous les intérêts personnels pour ne s'occuper que de l'intérêt public': idem, 'Sur les dangers de la patrie', ibid. viii. 390.

24 'Oublions tout individu, ne voyons que le salut de la république': idem, 'Sur les moyens de sauver la république', ibid. ix. 356.

25 N. Hampson, Saint-Just, Oxford 1991, 49.

That which constitutes a republic, it is the total destruction of that which is opposed to it. . . .

The first law of all laws is the conservation of the republic. . . .

It is difficult to establish a republic other than by the inflexible censure of all crimes.[26]

Despite the rhetoric, the Montagnard rise to power did not go unchallenged after the removal of the Girondins. Rather, they found themselves under attack, from both left and right, by members of the Cordeliers Club.

The *Enragés* and *Hébertists*: the new Cordeliers

Although it had continued to meet following the massacre on the Champ de Mars in July 1791, the Cordeliers Club changed significantly between then and late 1793. By the spring of that year, the Cordeliers were under the influence of the *Enragés* Jacques Roux, Jean-François Varlet and Théophile Leclerc.[27]

The *Enragés* rose to a position of influence in the midst of a shortage of basic commodities in Paris in February 1793. They were, for the most part, long-time members of the club and so it is not surprising that many of their ideas were typical of it. They were strongly opposed to the Brissotins/Girondins and their model of representative government and instead favoured the kind of democratic mechanisms advocated by members of the club since 1790. R. B. Rose suggests that several pamphlets produced by Varlet were aimed at reconciling 'abstract Rousseauist ideals . . . with the practical problems of governing revolutionary France . . . through means such as a binding mandate, the right of recall and the ratification of all laws by the primary assemblies'.[28] The economic ideas of the *Enragés* can also be seen as

---

[26] 'Vous avez donc moins à décider de ce qui importe à tel ou tel individu, qu'à décider de ce qui importe à la République; moins à céder aux vues privées, qu'à faire triompher des vues universelles. . . . Lorsqu'une République voisine des tyrans en est agitée, il lui faut des lois fortes; il ne lui faut point de ménagements contre les partisans de ses ennemis, contre les indifférents même. . . . Ce qui constitue une République, c'est la destruction totale de ce qui lui est opposé. . . . La première loi de toutes les lois est la conservation de la République. . . . Il est difficile d'établir une République autrement que par la censure inflexible de tous les crimes': Saint-Just, 'Rapport sur les personnes incarcérées', *Oeuvres complètes*, ii. 229–36.
[27] On the *Enragés* see Rose, *The Enragés*, and D. Richet, 'Enragés', in F. Furet and M. Ozouf (eds), *A critical dictionary of the French Revolution*, trans. A. Goldhammer, Cambridge, Mass. 1989, 337–41. Roux, Varlet and Leclerc themselves would not have accepted the label 'Enragés', which was generally used pejoratively at the time, but would simply have seen themselves as Cordeliers. The meaning and uses of the term are discussed in the introduction to Rose, *The Enragés*.
[28] Rose, *The Enragés*, 18.

having developed out of views that had long been expressed by Cordeliers Club members. Their attacks on speculators (*agioteurs*), monopolisers (*accapareurs*) and food hoarders, echo Rutledge's rhetoric during the 'boulanger affair'. *Enragé* calls for rigorous repression of such activities won them support from the *sans-culottes*. Despite their own comfortable backgrounds, they thus became the spokesmen of the ordinary people. Their ideas were most clearly set out in Roux's address to the Convention of 25 June 1793, which became known as the 'Manifest des Enragés'.[29] Roux gave his speech immediately following the voting of the constitution of 1793 on 24 June. He objected to that document on the grounds that it offered no solution to the economic problems facing the *sans-culottes*:

> The constitutional act is about to be presented for sanction by the sovereign; have you there prohibited speculation? No. Have you pronounced the punishment of death against monopolisers? No. Have you determined what liberty of commerce involves? No. Have you forbidden the sale of silver currency? No. Well then! We declare to you that you have not done everything possible for the happiness of the people.[30]

Roux was clear in his advice as to what the Convention should do: 'Well then! decree constitutionally that speculating, the sale of silver currency and monopolising are harmful to society.'[31]

As well as drawing on and developing traditional Cordelier ideas, the *Enragés* also responded to the specific circumstances of 1793. They accepted the justification of revolutionary necessity and the idea that the end justifies the means. They endorsed the need for public demonstrations and even bloodshed and ultra-terrorist measures. From May 1793 Varlet was advocating a programme of fifteen 'supreme measures of public safety' including the arrest of the Girondins and of all suspects, the extermination of all money speculators and food hoarders and the creation of a revolutionary army in every town.[32] Similarly, Roux advocated the use of 'draconian legislation and terroristic action' to bring about his political and economic goals.[33]

The Cordeliers Club disassociated itself from the *Enragés* in the summer of

29 The text has been printed in full by A. Mathiez in *Annales révolutionnaires* vii (1914), 547–60.
30 'L'acte constitutionnel va être présenté à la sanction du souverain; y avez-vous proscrit l'agiotage? Non. Avez-vous prononcé la peine de mort contre les accapareurs? Non. Avez-vous déterminé ce en quoi consiste la liberté du commerce? Non. Avez-vous défendu la vente de l'argent monnoyé? Non. Et bien! Nous vous déclarons que vous n'avez pas tout fait pour le bonheur du people': ibid. 548.
31 'Eh bien! décrétez constitutionnellement que l'agiotage, la vente de l'argent monnoie, et les accaparemens sont nuisibles à la société': ibid. 551.
32 Rose, *The Enragés*, 22.
33 Ibid. 45.

1793.[34] Yet this separation appears to have had more to do with personal animosity and ambition than ideas. On 27 June Roux went to the Cordeliers Club to tell them of the hostile reception of his speech (the 'Manifest des Enragés') by the nation's deputies. The Cordeliers expressed their support for him. They allegedly cried out 'Vive Jacques Roux! Vivent les sans-culottes' and they reiterated their endorsement of his speech.[35] However one or two club members, most notably Hébert, were disturbed by Roux's popularity and became determined to end his influence over the Cordeliers Club. Hébert had been a key spokesman for the club since the autumn of 1791. He was the author of the journal Le Père Duchesne, through which he exercised a significant influence over the sans-culottes; and he was keen that it should be him and his associates, rather than the Enragés, who took the lead in the club. On 30 June, having already attacked Roux in the commune two days earlier, Hébert secured the expulsion from the Cordeliers Club of Roux and Leclerc, and the suspension of Varlet pending further examination of his conduct. Hébert was supported by other Cordeliers, including Antoine François Momoro, and by a special delegation sent from the Jacobin Club – which included Robespierre.

It is ironic that Hébert and his associates, who were instrumental in expelling the Enragés from the club, went on to adopt many of their ideas and policies. Initially the Hébertists had been hostile to sans-culotte calls for price controls and ultra-terrorist measures.[36] In February 1793 Hébert had opposed an uprising led by the Enragés, and in his Le Père Duchesne he waged an ongoing campaign against the group.[37] At the same time Hébert and his friends pursued a policy of support for Robespierre and the Montagnards. However, the Hébertists gradually changed their views and by the winter of 1793–4 they had adopted many aspects of the Enragé programme.[38] At the same time, the Hébertists began to turn away from the Montagnards. As early as August 1793, Hébert began to withdraw his support for Montagnard policy. In early September he and his associates participated, alongside the sans-culottes, in a demonstration outside the National Convention. It was also Hébert who led the call for renewed militancy against all enemies of the republic. It was, in part, the pressure exerted by the Hébertists alongside, and as a mouthpiece for, the sans-culottes that led the National Convention to

---

[34] On this affair see Mathiez, Annales révolutionnaires, vii. 556–60 and Collot d'Herbois's account in Société des Jacobins, v. 281–3.

[35] Mathiez, Annales révolutionnaires, vii. 559.

[36] On the Hébertists see D. Richet, 'Hébertists', in Furet and Ozouf, Critical dictionary, 363–9, and M. Slavin, The Hébertists to the guillotine: anatomy of a 'conspiracy' in revolutionary France, Baton Rouge–London 1994. 'Hébertist' was not a contemporary label, but has been applied to the group by later writers. As with the Enragés, they would simply have seen themselves as Cordeliers.

[37] Slavin, The Hébertists to the guillotine, 17.

[38] Rose, The Enragés, 70.

increase the powers and workload of the Revolutionary Tribunal and to introduce Terror as 'the order of the day'.

The other key branch of *Hébertist* policy from late 1793 to 1794 concerned religion. During the autumn of 1793 a wave of dechristianisation swept across France: priests were forced to resign and even to marry, church buildings were looted and vandalised and Christian services and ceremonies were prohibited. In Paris, sectional committees closed the churches and the commune forbade their being reopened. Even Notre Dame was invaded and turned into a temple of reason.[39] The movement affected different areas of the country differently and to varying degrees. In Paris it was members of the commune, and particularly Hébert and Chaumette, who played a leading role. Chaumette (who had been one of the dissidents in the schism centred on Rutledge but had subsequently fallen out with the members of the new club; and who, by 1793, was a supporter of Hébert) travelled to Nevers in September, allegedly on family business. Once there he aided Joseph Fouché in organising a 'cult of reason', driving out priests and converting the churches into secular temples of reason.[40] Hébert demonstrated his support by publicly congratulating Chaumette for his actions. It was also Chaumette who gave a speech to the general council of the commune of Paris on 3 frimaire an II (23 November 1793) in which he put forward a five-point plan for dechristianisation:

> The council orders: 1. that all churches or temples of every religion and form of worship that exist in Paris will be closed straight away; 2. that all priests or ministers, of whatever form of worship, will remain personally and individually responsible for all the troubles that are the result of religious opinion; 3. that anyone who calls for the opening, either of a temple or of a church, will be arrested as a suspect; 4. that the revolutionary committees will be invited to watch carefully over all priests; 5. that a petition addressed to the Convention will be drawn up to invite them to pass a decree which excludes priests of all kinds from public functions, as well as from all employment in the manufacturing of arms.[41]

---

39 Palmer, *Year of the Terror*, 119.
40 Robertson, 'The society of the Cordeliers', 173.
41 'Le conseil arrête: 1. que toutes les églises ou temples de toutes religions et de tous cultes qui ont existé à Paris seront sur-le-champ fermées; 2. que tous les prêtres ou ministres, de quelque culte que ce soit, demeureront personnellement et individuellement responsables de tous les troubles dont la source viendrait d'opinions religieuses; 3. que celui qui demandera l'ouverture, soit d'un temple, soit d'une église, sera arrêté comme suspect; 4. que les comités révolutionnaires seront invités à surveiller de bien près tous les prêtres; 5. qu'il sera fait une pétition à la Convention pour l'inviter à porter un décret qui exclue les prêtres de toute espèce de fonction publique, ainsi que de tout emploi dans les manufactures d'armes': *Moniteur universel*, xviii. 506. Chaumette later lost his nerve and turned against the dechristianisation campaign. As a result he was expelled from the Cordeliers Club on 17 frimaire an II (7 Dec. 1793).

Owing to his emphasis on the role that religion could play in inculcating republican virtue, Robespierre was strongly opposed to dechristianisation and he worked hard to destroy the movement. On 18 floréal an II (7 May 1794) in his speech 'Sur les rapports des idées religieuses et morales avec les principes républicains et sur les fêtes nationales' he developed his attack. He began by presenting morality as the essential basis of society: 'Morality is the sole foundation of civil society.'[42] He went on to link religion to morality and, on this basis, he condemned atheism and supported religious liberty:

> Consult only the good of the *patrie* and the interests of humanity. All institutions, all doctrines that console and that raise up souls must be welcomed; reject all those that tend to degrade and corrupt them . . .

> The idea of the Supreme Being and of the immortality of the soul is a continual recall to justice; it is therefore both social and republican.[43]

While many in the Cordeliers Club came to support Hébert, there were some members who were opposed both to the dechristianisation campaign and to the idea of revolutionary necessity. Desmoulins's *Le Vieux Cordelier* is perhaps the most comprehensive statement of the position of members of this group.

The *Indulgents* and the background to Desmoulins's *Le Vieux Cordelier*

In the first issue of *Le Vieux Cordelier* Desmoulins launched an attack on the dechristianisation policies favoured by the *Hébertists*. It was not surprising, therefore, that Robespierre initially approved of the newspaper.[44] However, while Desmoulins and his fellow *Indulgents* shared Robespierre's opposition to Hébert they were certainly not unquestioning supporters of the revolutionary government. They continued to see the purpose of the Revolution as being to ensure the protection and promotion of the rights and liberties of individual citizens. On this basis they objected to appeals to the Revolution being used to justify the violation of the very principles it was supposed to be promoting. They argued that things had gone too far, and they called for clemency and for a relaxation of the Terror.[45]

---

[42] 'Le fondement unique de la société civile, c'est la morale': Robespierre, 'Sur les rapports des idées religieuses et morales', *Oeuvres*, x. 446.

[43] 'Ne consultez que le bien de la patrie et les intérêts de l'humanité. Toute institution, toute doctrine qui console et qui élève les âmes, doit être accueillie; rejettez toutes celle qui tendent à les dégrader et à les corrompre. . . . L'idée de l'Etre suprême et de l'immortalité de l'âme est un rappel continuel à la justice; elle est donc sociale et républicaine': ibid. x. 451–2.

[44] Robespierre was shown the proofs of some of the early issues and, according to Norman Hampson, he even borrowed phrases from the paper in a speech he made to the Jacobin Club a couple of days later: N. Hampson, *Danton*, Oxford 1978, 147; Palmer, *Year of the Terror*, 259.

[45] Desmoulins and the *Indulgents* had supported both the execution of the king and of the

This attitude on the part of Desmoulins had already led to Jacobin scrutiny of his conduct. His alleged 'indifference' to the progress of the Revolution had been noted, prior to the publication of the first issue of *Le Vieux Cordelier*, on the 11 frimaire an II (1 December 1793) when he was denounced by Hanriot Deschamps.[46] Concerns were raised again two weeks later. On 24 frimaire an II (14 December 1793) Desmoulins was asked about his relations with the soldier Arthur Dillon, who had been arrested for conspiracy at the end of June 1793, and about his alleged comment at the time of the execution of the Girondins that they had died as republicans. Desmoulins sought to justify himself, and then Robespierre spoke in defence of his childhood friend: 'Camille has developed since [school] the most ardent love for the republic; he is republican by instinct, by the simple impulse of his heart.'[47]

On the following day, 25 frimaire an II (15 December 1793), the third issue of *Le Vieux Cordelier* appeared. It was in this issue that Desmoulins began to voice his opposition to the revolutionary government. With its appearance, Robespierre's stance shifted. On 1 nivôse an II (21 December 1793) Desmoulins was denounced in the Jacobin Club by M. Nicolas.[48] This time Robespierre did not come to his defence. On the contrary, in his speech on the principles of revolutionary government on 5 nivôse an II (25 December 1793), which constituted his first open attack on the *Indulgents*, Robespierre offered what was in effect a direct response to Desmoulins's newspaper.[49] The main thrust of his argument was that Desmoulins had confused the principles of ordinary and extraordinary government. Under revolutionary circumstances, Robespierre claimed, it was necessary to introduce measures that would be unacceptable in a normal situation:

Girondins, so they were not entirely opposed to the use of Terror. Moreover, there are hints of support for terrorist policies in *Le Vieux Cordelier* itself. None the less, the overall thrust of the argument, and the reason why Desmoulins himself eventually became a victim of the Terror, was his suggestion that there was now a need for clemency.

[46] Deschamp's denunciation read as follows: 'I will make my observations on various other members . . . I accuse Camille Desmoulins as a man who, having served the revolution well, has ended up being, one can say, indifferent to its progress.' ('Je vais, faire mes observations sur différents autres membres . . . J'accuse Camille Desmoulins comme un homme qui, ayant bien servi la révolution, a fini par être on ne peut pas plus indifférent sur ses progrès.'): *Moniteur universel*, xviii. 572.

[47] 'Camille à développé depuis [collège] l'amour le plus ardent pour la République; il est républicain par instinct, par la simple impulsion de son coeur': Robespierre, 'Pour Camille Desmoulins', *Oeuvres*, x. 253. Robespierre and Desmoulins had both attended the exclusive *collège* Louis-le-Grand in Paris.

[48] The denunciation read as follows: 'I accuse him of having made a libel with criminal and counter-revolutionary intentions. I call to all those who have read it. Camille Desmoulins has for a long time been close to the guillotine!' ('Je l'accuse d'avoir fait un libelle avec des intentions criminelles et contre-révolutionnaires. J'en appelle à tous ceux qui l'ont lu. Camille Desmoulins frise depuis long-tems la guillotine!;'): quoted in Desmoulins, *Le Vieux Cordelier* (ed. Calvet), 110.

[49] Robespierre, 'Rapport sur les principes du gouvernement révolutionnaire', *Oeuvres*, x. 273–82.

The goal of constitutional government is to conserve the republic; that of rev-olutionary government is to establish it . . .

Revolutionary government has need of extraordinary action, precisely because it is at war . . .

Constitutional government concerns itself principally with civil liberty and revolutionary government with public liberty. Under a constitutional regime, it is sufficient to protect individuals against abuses of public power; under a revolutionary regime the public power itself is obliged to defend itself against all factions that attack it.[50]

Jacobin attacks on Desmoulins and his newspaper continued into 1794.[51] On 16 nivôse an II (5 January 1794) the commission that had been examining the accusations against Desmoulins, Pierre Philippeaux and François-Louis Bourdon 'de l'Oise' gave its report to the Jacobin Club. Speaking on behalf of the commission, Collot d'Herbois called for the exclusion of Philippeaux and the censure of *Le Vieux Cordelier*. Hébert took the stand to complain at the leniency of their decision against Desmoulins and a debate ensued between the authors of *Le Père Duchesne* and *Le Vieux Cordelier*. On 18 and 19 nivôse an II (7 and 8 January 1794) extracts from *Le Vieux Cordelier* were read to the club and Desmoulins was asked to account for his arguments. By this time Robespierre was strongly opposed at least to *Le Vieux Cordelier*, if not to its author. He claimed to be able to see the real aim of Desmoulins's newspaper:

He has claimed that the issues of his newspaper have been justified by the translation of some passages from Tacitus that he inserted into them. I ask whether these passages from Tacitus, who without doubt was more diplomatic than him, are not from his pen simply biting satires against the current gov-ernment of the Convention?

and he even went so far as to suggest that copies of the book be burned – although he did quickly retract that suggestion.[52] Desmoulins's uncompro-mising response – 'Well said Robespierre, but I respond to you as Rousseau

---

[50] 'Le but du gouvernement constitutionnel est de conserver la République; celui du gouvernement révolutionnaire est de la fonder. . . . Le gouvernement révolutionnaire a besoin d'une activité extraordinaire, précisément parce qu'il est en guerre. . . . Le gouvernement constitutionnel s'occupe principalement de la liberté civile: et le gouvernement révolutionnaire, de la liberté publique. Sous le régime constitutionnel, il suffit presque de protéger les individus contre l'abus de la puissance publique: sous le régime révolutionnaire, la puissance publique elle-même est obligée de se défendre contre toutes les factions qui l'attaquent': ibid. x. 274.

[51] My account of January 1794 is based on *Société des Jacobins*, v. 558–608, and Calvet, 'Hébert et Desmoulins devant les Jacobins', in Desmoulins, *Le Vieux Cordelier* (ed. Calvet), 172–7.

[52] 'Il a prétendu que ses numéros étaient justifiés par la traduction de quelques passages de Tacite, qu'il y a fait entrer. Je lui demande si ces passages de Tacite, qui sans doute était plus politique que lui, ne sont pas sous sa plume autant de satires piquantes du gouvernement actuel de la Convention?': *Société des Jacobins*, v. 598–600.

did: to burn is not to answer.' – rendered the break between the two men complete.[53] In a later speech entitled 'Pour rappeler Camille Desmoulins aux principes' Robespierre attacked Desmoulins himself: 'His writings are dangerous; they feed the hope of our enemies, and incite the public's sense of malice.'[54] Similarly, in his 'Sur les principes de morale politique', Robespierre made a scathing reference to the newspaper of his former friend:

> If we did not have a great task to fulfill, if it was a question here only of the interests of a faction or of a new aristocracy, we could have believed, as have certain writers more ignorant than depraved, that the plan of the French Revolution was written in full in the books of Tacitus and Machiavelli, and we would seek the duties of the representatives of the people in the histories of Augustus, Tiberius, or Vespasion, or even in that of certain French legislators; because, apart from nuances with respect to perfidy or cruelty, all tyrants resemble each other.[55]

On 21 nivôse an II (10 January 1794) Desmoulins's Jacobin opponents achieved their aim and his name was deleted from the list of club members. The next day he was struck off the list of Cordeliers, but he continued to use the title *Le Vieux Cordelier*, claiming that he associated himself not with the current club but with the district that had enjoyed a certain reputation in 1789 and 1790.[56] The execution of the *Hébertists* on 4 germinal an 2 (24 March 1794) was followed by the arrest of the *Indulgents*, including Desmoulins, on 9 and 10 germinal an II (29 and 30 March 1794) and their subsequent trial and execution. The Terror became more extreme and more brutal with the laws of 27 germinal an II (16 April 1794), 19 floréal an II (8 May 1794) and particularly the infamous law of 22 prairial an II (10 June 1794).

In spite of its apparent domination, the revolutionary government had effectively undermined its own position. It had been introduced and sustained on the foundation of groups such as the *Hébertists* and the

---

53 'C'est fort bien dit, Robespierre, mais je te répondrai comme Rousseau: brûler n'est pas répondre': Calvet, 'Hébert et Desmoulins devant les Jacobins', 174.

54 'Ses écrits sont dangereux; ils alimentent l'espoir de nos ennemis, et vorisent la malignité publique': Robespierre, 'Pour rappeler Camille Desmoulins aux principes', *Oeuvres*, x. 308.

55 'Si nous n'avions pas eu une plus grande tâche à remplir, s'il ne s'aggissoit ici que des intérêts d'une faction ou d'une aristocratie nouvelle, nous aurions pu croire comme certains écrivains, plus ignorans encore que pervers, que le plan de la Révolution française étoit écrit en toutes lettres dans les livres de Tacite et de Machiavel, et chercher les devoirs des représentants du peuple dans l'histoire d'Auguste, de Tibère ou de Vespasien, ou même dans celle de certains législateurs français; car, à quelques nuances près de perfidie ou de cruauté, tous les tyrans se ressemblent': idem, 'Sur les principes de morale politique', ibid. x. 351.

56 Desmoulins, *Le Vieux Cordelier* (ed. Calvet), 131. Interestingly, soon after Desmoulins's expulsion from the Cordeliers Club Jean Honoré Dunouy, Rutledge's former friend and associate, was also excluded: Robertson, 'The society of the Cordeliers', 191.

Indulgents, and the popular followings that they generated. In executing the leaders of these groups the government alienated its own supporters and, at the same time, divisions within the committee of public safety itself deepened. Collapse was bound to follow. In the aftermath of Robespierre's speech to the Convention (8 thermidor an II – 26 July 1794) in which he attacked his opponents and ordered the radicals Collot d'Herbois and Jacques Nicolas Billaud-Varenne to be expelled from the Jacobin Club, Robespierre himself, together with his collaborators Saint-Just, Georges Couthon, Philippe François Joseph Le Bas and Robespierre's own younger brother Augustin, were arrested. They were executed the next day.[57]

Against this background, the traditional argument has been that Desmoulins's *Le Vieux Cordelier* was inspired by the personal animosities and political rivalries of late 1793 and early 1794. It has been suggested that Desmoulins wrote the newspaper in order to defend himself and his fellow *Indulgents* and to further their campaign against both the *Hébertists* and the revolutionary government. While this contemporary political context makes some sense of Desmoulins's text, it does not explain everything. In particular, there is the issue of why Desmoulins quoted long passages apparently taken from the works of Tacitus. It was not unusual for French revolutionary orators (especially those educated at Louis-le-Grand) to hark back to the ancient writers,[58] but, as a twentieth-century editor of *Le Vieux Cordelier* (Henri Calvet) realised, Desmoulins was not quoting Tacitus himself, but rather the French translation of Thomas Gordon's *Discourses on Tacitus*.[59] Calvet, however, did not attempt to explain why Desmoulins did this, or how he had come across Gordon's work. By contrast, another commentator, Jaikur Ramaswamy, aware of Gordon's role as a British commonwealthman or eighteenth-century republican, has suggested that Desmoulins's knowledge of English republicanism (and thus of Gordon) arose either from his involvement in the salon of the baron d'Holbach, or from his association with the republican circle of Thomas Hollis and Catharine Macaulay.[60] While Desmoulins's pre-revolutionary connections, as well as the contemporary political debates in which he was engaged, were undoubtedly influential in

---

[57] Le Bas was not executed with the others; he had already committed suicide.

[58] See Parker, *The cult of antiquity*.

[59] T. Gordon, *The works of Tacitus . . . to which are prefixed political discourses upon that author*, London 1728–31, and *Discours sur Tacite*. Desmoulins also referred to Daudé's translation of Gordon's *Discourses on Sallust: the works of Sallust translated into English with political discourses upon that author*, London 1744, and *Discours sur Salluste*.

[60] Ramaswamy, 'Reconstituting the "liberty of the ancients"', 199n. See also M. Sonenscher, 'Artisans, sans-culottes and the French Revolution', in A. Forrest and P. Jones (eds), *Reshaping France: town, country and region during the French Revolution*, Manchester 1991, 105–18. D'Holbach had translated Trenchard and Gordon's *The independent Whig* under the title *L'Esprit du clergé* in 1767. Catharine Macaulay's republican history of seventeenth-century England was translated into French by Mirabeau in 1791–2.

shaping his ideas, *Le Vieux Cordelier* must also be understood in the context of the position of the Cordeliers (both the district and the club) between 1789 and 1794.

Le Vieux Cordelier: principles and sources

Though published in 1793–4, *Le Vieux Cordelier* was driven by the same key ideas of individual rights, liberty and democracy that had inspired Desmoulins and his fellow Cordeliers in 1789–91. Indeed the title *Le Vieux Cordelier* implicitly invoked old Cordeliers values against the newly dominant voices in the club. The seventh, posthumous, issue of the newspaper included a conversation between two old Cordeliers – Desmoulins himself and an unnamed interlocuter: '[An] old priest of the Cordeliers district, who entered my house, and came to see whether I would speak with dignity of the chapter in my issue VII, and whether I would not step back from the fight.'[61] The two of them discuss various topics, including the respective merits of the French and English systems of government and the importance of the liberty of the press. The issue ends with them agreeing on the necessity of a free press and the dangers that can ensue if it is not protected. As we have seen, from the third issue onwards *Le Vieux Cordelier* not only constituted an attack on the *Hébertists* but also offered a critique of the reign of Terror and thus of the revolutionary government itself. Desmoulins was therefore asserting old Cordeliers ideas not just against Hébert and the new Cordeliers, but also against the policies of the revolutionary government.

Desmoulins objected to Robespierre's appeal to revolutionary necessity, and against it he asserted the traditional Cordeliers emphasis on the need to protect and defend the rights of individuals as set out in the *Declaration des droits*: 'We fight to defend the goods that are possessed when they are invoked. These goods are the declaration of rights, the gentleness of republican maxims, fraternity, holy equality, the inviolability of principles.'[62] He particularly emphasised the importance of the liberty of the press and freedom of speech for deputies, as means of protection against tyranny: 'As long as the unlimited liberty of the press has existed, it has been easy for us to anticipate and to prevent everything.'[63] In the seventh issue the same idea was still being expressed:

---

61 'Vieux prêtre de l'ancien district des Cordeliers, qui entre chez moi, et vient voir si je fais parler dignement le chapitre dans mon numéro VII, et si je ne fais pas reculer la bannière': Desmoulins, *Le Vieux Cordelier* (ed. Calvet), 204n.
62 'Nous combattons pour défendre des biens dont elle met sur le champ en possession ceux qui l'invoquent. Ces biens sont la déclaration des droits, la douceur des maximes républicaines, la fraternité, la sainte égalité, l'inviolabilité des principes': ibid. 114.
63 'Tant que la liberté indéfinie de la presse a existé, il nous a été facile de tout prévoir, de tout prévenir': ibid. 87.

What is the last retrenchment against despotism? It is the liberty of the press. And then the best? It is the liberty of the press. And after the best? It is still the liberty of the press . . .

What is it that distinguishes a republic from a Monarchy? It is a single thing, the liberty of speaking and of writing.[64]

Against Robespierre Desmoulins even insisted that it was the liberty of the press and the form of government, rather than virtue, that was the essential basis of a republic:

But to return to the question of the liberty of the press, without doubt it must be unlimited; without doubt republics must have as their base and foundation the liberty of the press, not this other base that Montesquieu has given them. [If virtue was the only spring of government, if you suppose all men to be virtuous, the form of government is of no importance and all are equally good. Why therefore do we have some governments that are detestable and others that are good? Why do we have a horror of monarchy and cherish republics? It is, one supposes with reason, that men are not all equally virtuous, the goodness of the government must supplement virtue and the excellence of a republic consists precisely in this that it supplements virtue . . .

This series of simple and incontestable principles renders palpable the error of *Montesquieu*. Virtue is not the foundation of a republic. What does the form of government matter, and what is the need of a republic, if all the citizens are virtuous? But the republic is the supplement of virtue][65]

Not only does this passage read as an almost direct response to Robespierre's discussion of virtue in his speech 'Sur les principes de morale politique' which is quoted above, but it also suggests that Desmoulins shared Rutledge's pessimistic (Harringtonian) view as to the possibility of virtue and its place within

[64] 'Quel est le dernier retranchement contre le despotisme? C'est la liberté de la presse. Et ensuite le meilleur? C'est la liberté de la presse. Et après le meilleur? C'est encore la liberté de la presse. . . . Qu'est-ce qui distingue la république de la Monarchie? c'est une seule chose, la liberté de parler et d'écrire': ibid. 206–7.
[65] 'Mais pour nous renfermer dans la question de la liberté de la presse, sans doute elle doit être illimitée; sans doute les républiques ont pour base et fondement la liberté de la presse, non pas cette autre base que leur a donnée Montesquieu. [Si la vertu était le seul ressort du gouvernement, si vous supposez tous les hommes vertueux, la forme du gouvernement est indifférente et tous sont également bons. Pourquoi donc y a-t-il des gouvernements détestables et d'autres qui sont bons? Pourquoi avons-nous en horreur la monarchie et chérissons-nous la république? C'est qu'on suppose avec raison que les hommes n'étant pas tous également vertueux, il faut que la bonté du gouvernement supplée à la vertu et que l'excellence de la république consiste en cela précisément qu'elle supplée à la vertu. . . . Cette série de propositions simples et incontestables rend palpable l'erreur de *Montesquieu*. La vertu n'est point le fondement de la république. Qu'importe la forme du gouvernement, et qu'est-il besoin de république, si tous les citoyens sont vertueux? Mais la république est le supplément de la vertu]': ibid. 237–8. Robespierre himself had initially been an ardent supporter of the liberty of the press. However his opinions began to change following the collapse of the monarchy in the summer of 1792 when a number of royalist pamphlets were censored.

a republic.[66] Desmoulins also continued, as in his earlier works, to defend the existence of a democratic republican constitution. For example, the third issue of *Le Vieux Cordelier* opened with an assertion of his preference for republican, or even democratic, over monarchical government. And in the sixth issue he referred back to his earlier work, claiming that just as he had written in *La France Libre* he still believed 'That popular government or democracy is the only constitution that suits France, and all those who are not unworthy of the name of men.'[67]

It was not just old Cordeliers principles that Desmoulins revived in the later issues of his newspaper. The sources on which he based his argument were also those of the old Cordeliers. At the end of the first issue of *Le Vieux Cordelier*, Desmoulins explained that he was going to present lessons drawn from history in the councils of Tacitus and Machiavelli, whom he described as 'the greatest politicians ever to have existed'.[68] Citations from Machiavelli's *Discourses* are prominent in *Le Vieux Cordelier*. For example the epigraph of the first three issues was drawn from the *Discourses*: 'From the time that those who govern come to be hated, their rivals are soon admired.'[69] Calvet noted that this quotation does not appear to be in the French version of Machiavelli's *Discourses* held in Desmoulins's library.[70] He suggested that Desmoulins perhaps borrowed the phrase from Pierre Daudé's French transla- tion of Thomas Gordon's *Discourses on Tacitus*, which included the following passages:

> Machiavelli said that when a prince has once incurred public hatred, he must fear everything . . .
>
> A prince who neglects his affairs . . . from the moment that he is scorned, he ceases to be secure. The people then turn . . . their affections towards his successors . . .
>
> When a prince begins to become infirm, everyone turns their eyes . . . towards his successor'.[71]

---

66 Robespierre, 'Sur les principes de morale politique', *Oeuvres*, x. 353. On Rutledge's views on virtue see chapter 3 above.

67 'Que le gouvernement populaire et la démocratie est la seule constitution qui convienne à la France, et à tous ceux qui ne sont pas indignes du nom d'hommes': Desmoulins, *Le Vieux Cordelier* (ed. Calvet), 181. For the original statement see Desmoulins, *La France libre*, 45.

68 'les plus grands politiques qui aient jamais existé': Desmoulins, *Le Vieux Cordelier* (ed. Calvet), 48.

69 'Dès que ceux qui gouvernent seront haïs, leurs concurrens ne tarderont pas à être admirés': ibid. 41, 51, 67.

70 Ibid. 41n. The catalogue of Desmoulins's library can now be found among his papers, which are held by the BHVP, Rés. 24, 25, 26.

71 'Machiavel dit que lorsqu'un prince a une fois encouru la haine publique, il n'est rien qu'il ne doive craindre. . . . Un prince qui néglige ses affaires . . . du moment qu'il est méprisé, cesse d'être en sûreté. Les peuples tournent alors . . . leurs affections vers les

Whether or not Gordon was the source of Desmoulins's Machiavellian quotation, he certainly provided the Tacitean references. The third issue of Desmoulins's newspaper opened with a discussion of the advantages of republican over monarchical government, and, in particular, the fact that in the former merit is usually the basis of success. But, Desmoulins insisted, in order to make a sound judgement between the two it is necessary to look back through history at the examples it provides:

> We are now in the midst of a fight to the death between the republic and the monarchy. In this fight it is inevitable that either one or the other will win a bloody victory. But who could object to the triumph of the republic, after having seen the historical evidence left to us by the triumph of monarchy [Who could oppose the republic] after glancing at the debauched and grotesque scenes of Tacitus, that I am going to present to the honourable circle of my subscribers?[72]

There then follows several pages-worth of text drawn, not directly from Tacitus, but from Daudé's translation of Gordon's *Discourses on Tacitus*.

Thomas Gordon was born in 1684 in Scotland. Alone, and also in collaboration with John Trenchard, he produced some of the central works of the British commonwealth tradition. The connections between seventeenth-century English republicanism and its eighteenth-century descendant have been examined in detail in Caroline Robbins's *The eighteenth-century commonwealthman* and J. G. A. Pocock's *The Machiavellian moment*. Gordon's *Tacitus* consisted of English translations of Tacitus's works. Each of the two volumes was prefaced by a series of discourses by Gordon himself.[73] In those discourses he highlighted and discussed various ideas raised by Tacitus. Gordon's praise of that author and his works was based on his emphasis on liberty and virtue, and his opposition to corruption and tyranny:

> As obvious too as his other great qualities, is the love of Mankind, of Civil Liberty, and of private and publick Virtue. His book is a great tablature of the ugliness and horrors of Tyranny; of the loveliness of virtue and a free spirit; of the odiousness of vice and sycophancy.[74]

---

successeurs. . . . Quand un prince commence à devenir infirme, tout le monde tourne les yeux . . . vers son successeur': Gordon, *Discours sur Tacite*, i. 217; ii. 111; i. 73.

[72] 'Dans le combat à mort que se livrent, au milieu de nous, la république et la monarchie, et dans la nécessité que l'une ou l'autre remportât une victoire sanglante, qui pourra gémir du triomphe de la République, après avoir vu la description que l'histoire nous a laissée du triomphe de la monarchie; après avoir jeté un coup-d'oeil sur la copie ébauchée et grossière des tableaux de Tacite, que je vais présenter à l'honorable cercle de mes abonnés?': Desmoulins, *Le Vieux Cordelier* (ed. Calvet), 70.

[73] The French translation by Daudé was just of Gordon's discourses not his translation of Tacitus. Thus what Desmoulins quoted was in fact by Gordon not Tacitus.

[74] Gordon, *The works of Tacitus*, i. 15.

Gordon favoured free over un-free government and, while he accepted the place of a single ruler within a state, he insisted that that ruler should rule not by his will but according to the laws. It was this that distinguished kings from tyrants. Any move towards tyranny, and the rule of will, would be disastrous for the people and the state:

> As tyranny produces abject fear and anxiety in particulars for themselves, so from this selfish fear and anxiety comes the beginning and progress of universal servitude, the extinction of all Patriotism and honest zeal, the power of corruption, and the symptoms of a state hastening to ruin and desolation.[75]

Gordon drew a parallel between republican and imperial Rome, on the one hand, and the eighteenth-century English and French monarchies, on the other. In Rome, the shift from republic to empire had been preceded by an expansion of the treason laws, which thus gave the dictators the ability to alienate the sovereignty of the people in order to secure their own authority. Gordon likened these treason laws to the powers of arbitrary arrest and imprisonment that had existed in the system of *lettres de cachet* under the French monarchy. This system contrasted sharply, in Gordon's eyes, with the English monarchy under which there were provisions – such as *habeas corpus*, the freedom of the press and the right to trial by jury – which ensured that the government was restricted from exercising any extraordinary authority beyond that which was necessary for public safety.

Gordon's work proved popular in Britain. Knowledge of it passed to France *via* the francophone Huguenot press, and in 1742 it was translated into French by a Protestant minister, Pierre Daudé, who had met Gordon in England. Daudé was said to have been inspired to make the translation by his respect for the work and its author, and in order 'To enrich the public in its reflections useful to the study of healthy politics and the government of free States.'[76] The work apparently circulated under the *ancien régime*, but illegally owing to the fact that it upheld liberty and criticised the despotism of Church and State. In contrast with its clandestine reputation under the *ancien régime*, the outbreak of Revolution in France and the establishment of the first French republic made Daudé's translation of Gordon appear much more relevant to the French. It was republished by François Buisson in l'an II (1794) and in his 'Avis' the editor insisted that the utility of the work lay in its support for republicanism and its advice on how to avoid the errors and faults of the ancient republics.[77]

Daudé's translation of Gordon's *Discourses on Tacitus* was held in Desmoulins's library and it was clearly made use of in the writing of *Le Vieux Cordelier*. Desmoulins criticised the Terror for the same reasons that Gordon

---

[75] Ibid. i. 97.
[76] 'A enrichir le public de ses réflexions utiles à l'étude de la saine politique et du gouvernement des etats libres': idem, *Discours sur Tacite*, i, p. vii.
[77] Idem, *Discours sur Tacite et sur Salluste*, i, p. vi.

had criticised the French monarchy and the Roman empire. He drew a parallel between the tyranny that had existed under the reign of the Caesars, as described by Tacitus, and that of the contemporary revolutionary government: 'The committee of public safety has felt strongly, and has believed, that to establish a republic, it has need, for a moment, of the jurisprudence of despots.'[78] And, having been denounced, he criticised his attackers by claiming 'Is this not the ridiculous crime of which Tacitus speaks?'[79] He insisted that the unbridled authority that was being exercised by the government in the name of revolutionary necessity was not, as Robespierre and Saint-Just claimed, the means to produce a stable republican regime; rather, it would lead to tyranny. To bring an end to the existing situation he called for the establishment of a committee of clemency, and insisted on the need for procedural mechanisms to limit excessive authority if popular sovereignty was to be conserved: 'I think very differently from those who say that terror must be left as the order of the day. I am certain, to the contrary, that liberty will be consolidated, and Europe vanquished if there is a committee of clemency.'[80]

Gordon's *Discourses* clearly spoke to Desmoulins in the winter of 1793–4; and he saw them as ideal material to support his own attack on the *Hébertists* and the revolutionary government. In doing so, Desmoulins was in many ways following the practice of Mandar and Rutledge who had used the works of Nedham and Harrington respectively to justify their own ideas earlier in the 1790s. While Gordon was not a contemporary of Nedham and Harrington, he drew heavily on their writings and all are part of the same English republican tradition.

We know, from his *Révolutions de France et de Brabant*, that Desmoulins was aware of, and frequently drew on, ideas from the English republican tradition. In that newspaper he had made frequent references to the events and writings of mid seventeenth-century England. He referred to John Milton and Algernon Sidney, both of whom he described as 'republicans'.[81] His references to Sidney are, for the most part, little more than a reflection of the myth that had built up following his execution.[82] In the case of Milton, however, Desmoulins was clearly closely acquainted with his writings. The

---

[78] 'Le comité de salut public l'a bien senti, et il a cru que, pour établir la république, il avoit besoin un moment de la jurisprudence des despotes': Desmoulins, *Le Vieux Cordelier* (ed. Calvet), 89.
[79] 'N'est-ce pas là le crime ridicule dont parle Tacite?': ibid. 133.
[80] 'Je pense bien différemment de ceux qui vous disent qu'il faut laisser la terreur à l'ordre du jour. Je suis certain au contraire, que la liberté seroit consolidée, et l'Europe vaincue, si vous aviez un comité de clémence': ibid. 119.
[81] Desmoulins, *Révolutions de France et de Brabant*, iv. 405 and v. 535 (Milton); iv. 447 and vi. 272 (Sidney).
[82] Ibid. iii. 342; iv. 178, 447. On the 'myth' surrounding Sidney see Karsten, *Patriot-heroes*, and Worden, *Roundhead reputations*, chs v, vi, vii.

fourth issue of *Révolutions de France et de Brabant* included a detailed review of the recent publication by the comte de Mirabeau of *Théorie de la royauté après la doctrine de Milton*.[83] Paraphrasing the work, Desmoulins acknowledged that Milton was only known in France as a poet, despite the fact that he was also a 'great polemical writer' and an 'ardent defender of liberty'.[84] Desmoulins also referred to Toland's *Life of Milton*, and to various works by Milton including: *Areopagitica* and *The readie and easie way*, from which he quoted a long passage on the importance of a nation maintaining its liberty. In his newspaper Desmoulins also offered praise for those men whom Caroline Robbins has described as the third generation of eighteenth-century commonwealthmen: 'Already the tower of London shakes in its foundations. Price, Williams, Priestley, Horne Tooke, Paine, call the three realms to liberty.'[85]

As a member of the Cordeliers Club Desmoulins mixed with others who were making use of English republican ideas to further their revolutionary aims. Furthermore, we know that there was a direct connection between Desmoulins and Rutledge as early as 1789, when both men were involved in the 'boulanger affair'.[86] It therefore seems likely that Desmoulins's knowledge of English republican works (including those of Gordon) came not simply from his pre-revolutionary associations, but from within the Cordeliers Club itself. Desmoulins, like Mandar and Rutledge before him, used English republican ideas to support the values and aims of the old Cordeliers.

There are, however, obvious differences between Desmoulins's use of English republican ideas in 1793–4 and that of his Cordeliers predecessors in 1790–2. First, as has already been suggested, there is the fact that where Mandar and Rutledge had drawn on seventeenth-century English republican writings, Desmoulins turned to the eighteenth-century commonwealth works of Thomas Gordon. The reason for this no doubt lies in the particular task that Desmoulins was seeking to perform in *Le Vieux Cordelier*. His concern was not the same as that of Mandar and Rutledge. They had been trying to answer the question of how to establish a democratic republic in a large modern state such as France. By late 1793 the possibility of a French republic

---

83 Desmoulins, *Révolutions de France et de Brabant*, i. 180–7. The fact that Desmoulins himself had worked for Mirabeau, coupled with his detailed knowledge of Milton's works, raises the possibility that he was involved with Mirabeau's translations of Milton: Janssens, *Camille Desmoulins*, 184–98. There are also obvious parallels between Milton's *Areopagitica* (translated by Mirabeau in 1788) and Desmoulins's insistence on the importance of the liberty of the press.

84 Desmoulins, *Révolutions de France et de Brabant*, i. 180.

85 'Déjà le tour de Londre s'ébranle dans ses fondemens. Les Price, les Williams, les Priestley, les Horne-Toocke, les Payne, appellent les trois royaumes à la liberté': ibid. vi. 351.

86 See chapter 3 above. The 'boulanger affair' also featured in Desmoulins's *Révolutions de France et de Brabant*, and in that work Desmoulins made a number of references to Rutledge, even including a whole series of letters from him in which he defended his role in that and other debates: ibid. ii. 336n; iii. 531, 549, 735; iv. 35.

was no longer in question, the key debate then was how a republic should behave in conditions of crisis, and particularly whether it was necessary to resort to appeals to 'revolutionary necessity', and to advocate the sacrificing of individual rights to the public good. On this question Gordon proved more appropriate than his seventeenth-century predecessors. Secondly, Desmoulins's opponents in 1793–4 were very different from those of 1790–2. Mandar and Rutledge had been writing on behalf of the club as a whole and had been expressing fairly standard Cordeliers ideas of support for a republic against constitutional monarchy, as favoured by the authorities of the time, and for democracy against the modern representative republicanism of many other revolutionaries. By contrast, in *Le Vieux Cordelier* Desmoulins was writing against other more democratic forms of republicanism advocated by his former associates within the Jacobin Club – particularly Robespierre – and by his fellow Cordeliers – notably Hébert.

Conclusion

Throughout their existence the old Cordeliers remained committed to the rights of man and of the citizen. The enforcement and protection of those rights, so they believed, would secure liberty against tyranny and oppression. However, from as early as 1789 these revolutionaries were convinced that those rights (and therefore liberty) could only be secured under a republican form of government. As Desmoulins and Robert proclaimed in their pamphlets, and as Mandar explained in detail in his translation of Nedham's *The excellencie of a free state*, monarchical government was, by its very nature, tyrannical.

It was in their calls for the establishment of a republic that the Cordeliers became associated with the Brissotins. Both Desmoulins and Mandar attended meetings of the *Confédération des amis de la vérité*; Desmoulins, Mandar and La Vicomterie all published works with the Cercle Social publishing house; and the two groups collaborated in the republican campaign of June 1791.[1] Yet there were important differences in the kind of republicanism that was advocated by members of these two groups. These had first been made apparent when the Cordeliers District came into conflict with Brissot and his associates on the Parisian communal assembly in the summer of 1789, but they continued to prove important after the abolition of the districts and the creation of the Cordeliers Club.

Both the Brissotins and the Cordeliers were familiar with the views of Montesquieu and Rousseau concerning republican government. Moreover, both groups rejected the suggestion of these great political thinkers that republican government was not appropriate to the nations of modern Europe. Where the Brissotins and the Cordeliers differed was in their proposals as to how republican government could be made compatible with contemporary circumstances and in exactly what kind of republican government they wished to implement in France. The Brissotins developed their form of 'modern republicanism' as a response to the problem of how to make republican government workable in the large states of contemporary Europe. Central to the achievement of this aim was their adoption (against the warnings of Rousseau, but following the model of the young American republic) of a system of representative government. Drawing on their own experiences of politics in Paris in 1789 the Cordeliers took more seriously Rousseau's indictment of representative government and rejected it in favour of democracy.

---

1 For a list of those who attended one or more meetings of the *Confédération des amis de la vérité* see appendix A in Kates, *The* Cercle Social, 277–81. For a list of authors who published with the *imprimerie du Cercle Social* see appendix C, pp. 292–4.

While accepting the impossibility of implementing ancient-style direct democracy (in which all citizens would gather together on a regular basis in order to make political decisions), the Cordeliers sought a compromise. They advocated a mixture of delegate and semi-direct democracy. Under this system deputies were to be considered as delegates rather than representatives and, at both local and national level, their decisions and actions were to be kept firmly under the control of the people who had elected them. This was to be achieved by means of short terms of office and the use of binding mandates. In addition, the Cordeliers also adopted the radical proposal that all laws should be ratified by the citizens of the state, gathered in their local assemblies.

Both the Brissotins and the Cordeliers also addressed the question of the role played by civic virtue within a republican state. The Brissotins believed that citizens had to be virtuous in order for a republic to function successfully. They thus placed great emphasis on the inculcation of republican manners through education and other means. At times this assumption even led the Brissotins to question whether France was yet ready for republican government. The Cordeliers adopted a different approach. Following Harrington, Rutledge was sceptical about the human capacity for virtue. Thus, instead of relying on it, he adopted the various constitutional mechanisms that had been proposed by Harrington as a means of ensuring that, though the people acted in their own interests, the outcome of their actions would be 'virtuous'. This same idea is also evident in Desmoulins's critique, in *Le Vieux Cordelier*, of Montesquieu's (and by implication Robespierre's) emphasis on virtue.

In addition to addressing the concerns expressed by Montesquieu and Rousseau, the Brissotins had also sought to make republican government compatible with commercial society. The Cordeliers, who were undoubtedly less sophisticated than the Brissotins in their understanding of political economy, continued to believe that land and agricultural production formed the essential foundation for a successful republic.

It is difficult to determine whether members of the Cordeliers Club drew on English republicanism in order to support their existing ideas or whether those ideas developed on the basis of their knowledge of English republicanism. In reality, it was probably a mixture of the two. Certainly, members of the club drew heavily on English republican works in order to respond to the scepticism of Montesquieu and Rousseau, and to counter the 'modern republicanism' of the Brissotins. Nedham's *The excellencie of a free state* provided an anti-monarchical and potentially democratic definition of a free state. Harrington's works demonstrated the economic underpinning of political power, and emphasised the importance of land as the foundation of the republic. Moreover, both works suggested a number of mechanisms designed to make democratic government viable in the circumstances of the modern world – including rotation of office, an agrarian law, the separation of discussion of policy from decision-making and the Venetian ballot.

While members of the Cordeliers Club clearly made much use of the works of Nedham and Harrington, they were not averse to adapting the ideas of those writers so as to make them better fit their own circumstances and concerns. In particular, in their borrowings and translations they adapted the English originals so as to make them more democratic (and therefore more in line with their own views) than their seventeenth-century English authors had intended. In Mandar's *De la Souveraineté* and in *Idées sur l'espèce du gouvernement populaire* we see a systematic democratisation of the works of Nedham and Harrington.

By late 1793 circumstances had changed, together with the debates and issues at stake. The French had succeeded in establishing a republic and the king had been dethroned and executed; but the country now faced problems of war abroad and civil unrest at home. Debate thus centred on the question of how the new republic ought to behave under these revolutionary conditions. With the Brissotins/Girondins out of the way, the old Cordeliers now found themselves at odds both with the Jacobins and with newer members of the Cordeliers Club. Despite the change in circumstances, Desmoulins continued to assert traditional Cordeliers principles. He also continued to have recourse to English republican sources. When attacking the revolutionary government, and its appeal to revolutionary necessity, in late 1793 and early 1794, Desmoulins turned to the writings of one of the eighteenth-century intellectual descendants of Nedham and Harrington: Thomas Gordon.

Desmoulins's devotion to old Cordeliers principles ultimately cost him his life. Rutledge also died in the spring of 1794.[2] Nor did the Cordeliers Club itself survive for much longer. It was closed down at the end of May 1795, though it had declined in power and influence well before that point.

Yet, while the old Cordeliers were no longer active beyond the spring of 1794, their ideas did not die with them. English republicanism appears to have continued to generate interest in France in the mid-1790s. A number of histories of the English Revolution and republic were produced, including the one based explicitly on Ludlow's *Memoirs* and another produced by Sieyès's friend Boulay de la Meurthe.[3] Translations of English republican works also proved popular, with the republication of Sidney's *Discourses* and Gordon's *Discourses on Tacitus and Sallust* in 1794, and the 1795 editions of Harring-

---

[2] Peyronnet, 'J. J. Rutlidge', 341. Peyronnet points out that both J. G. Alger in the *Dictionary of national biography* and Rutledge's biographer, R. Las Vergnas, are wrong in suggesting that Rutledge died in prison. In fact, he died on the rue Martin on either 30 or 31 March 1794.

[3] *Histoire de la république d'Angleterre d'après les Mémoires d'Edmond Ludlow*; A. J. C. J. Boulay de la Meurthe, *Essai sur les causes qui en 1649 amènerent en Angleterre l'établissement de la république; sur celles qui deviaient l'y consolider, sur celles qui l'y firent périr*, Paris l'an VII [1799]. On classical republicanism in France post-Thermidor see Jainchill, 'Constitution of the year III', 399–435.

ton's political works.[4] Moreover, we have at least some indication that the latter was prompted by and generated specific interest. In July 1794 a librarian at the Bibliothèque Nationale, L. Villebrune, had written an article for *Le Moniteur*, in which he had called for a translation of Harrington's works.[5] He referred to the petition presented to the English Parliament on 6 July 1659, which had urged that monarchical government should not be re-established. The petition was presented, Villebrune claimed, 'by many persons who, like Harrington, wanted England to adopt a purely democratic government'.[6] Presumably having read Desmoulins's newspaper, Villebrune went on to draw a comparison between the ideas of Harrington and those of Gordon. In another letter to *Le Moniteur* in March 1796, Goupil-Préfeln – a member of the council of elders – explained that he had just finished reading the recent translation of Harrington's political works. He claimed that he had been struck by Harrington's plea to revive ancient prudence and his apparent belief that France was ripe for such a revival, and he urged others to read the works for themselves.[7]

The Cordeliers interest in the English republican tradition can also be contrasted with uses made of that same tradition in pre-revolutionary France. Understandably, French translators and advocates of English republican ideas under the *ancien régime* tended to downplay the republican implications of these works. Boulainvilliers, Montesquieu and Mably did not explicitly call for the abolition of the monarchy. Moreover, these thinkers and their contemporaries tended to draw on the works of British commonwealthmen – who had themselves adapted the seventeenth-century ideas to fit a monarchical context – rather than on the original seventeenth-century writings. It is particularly striking that the texts on which members of the Cordeliers Club primarily drew (those of Nedham and Harrington) had been almost unknown in France until the 1770s. At the same time, it is possible to see the Cordeliers as marking the culmination of the eighteenth-century French interest in English republican ideas. There is a clear trend evident in the gradual movement from the *thèse nobiliaire* of Boulainvilliers and the monarchical democracy of d'Argenson, via Montesquieu and Mably, to the ideas of the Cordeliers. The Revolution undoubtedly played a key role in moving things forward, but the members of the Cordeliers Club were certainly building on what had gone before. Wright has argued that Mably 'democratised' this tradition in France through his removal of 'the aristocratic and nostalgic cast given it by Boulainvilliers and Montesquieu'.[8] Members of the Cordeliers Club continued that process of democratisation, not only in their

---

4 Sidney, *Discours sur le gouvernement, par Algernon Sidney*; Gordon, *Discours sur Tacite et sur Salluste*; Harrington, *Oeuvres politiques de James Harrington*, and *Aphorismes politiques*.
5 *Moniteur universel*, xxi. 123.
6 Ibid. xxi. 123.
7 Ibid. xxvii. 658–9. Both articles are referred to in Liljegren, *A French draft constitution*, 32–4, and in Russell Smith, *Harrington and his* Oceana, 203–4.
8 Wright, *A classical republican*, 203. See also idem, 'Republican constitution'.

use of explicitly republican works by Nedham and Harrington, but also in the democratic additions and alterations that they made to those works.

This account of the republicanism of the Cordeliers Club has implications for our understanding of both the French Revolution and the wider republican tradition. It challenges the preponderant role that has been attributed to the Jacobins, and especially to Jacobin republicanism, in shaping the Revolution and subsequent French history. Despite their importance, the Jacobins were not the only group to develop a sophisticated theory of republicanism in the early 1790s. Nor, indeed, were they the first, or the most dedicated, advocates of republican government. Owing to the work of Whatmore and Livesey we now know a great deal about the development of modern republicanism in revolutionary France. The case of the Cordeliers Club adds another dimension to this complex story. The French Revolution did not simply mark the defeat of the ancient republican tradition – through the Jacobin association between virtue and terror – and its replacement by modern republicanism. Rather, the period witnessed a series of profound and complex debates concerning the best kind of republicanism for the circumstances, and the means by which such a system could be implemented.

An understanding of Cordeliers republicanism also raises questions about, or at least complicates, Rousseau's totemic status as a major influence on the political thought of the Revolution. Not only did some revolutionaries draw extensively on non-francophone sources in constructing their revolutionary language – in this case English republicanism – but for many the contribution of Rousseau (and Montesquieu) was to identify the problems (perhaps the most important being how to create a republic in a large, modern, state) and to provide the terms in which those problems were discussed. For solutions to those problems, however, the revolutionaries sometimes turned to other thinkers and ideas.

Moreover, it seems clear that English ideas played a more important role in the French Revolution than has previously been acknowledged. The *Monarchien* debt to English constitutional ideas has long been recognised, but it has often been assumed that their fall from power marked the end for English political ideas in France. As this study has demonstrated, English ideas continued to prove influential in France beyond 1789, and the constitution admired by the *Monarchiens* was not the only English model that was of interest to the French.

An appreciation of Cordeliers republicanism also adds breadth to the historiography of the republican tradition. Contrary to the conventional view, English republican ideas did not simply abandon Europe for North America in the 1770s and 1780s. Cordeliers such as Mandar and Desmoulins clearly saw themselves as the inheritors of a tradition that had been passed on to them by the commonwealthmen of seventeenth- and eighteenth-century Britain. Indeed, the uses to which those republican ideas were put by members of the Cordeliers Club should perhaps be seen as marking the apogee of the early modern republican tradition which, in its anglophone form, had proved such a pervasive force in seventeenth- and eighteenth-century Britain and North America.

In revolutionary America, as in revolutionary France, republicanism took a variety of forms, and English republican texts and ideas were put to various uses by a diverse range of revolutionaries. None the less, parallels can be drawn between features adopted by individuals and groups within America and those favoured by members of the Cordeliers Club. John Adams shared Rutledge's respect for the ideas of Harrington. He is said to have owned two copies of Harrington's works and the Englishman's influence is clearly evident in works such as his *Thoughts on government* (1776).[9] In that work, written in response to requests for advice on the framing of the state constitutions, Adams adopted Harrington's definition of a republic as an 'empire of laws, and not of men' and went on to recommend the adoption of several Harringtonian features including a ballot, annual elections, the rotation of offices and a citizen militia. However, in another respect his use of Harrington pointed in a completely different direction from that of Rutledge and his colleagues. Where they had emphasised the democratic aspects of Harrington's theory, and had sought to push the democratic conclusions of that theory further than Harrington himself had intended, Adams's vision was more hierarchical and elitist. Recognising that in a large nation all cannot gather together to make the laws he continued 'The first necessary step, then, is to depute power from the many to a few of the most wise and good.'[10] He acknowledged that care should be taken over the choice of these representatives, but he said nothing about the need for constituents to retain control over their representatives once they had been elected. In contrast to Rutledge, Adams placed great emphasis on Harrington's notion of a 'natural aristocracy'. There were others among the American revolutionaries who did share the Cordeliers belief in delegate democracy, and the need for the people to control those who elected them. Such democratic ideas were endorsed by a number of anti-federalist writers and by figures such as Thomas Jefferson.[11] Jefferson also shared the Cordeliers emphasis on land as the essential basis of a successful republic. However, these revolutionaries were much less directly influenced by the writings of seventeenth and eighteenth-century English

---

[9]   J. Adams, 'Thoughts on government: applicable to the present state of the American colonies', in *The revolutionary writings of John Adams*, ed. C. Bradley Thompson, Indianapolis 2000, 287–93. On Adams's use of Harrington see Russell Smith, *Harrington and his Oceana*, ch. viii.

[10] *Revolutionary writings of John Adams*, 288.

[11] For a detailed study of the anti-federalists and their ideas see S. Cornell, *The other founders: anti federalism and the dissenting tradition in America, 1788–1828*, Chapel Hill 1999. Some sense of Jefferson's views can be gleaned from his *Political writings*, ed. J. O. Appleby and T. Ball, Cambridge 1999.

republicans, and particularly by those of Harrington.[12] Consequently they tended to be much more optimistic about the possibility of civic virtue and continued to insist that it was essential to the success of republican government.[13]

Republicans in late eighteenth-century America and France faced the same crucial obstacles to the construction of a republic: the large size of modern states, the apparent lack of the requisite civic virtue among the population and the existence of commercial society. They also had the same models on which to draw. Yet the solutions that were found to these problems and the particular ways in which the existing models were drawn upon (and new ones created) varied. The debate between the Brissotins and the Cordeliers, and that between the old Cordeliers and the Jacobins, cannot easily be mapped on to the debates between federalists and anti-federalists and Democrats and Republicans. While the terminology used was often the same, the different circumstances meant that the focus of the debates, and their outcomes, were different.

The old Cordeliers were not as influential as either the Brissotins and Jacobins in France, or Adams and Jefferson in America; but their political thought was of fundamental importance. They may have been the last exponents of that early modern republican tradition that had been developed in seventeenth-century England. They were also among the first self-confessed democrats of the modern world.

[12] Jefferson did demonstrate a certain interest in the works and writings of John Milton: Davies, 'Borrowed language: Milton, Jefferson, Mirabeau', 257–65.
[13] There has been much debate as to whether Jefferson is best characterised as a republican or a Lockean liberal: Appleby, *Liberalism and republicanism*.

Bibliography

Unpublished primary sources

Paris, Archives Nationales (AN)
Dossier Y10504 Unpublished material relating to the 'boulanger affair'
DXXIXbis 12, no. 130 J. J. Rutledge, *Réquète du sieur de Rutlidge aux comités des rapports et des recherches, de mandant qu'on pris des mesures pour mettre obstacle à la suite présumable de M. Necker*, 8 sept. 1790
C158 no. 332 (46), C192 no. 160 (19) 'Ordre du jury spécial d'accusation du tribunal du 17 août'
F7 4775/8 dossier 2 Documents concerning the arrest of Jean Jacques Rutledge in brumaire an II including Théodore Le Sueur's defence of Rutledge's character, 31 Oct. 1793

Paris, Bibliothèque Historique de la Ville de Paris (BHVP)
Rés 24, 25, 26 Correspondence and papers of Camille Desmoulins

Published primary sources

Contemporary publications

Petitions, speeches, pamphlets and books
Assemblée des représentans de la commune de Paris, *Extrait du procès-verbal de l'assemblé des représentans de la commune de Paris, du 30 août 1789*, Paris 1789 [BL, F. 9*. (7**.)]
[Aubert de Vitry, F. J. P.], *Jean Jacques Rousseau à l'assemblée nationale*, Paris 1789
Bancal des Issarts, J. H., *Secondes Réflexions sur l'institution du pouvoir executive: lues à la Société des amis de la constitution de Clermont-Ferrand, le 3 juillet 1791*, Clermont-Ferrand 1791
Bolingbroke, Henry St John, viscount, *Des Devoirs d'un roi patriote, et portrait des ministres de tous les temps: ouvrage traduit de l'anglois de Bolingbroke*, Paris 1790
———— 'A dissertation upon parties', in *The works of the late right honourable Henry St. John, Lord viscount Bolingbroke*, London 1809, iii. 3–311
———— 'The idea of a patriot king', *Works of Bolingbroke*, iv. 225–334
Boucher Saint-Sauveur, A. S., *Déclaration du citoyen Boucher Saint-Sauveur (au sujet d'un dénonciation faite contre Rutledge)*, Paris 1793 [BN, Lb41 903]
Boulay de la Meurthe, A. J. C. J., *Essai sur les causes qui en 1649 amènerent en Angleterre l'établissement de la république; sur celles qui deviaient l'y consolider, sur celles qui l'y firent périr*, Paris l'an VII [1799]
Brissot de Warville, J. P., *Plan de conduite pour les députés du peuple aux états-généraux de 1789*, Paris 1789
———— *Motifs des commissaries, pour adopter le plan de municipalité qu'ils ont*

présenté à l'assemblée générale des représentans de la commune: lues à l'assemblée-générale, par J. P. Brissot de Warville, représentant de la commune, suivis du projet du plan de municipalité, Paris 1789 [BL, F. 9*. (7.)]

———— *Discours sur les conventions*, Paris 1791

———— 'Sur les motifs de ceux qui défendent la monarchie et qui calomnient le républicanisme', in N. Bonneville (ed.), *La Chronique du mois*, Paris 1791–3 (Oct. 1792)

———— and E. Clavière, *De la France et des États-Unis, ou de l'importance de la revolution de l'Amérique pour le bonheur de la France: des rapports de ce royaume & des États-Unis, des avantages réciproques qu'ils peuvent retirer de leurs liaisons de commerce, & enfin de la situation actuelle des États-Unis*, 2nd edn, Paris 1791 (1st edn. 1787)

———— and E. Clavière, *Nouveau Voyages dans l'États-Unis de l'Amérique septentrionale, fait en 1788*, Paris 1791

Collection complète des oeuvres de l'abbé de Mably, Paris l'an III [1794–5]

Condorcet, M. J. A. N. de Caritat, marquis de, *Essai sur l'application de l'analyse à la probabilité des décisions rendues à la pluralité des vois*, Paris 1785

———— *Sentiments d'un républicain sur les assemblées provinçales et les états-généraux*, Paris 1788

Défense du peuple anglais sur le jugement et la condamnation de Charles premier, roi d'Angleterre: par Milton: ouvrage propre à éclairer sur la circonstance actuelle où se trouve la France, réimprime aux frais des administrateurs du Département de la Drôme, Valence 1792

D'Eon de Beaumont, *Les Loisirs du chevalier d'Eon de Beaumont ancien ministre plénipotentiaire de France, sur divers sujets importans d'administration, &c. pendant son séjour en Angleterre*, Amsterdam 1774

Desmoulins, C., *La France libre*, Paris 1789

———— *Réplique aux deux mémoires des sieurs Leleu*, Paris 1789

———— *Jean-Pierre Brissot démasqué*, Paris 1792

———— *Histoire des Brissotins: fragment de l'histoire secrete de la Révolution, et des six premiers mois de la république*, Paris 1793

District des Cordeliers, *Extrait des registres de l'assemblée générale du district des Cordeliers, du premier juillet mil sept cent quatre-vingt-dix*, Paris 1790 [BL, F. 13* (16.)]

———— *Extrait des registres des délibérations de l'assemblée du district des Cordeliers, du 28 juin 1790*, Paris 1790 [BL, R.229 (17.)]

Dumont, E., *Souvenirs sur Mirabeau et sur les deux premières assemblées legislatives*, Paris 1832

Dunouy, J. H., *Vérités incontestables*, Paris 1794 [BN, Lb41 923]

Essai d'une déclaration des droits de l'homme et du citoyen and *Quelques Pensées sur l'unité du législateur, par l'auteur des Idées sur la constitution populaire etc.*, Paris l'an I [1792]

Ferrières, J. A., *Plan d'un nouveau genre de banque nationale et territoriale*, Paris 1789

Girardin, R., *Discours sur l'institution de la force publique, par Réné Girardin, commandant de la guard nationale d'Erménonville*, Paris [1791]

———— *Discours de René Girardin sur la nécessité de la ratification de la loi, par la volonté générale*, Paris [1791]

Gordon, T., *The works of Tacitus . . . to which are prefixed political discourses upon that author*, London 1728–31

———— *Discours historiques, critiques et politiques sur Tacite*, trans. P. Daudé, Amsterdam 1742

———— *The works of Sallust translated into English with political discourses upon that author*, London 1744

———— *Discours historiques et politiques sur Salluste: par feu Mr. Gordon, traduits de l'anglois, par un de ses amis* [P. Daudé], [Paris] 1759

———— *Discours historiques, critiques et politiques de Thomas Gordon, sur Tacite et sur Salluste, traduits de l'anglois* [by P. Daudé], nouvelle édition, corrigée, Paris l'an II [1794]

Guy-Kersaint, A., 'De la constitution et du gouvernement qui pourroient convenir à la république française', in N. Bonneville (ed.), *La Chronique du mois*, Paris 1791–3 (Feb. 1793, supplement)

Harrington, J., *Aphorismes politiques*, trans. P. F. Aubin, Paris 1795

———— *Oeuvres politiques de James Harrington*, trans. P. F. Henry, Paris l'an III [1795]

Histoire de la république d'Angleterre d'après les Mémoires d'Edmond Ludlow l'un des principaux chefs des républicains anglais: contenant la narration des faits qui ont précédé accompagné et suivi ces momens lucides de la nation anglaise, par un républicain, Paris l'an II [1794]

[Holbach, Baron P. H. D. von], *L'Esprit du clergé, ou le christianisme primitif vengé des entreprises & des excès de nos prêtres modernes, traduit de l'anglois*, London [Amsterdam] 1767

Idées sur l'espèce de gouvernement populaire qui pourrait convenir à un pays de l'étendue et de la population présumée de la France, Paris 1792

[Keralio, L.], *Les Crimes des reines de France, depuis le commencement de la monarchie jusqu'à la mort de Marie-Antoinette: avec les pièces justicatives de son procès*, Paris 1791

La Vicomterie de Saint-Samson, L. de, *Du Peuple et des rois*, Paris 1790

———— *Des Crimes des rois de France depuis Clovis jusqu'à Louis seize*, Paris 1791

———— *Les Droits du peuple sur l'assemblée nationale*, Paris 1791

———— *République sans impôt*, Paris 1792

Leleu, E. L. and D. C. Leleu, *Compte rendu au public par les sieurs Eloi-Louis & Dominique-César Leleu, négocians; sur l'établissement des moulins de Corbeil*, Paris 1789

———— *Observations des sieurs Eloy-Louis and Dominique-César Leleu, frères, négocians; sur un écrit intitulé: 'Second Mémoire pour les maîtres boulangers, lu au bureau des subsistances de l'assemblée nationale'*, Paris 1789

Lettre de felicitation de milord Sidney aux parisiens et à la nation françoise: ou résurrection de milord Sidney second coup de griffe aux renards de toute couleur, Paris 1789

Ludlow, E., *Les Mémoires d'Edmond Ludlow, . . . contenant ce qui c'est passé de plus remarquable sous le règne de Charles I jusqu'à Charles II . . . traduit de l'anglois*, Amsterdam 1699

Mably, G. B., 'Du Gouvernement et des lois de Pologne', in *Collection complète*, viii. 1–336

———— 'Observations sur le gouvernement et les lois des États-Unis d'Amérique', *Collection complète*, viii. 337–485

Mandar, T., *De la Souveraineté du peuple, et de l'excellence d'un état libre, par Marchamont Needham, traduit de l'anglois et enrichi de notes de J. J. Rousseau, Mably, Bossuet, Condillac, Montesquieu, Letrosne, Raynal, etc., etc., etc.*, Paris 1790

———— *Des Insurrections: ouvrage philosophique et politique sur les rapports des insurrections avec la prospérité des empires*, Paris 1793

[Marat, J. P.], *The chains of slavery: a work wherein the clandestine and villainous attempts of princes to ruin liberty are pointed out, and the dreadful scenes of despotism disclosed, to which is prefixed, an address to the electors of Great Britain, in order to draw their timely attention to the choice of proper representatives in the next parliament*, London 1774

———— *Les Chaines de l'esclavage, ouvrage destiné à développer les noirs attentats des princes contre les peuples; les ressorts secrets, les ruses, les menées, les artifices, les coups d'état qu'ils emploient pour détruire la liberté, et les scènes sanglantes qui accompagnent le despotisme*, Paris l'an I [1793]

Mirabeau, H. G., comte de, *De la Liberté de la presse: imité de l'anglais de Milton*, Paris 1788

———— *Théorie de la royauté après la doctrine de Milton*, Paris 1789

———— *Histoire de l'Angleterre, depuis l'avènement de Jacques Ier jusqu'à la révolution, par Catharine Macaulay Graham, traduit en français et augmentée d'un discours préliminaire contenant un précis de l'histoire de l'Angleterre jusqu'à l'avènement de Jacques I, et enrichie de notes*, Paris 1791–2

[Moyle, W.], *Essai sur le gouvernement de Rome, traduit de l'anglois* [by B. Barrère de Vieuzac], Paris 1801

Nedham, M., *The excellencie of a free state*, London 1767

Pièces justificatives: exposé de la conduite et des motifs du district des Cordeliers concernont le décret de prise de corps prononcé par le Châtelet contre le sieur Marat, le 8 octobre 1789 et mis à exécution le 22 janvier 1790, Paris [1790] [BL, F.R. 63. (36.)]

Pièces qui établissent l'illégalité de l'arrêté des mandataires provisoires de l'Hôtel de Ville, relativement aux cinq mandataires particuliers du district des Cordeliers, 12 septembre–22 novembre 1789, Paris [1789] [BL, F.620. (22.)]

'Procès-verbal de la formation et des opérations du comité militaire de la ville de Paris', Paris 1790 [BN, Lf 133 122]

Robert, F., *Le Droit de faire la paix et la guerre appartient incontestablement à la nation*, Paris 1790

———— *Le Républicanisme adapté à la France*, Paris 1790

———— *Avantages de la fuite de Louis XVI, et nécessité d'un nouveau gouvernement: second édition du Républicanisme adapté à la France*, Paris 1791

[Rutledge, J. J.], *Essai sur le caractère et les moeurs des françois comparés à ceux des anglois*, London 1776

M. R. C. B. [J. J. Rutledge], *Essais politiques sur l'état actuel de quelques puissances*, London [Geneva] 1777

Rutledge, J. J., *Éloge de Montesquieu*, London 1786

———— *Mémoire pour la communauté des maîtres boulangers de la ville et faubourgs de Paris*, Paris 1789

———— *Second Mémoire pour les maîtres boulangers: lu au bureau des subsistances de l'assemblée national par le chevalier Rutledge*, Paris 1789

—— *Dénonciation sommaire, faite au comité des recherches de l'assemblée nationale contre M. Necker, ses complices, fauteurs, et adheréns*, Paris 1790

—— *Mémoire au roi par le clier. Rutledge, Bnet*, Paris 1790

—— *Procès fait au chevalier Rutledge, baronet, avec les pièces justificatives, et sa correspondence avec M. Necker*, Paris [1790]

—— *Projet d'une législation des subsistances, composée pour M. Necker*, Paris 1790

—— *Rappel des assignats à leur véritable origine: ou démonstration d'un plagiat dangereux du premier ministre et comité des finances*, Paris 1790

—— *Sommaire d'une discussion importante (relative au plan de banque territoriale du modeste M. de Ferrières)*, [Paris] 1790

—— *La Vie privée et ministérielle de M. Necker, directeur général des finances, par un citoyen*, Geneva 1790

Rutolfe de Lode [J. J. Rutledge], *L'Astuce dévoilé* [sic]: *ou origine des maux de la France perdue, par les manoeuvres du ministre Necker, avec des notes et anecdotes sur son administration*, n.p. 1790

Sidney, A. *Discours sur le gouvernement, par Algernon Sidney, . . . publiez sur l'original manuscrit de l'auteur, traduits de l'anglois par P. A. Samson*, The Hague 1702 (repr. 1755)

—— *Discours sur le gouvernement, par Algernon Sidney, traduits de l'anglais par P. A. Samson: nouvelle édition conforme à cette de 1702*, Paris 1794

Toland, J., *The Oceana of James Harrington, and his other works . . . with an exact account of his life prefix'd by John Toland*, London 1700

Turgot, A. R. J., 'Mémoire au roi sur les municipalités, sur la hiérarchie qu'on pourroit établir entre elles et sur les services que le gouvernement en pourroit tirer', in *Oeuvres de M. Turgot*, Paris 1809

Newspapers and journals

Bulletin des amis de la vérité, publie par les directeurs de l'imprimerie du Cercle social, Paris 1793 [l'an II]

Histoires des ouvrages des savans par M. Monsr B*** docteur en droit, Rotterdam 1702

Le Républicain: ou le défenseur du gouvernement représentatif, par un société de républicains, Paris 1791

Bernard, J. (ed.), *Les Nouvelles de la république*, Amsterdam 1700

Bonneville, N. (ed.), *La Bouche de fer*, Paris 1790–1

—— *La Chronique du mois: ou les cahiers patriotiques de E. Clavière, Condorcet, L. Mercier, A. Auger, J. Oswald, N. Bonneville, J. Bidderman, A. Broussonet, A. Guy-Kersaint, J. P. Brissot, J. Ph. Garan de Coulon, J. Dussaulx, F. Lanthenas, Collot d'Herbois*, Paris 1791–3

Desmoulins, C., *Révolutions de France et de Brabant*, Paris 1789–91

Kemp, P. and others (ed.), *Bibliothèque britannique*, The Hague 1737

Keralio, L. (ed.), *Mércure national et révolutions de l'Europe: journal démocratique*, Paris 1791

Momoro, A. F. (ed.), *Journal du Club des Cordeliers*, Paris 1791

[Rutledge, J. J.], *Calypso, ou les babillards: par une société de gens du monde et de gens de lettres*, Paris 1785

—— *Le Creuset: ouvrage politique et critique*, Paris 1791

Modern editions

Actes de la commune de Paris pendant la Révolution, ed. S. Lacroix, 1st ser., Paris 1894–8 (repr. New York 1974)
Actes de la commune de Paris pendant la Révolution, ed. S. Lacroix, 2nd ser., Paris 1900–14
Adams, J, *The revolutionary writings of John Adams*, ed. C. Bradley Thompson, Indianapolis 2000
Archives parlementaires, 1787–1860, ed. M. Madival and E. Laurent, 1st ser., Paris 1879–1914
Aubrey, J., *Brief lives*, ed. R. Barber, Woodbridge 1982
Braesch, F., *Papiers de Chaumette*, Paris 1908
Brissot de Warville, J. P., 'Discours sur la question de savoir si le roi peut être jugé, prononcé à l'assemblée des amis de la constitution, dans la séance du 10 juillet 1791', repr. in *Archives parlementaires*, xxviii. 338–45
———— *Le Patriote français: journal libre, impartial et national*, Frankfurt-am-Main 1989
Condorcet, M. J. A. N. de Caritat, marquis de, 'De la République ou un roi est-il nécessaire à la conservation de la liberté', repr. in *Archives parlementaires*, xxviii. 336
Constant, B., 'The liberty of the ancients compared with that of the moderns: speech given at the Athénée Royal in Paris', in *Constant: political writings*, ed. B. Fontana, Cambridge 1988, 307–28
Les Cordeliers: documents pour servir à l'histoire de la Révolution française, ed. A. Bougeart, Caen 1891
'Défense du peuple anglais, sur le jugement et la condamnation de Charles premier, roi d'Angleterre', in C. Tournu (ed.), *Milton et Mirabeau: rencontre révolutionnaire*, n.p. 2002, 93–158
Desmoulins, C., *Le Vieux Cordelier*, ed. H. Calvet, Paris 1936
———— *Le Vieux Cordelier*, ed. P. Pachet, Paris 1987
———— *Les Révolutions de France et de Brabant*, ed. G. Kates, Frankfurt-am-Main 1989
Duchastelet, A., 'Trente millions à gagner', repr. in *Actes de la commune de Paris*, v. 376–7
A French draft constitution of 1792 modelled on James Harrington's Oceana, ed. S. B. Liljegren, Lund 1932
Harrington, J., *Political works of James Harrington*, ed. J. G. A. Pocock, Cambridge 1977
Hume, D., 'Of civil liberty', in D. Hume, *Essays moral, political and literary*, ed. E. F. Miller, revised edn, Indianapolis 1987, 87–96
Jaucourt, le chevalier de, 'Rutland', *Encyclopédie: ou dictionnaire raisonné des sciences arts et des métiers, par une société des gens de lettres*, Stuggart 1967
Jefferson, T., *Jefferson: political writings*, ed. J. Appleby and T. Ball, Cambridge 1999
John Law's 'Essay on a land bank', ed. A. Murphy, Dublin 1994
Ludlow, E., *A voyce from the watch tower, V: 1660–1662*, ed. B. Worden, London 1978
Mably, G. B., *Des Droits et des devoirs du citoyen*, ed. J. L. Lecercle, Paris 1972

Madison, J., A. Hamilton and J. Jay, *The federalist papers*, ed. I. Kramnick, Harmondsworth 1987

Marat, J. P., *Marat dit l'Ami du peuple*, Tokyo 1967

—— *Les Chaînes de l'esclavage 1793 The chains of slavery 1774*, ed. C. Goëtz and J. De Cock, Brussels 1995

Mirabeau, H. G., comte de, 'Sur la liberté de la presse', in C. Tournu (ed.), *Milton et Mirabeau: rencontre révolutionnaire*, n.p. 2002, 55–92

Moniteur universel: réimpression de l'ancien Moniteur; seule histoire authentique et inaltéré de la Révolution française; depuis la réunion des états-généraux jusqu'au consulat (mai 1789 – novembre 1799), Paris 1847–79

Montesquieu, Charles Louis, *The spirit of the laws*, ed. A. Cohler, B. Miller and H. Stone, Cambridge 1989

Neville, H., 'Plato redivivus', in C. A. Robbins (ed.), *Two republican tracts*, Cambridge 1969

Political pamphlets of the American Revolution, 1750–1776, ed. B. Bailyn, Cambridge, Mass. 1965, i

Robespierre, M., *Oeuvres, IV, V: Les Journaux, lettres à ses commettants*, ed. G. Laurent, Gap 1961

—— *Oeuvres de Maximilien Robespierre, VI–X: Discours*, ed. M. Bouloiseau and A. Soboul, Paris 1950–67

Roland, M., *Mémoires de Madame Roland*, ed. S. A. Berville and J. F. Barrière, 2nd edn, Paris 1821

Rousseau, J. J., *Oeuvres complètes de Jean Jacques Rousseau*, ed. B. Gagnebin and M. Raymond, Paris 1959–64

—— 'Considérations sur le gouvernement de Pologne et sur sa réformation projettée', *Oeuvres complètes*, iii. 951–1041

—— 'Discours sur l'économie politique', *Oeuvres complètes*, iii. 239–78

—— *Correspondence complète de Jean Jacques Rousseau*, ed. R. A. Leigh, Oxford 1979

—— *The social contract and other later political writings*, ed. V. Gourevitch, Cambridge 1997

Roux, J., ['Manifest des Enragés'], repr. in A. Mathiez, *Annales révolutionnaires* vii (1914), 547–60

Rutledge, J. J., *Les Comédiens ou le foyer*, ed. P. Peyronnet, Paris 1999

Saint-Just, A. *Oeuvres complètes de Saint-Just*, ed. C. Vellay, Paris 1908

Sidney, A., *Discourses concerning government*, ed. T. G. West, Indianapolis 1996

La Société des Jacobins: recueil de documents pour l'histoire du club des Jacobins de Paris, ed. A. Aulard, Paris 1889–97

Toland, J., 'The Life of James Harrington', in Borot, *The Oceana of James Harrington*, 23–80

Voltaire, *Letters concerning the English nation*, Oxford 1994

Voyer de Paulmy, R. L. de, marquis d'Argenson, *Mémoires*, ed. P. Jannet, Paris 1858

Wood, A. A., *Athenae oxoniensis: an exact history of all the writers and bishops who have had their education in the University of Oxford*, ed. P. Bliss, London 1817

Works of reference

Biographie universelle ancienne et moderne, ed. J. F. Michaud, Paris 1843–65
Dictionary of national biography, ed. L. Stephen and S. Lee, London 1908–9 (repr. of 1895–1900 edn)
Caillet, P., *Comité des recherches de l'assemblée nationale, 1789–1791: inventaire analytique de la sous-série Dxxix bis*, Paris 1993
Furet, F. and M. Ozouf (eds), *A critical dictionary of the French Revolution*, trans. A. Goldhammer, Cambridge, Mass. 1989
Hunter, W. B. and others (eds), *Milton encyclopaedia*, Lewisburg, 1978–83
Sgard, J. (ed.), *Dictionnaire des journaux, 1600–1789*, Paris–Oxford 1991
——— *Dictionnaire des journalistes, 1600–1789*, Oxford 1999
Tourneux, M., *Bibliographie de l'histoire de Paris pendant la Révolution*, Paris 1906
Tuetey, A., *Répertoire général des sources manuscrites de l'histoire de Paris pendant la Révolution française*, Paris 1890
Walter, G., *Catalogue de l'histoire de la Révolution française*, Paris 1941

Secondary sources

Acomb, F., *Anglophobia in France, 1763–89: an essay in the history of constitutionalism and nationalism*, Durham, NC 1950
Alger, J. G., *Englishmen in the French Revolution*, London 1889
——— 'Rutledge, James or John James', in *Dictionary of national biography*, l. 518–19
Andress, D., *Massacre at the Champ de Mars: popular dissent and political culture in the French Revolution*, Woodbridge 2000
Antheunis, L., *Le Conventionnel belge François Robert (1768–1826) et sa femme Louise de Keralio (1758–1882 [sic recte 1822])*, Wetteren 1955
Appleby, J. O., 'America as a model for the radical French reformers of 1789', *WMQ* (1971), 267–86
——— *Liberalism and republicanism in the historical imagination*, Cambridge, Mass. 1992
Aulard, A., *Études et leçons sur la Révolution française*, 4th ser., Paris 1904
——— 'Danton au Club des Cordeliers et au département de Paris', in Aulard, *Études et leçons*, 128–52
——— 'Danton au District des Cordeliers et à la commune de Paris', in Aulard, *Études et leçons*, 90–127
——— *The French Revolution: a political history, 1789–1804*, trans. B. Miall, London 1910, i
Bailyn, B., *The ideological origins of the American Revolution*, Cambridge, Mass. 1967
Baker, K. M., *Condorcet: from natural philosophy to social mathematics*, Chicago 1975
——— 'A script for a French Revolution: the political consciousness of the *abbé* Mably', *Eighteenth-Century Studies* xiv (1981), 235–63
——— 'Representation', in Baker, *The French Revolution*, 469–92
——— *Inventing the French Revolution: essays on French political culture in the eighteenth century*, Cambridge 1990

—— 'Transformations of classical republicanism in eighteenth-century France', *JMH* lxxiii (2001), 32–53

—— (ed.), *The French Revolution and the creation of modern political culture*, I: *The political culture of the old regime*, Oxford 1987

—— *The French Revolution and the creation of modern political culture*, IV: *The Terror*, Oxford 1994

Barny, R., *L'Éclatement révolutionnaire du Rousseauisme*, Paris 1988

Baron, H., *The crisis of the early Italian Renaissance: civic humanism and republican liberty in an age of classicism and tyranny*, 2nd edn, Princeton 1966

Bénétruy, J., *L'Atelier de Mirabeau: quatre proscrits génevois dans la tourmente revolutionnaire*, Paris 1962

Blitzer, C., *An immortal commonwealth: the political thought of James Harrington*, New Haven 1960

Blum, C., *Rousseau and the republic of virtue: the language of politics in the French Revolution*, Ithaca 1986

Bonno, G., *La Constitution britannique devant l'opinion française de Montesquieu à Bonaparte*, Paris 1931

Borot, L. (ed.), *The Oceana of James Harrington and the notion of commonwealth* (Collection Astraea 6), Montpellier 1998

Bourdin, I., *Les Sociétés populaires à Paris pendant la Révolution*, Paris 1937

Bourne, H. E., 'Improvising a government for Paris in July, 1789', *AHR* x (1905), 280–308

—— 'Municipal politics in Paris in 1789', *AHR* xi (1906), 263–86

Brinton, C. C., *The Jacobins: an essay in the new history*, New York 1961

Brucker, G. A., *Jean-Sylvain Bailly: revolutionary mayor of Paris*, Urbana 1950

Burtt, S., *Virtue transformed: political argument in England, 1688–1740*, Cambridge 1992

Calvet, H., 'Hébert et Desmoulins devant les Jacobins', in Desmoulins, *Le Vieux Cordelier* (ed. Calvet), 172–7

Censer, J. R., *Prelude to power: the Parisian radical press, 1789–1791*, Baltimore–London 1976

Clapham, J. H., *The abbé Sieyès*, Westminster 1912

Clark, A., 'The chevalier d'Eon and Wilkes: masculinity and politics in the eighteenth century', *Eighteenth-Century Studies* xxxii (1998), 19–48

Cobban, A., *The social interpretation of the French Revolution*, Cambridge 1964

—— *Aspects of the French Revolution*, London 1968

Collini, S., R. Whatmore and B. Young (eds), *Economy, polity, and society: essays in British intellectual history, 1750–1950*, Cambridge 2000

—— *History, religion, and culture: essays in British intellectual history, 1750–1950*, Cambridge 2000

Comninel, G. C., *Rethinking the French Revolution: Marxism and the revisionist challenge*, London–New York 1987

Cornell, S., *The other founders: anti-federalism and the dissenting tradition in America, 1788–1828*, Chapel Hill 1999

Davies, T., 'Borrowed language: Milton, Jefferson, Mirabeau', in D. Armitage, A. Himy and Q. Skinner (eds), *Milton and republicanism*, Cambridge 1995, 254–71

De Cock, J., *Les Cordeliers dans la Révolution française*, I: *Lineaments*, Lyon 2001

Dedieu, J., *Montesquieu et la tradition politique anglaise en France*, Geneva 1971 (repr. of 1909 edn)

Dodge, G. H., *The political theory of the Huguenots of the dispersion with special reference to the thought and influence of Pierre Jurieu*, New York 1947

Doyle, W., *Origins of the French Revolution*, 3rd edn, Oxford 1999

Dunn, J. (ed.), *Democracy: the unfinished journey 508BC – AD1993*, Oxford 1992

Dziembowski, E., 'The English political model in eighteenth-century France', *Historical Research* lxxiv (2001), 151–71

Echeverria, D., *The Maupeou revolution: a study in the history of libertarianism, France, 1770–1774*, Baton Rouge 1985

Egret, J., *La Révolution des notables: Mounier et les monarchiens, 1789*, Paris 1950

Ellis, H., *Boulainvilliers and the French monarchy: aristocratic politics in early eighteenth-century France*, Ithaca 1988

Erdman, D. V., *Commerce des lumières: John Oswald and the British in Paris, 1790–1793*, Columbia 1986

Fehér, F., *The frozen revolution: an essay on Jacobinism*, Cambridge 1987

Fink, Z., *The classical republicans: an essay in the recovery of a pattern of thought in seventeenth-century England*, Evanstan 1945

Flammermont, J., *Le Chancelier Maupeou et les parlements*, Paris 1883

Fletcher, D. J., 'The fortunes of Bolingbroke in France in the eighteenth century', in T. Besterman (ed.), *Studies on Voltaire and the eighteenth century*, Geneva 1966, 207–32

Fontana, B., *The invention of the modern republic*, Cambridge 1994

Forsyth, M., *Reason and revolution: the political thought of the abbé Sieyès*, Leicester 1987

Frank, J., *Cromwell's press agent: a critical biography of Marchamont Nedham, 1620–1678*, n.p. 1980

Friguglietti, J., *Albert Mathiez historien révolutionnarie (1874–1932)*, Paris 1974

Fukuda, A., *Sovereignty and the sword: Harrington, Hobbes and mixed government in the English civil wars*, Oxford 1997

Furet, F., *Interpreting the French Revolution*, trans. E. Forster, Cambridge 1981

———— ' "Jacobin" fortune et infortunes d'un mot', in M. Ozouf (ed.), *L'Ecole de la France: essai sur la révolution, l'utopie et l'enseignement*, Paris 1984, 82–4

———— *Revolutionary France, 1770–1880*, trans. A. Nevill, Oxford 1992

———— and M. Ozouf, 'Two historical legitimations of eighteenth-century French society: Mably and Boulainvilliers', in F. Furet, *In the workshop of history*, trans. J. Mandelbaum, Chicago–London 1984, 125–39

———— and M. Ozouf (eds), *The French Revolution and the creation of modern political culture*, III: *The transformations of political culture, 1789–1848*, Oxford 1990

———— and M. Ozouf (eds), *Terminer la Révolution: Mounier et Barnave dans la Révolution française*, Grenoble 1990

———— and M. Ozouf (eds), *La Gironde et les Girondins*, Paris 1991

———— and M. Ozouf (eds), *Le Siècle de l'avènement républicain*, Paris 1993

Genty, M., 'Mandataires ou représentants: un problème de la démocratie municipale à Paris, en 1789–1790', *AHRF* ccvii (1972), 1–27

———— 'Pratique et théorie de la démocratie directe: l'exemple des districts parisiens (1789–1790)', *AHRF* cclix (1985), 8–24

———— *L'Apprentissage de la citoyenneté: Paris, 1789–1795*, Paris 1987

Gibson, A., 'Ancients, moderns and Americans: the republicanism–liberalism debate revisited', *History of Political Thought* xxi (2000), 261–307

Gilbert, F., *Machiavelli and Guicciardini: politics and history in sixteenth-century Florence*, Princeton 1965

Glover, S. D., 'The Putney debates: popular versus elitist republicanism', *P&P* clxiv (1999), 47–80

Goldie, M., 'The unacknowledged republic: officeholding in early modern England', in T. Harris (ed.), *The politics of the excluded, c. 1500–1850*, Basingstoke 2001, 153–94

Goldsmith, M. M., 'Liberty, virtue, and the rule of law, 1689–1770', in Wootton, *Republicanism, liberty, and commercial society*, 197–232

Goodale, J. R., 'J. G. A. Pocock's new-Harringtonians: a reconsideration', *History of Political Thought* i (1980), 237–59

Goodwin, A., *The friends of liberty: the English democratic movement in the age of the French Revolution*, Cambridge, Mass. 1979

Gordon, D., *Citizens without sovereignty: equality and sociability in French thought, 1670–1789*, Princeton 1994

Gottschalk, L. R., *Jean-Paul Marat: a study in radicalism*, Chicago 1967

Goulemot, J. M., 'Du Républicanisme et de l'idée républicaine au XVIIIe siècle', in Furet and Ozouf, *Le Siècle de l'avènement républicain*, 25–56

Grieder, J., *Anglomania in France, 1740–1789: fact, fiction and political discourse*, Geneva–Paris 1985

Griffiths, R., *Le Centre perdu: Malouet et les 'monarchiens' dans la Révolution française*, Grenoble 1988

Gueniffey, P., 'Girondins and Cordeliers: a prehistory of the republic?', trans. L. Mason, in Fontana, *Invention of the modern republic*, 86–106

——— *La Politique de la Terreur: essai sur la violence révolutionnaire, 1789–1794*, Paris 2000

Guilhaumou J. and R. Monnier, 'Les Cordeliers et la république de 1793', in Vovelle, *Révolution et république*, 200–12

Haitsma Mulier, E., *The myth of Venice and Dutch republican thought in the seventeenth century*, Assen 1980

——— 'The language of seventeenth-century republicanism in the United Provinces: Dutch or European?', in Pagden, *Languages of political theory*, 179–95

Halévi, R., 'Les Girondins avant la Gironde: esquisse d'une éducation politique', in Furet and Ozouf, *La Gironde et les Girondins*, 137–68

Hammersley, R., 'English republicanism and the French Revolution: the case of Jean Jacques Rutlidge', in E. Tuttle (ed.), *Confluences XVII: républic anglais et idée de tolerance*, Paris 2000, 169–83

——— 'Camille Desmoulins's *Le Vieux Cordelier*: a link between English and French republicanism', *History of European Ideas* xxvii (2001), 115–32

Hampson, N., *Danton*, Oxford 1978

——— *Will and circumstance: Montesquieu, Rousseau and the French Revolution*, London 1983

——— *Saint-Just*, Oxford 1991

——— *The perfidy of Albion: French perceptions of England during the French Revolution*, London 1998

Haydon, C. and W. Doyle (eds), *Robespierre*, Cambridge 1999

Hesse, C., *The other Enlightenment: how French women became modern*, Oxford–Princeton 2001

Higonnet, P., 'The social and cultural antecedents of a revolutionary discontinuity: Montagnards and Girondins', *EHR* (1985), 513–44

—————— *Sister republics: the origins of French and American republicanism*, Cambridge, Mass. 1988

—————— *Goodness beyond virtue: Jacobins during the French Revolution*, Cambridge, Mass. 1998

Hill, B., *The republican virago: the life and times of Catharine Macaulay, historian*, Oxford 1992

Hirschman, A. O., *The passions and the interests: political arguments for capitalism before its triumph*, Princeton 1977

Hont, I., 'The permanent crisis of a divided mankind: "contemporary crisis of the nation state" in historical perspective', *Political Studies* xlii (1994), 166–231

Hope Mason, J., 'Individuals in society: Rousseau's republican vision', *History of Political Thought* x (1989), 89–112

Houston, A. C., *Algernon Sidney and the republican heritage in England and America*, Princeton 1991

Hulling, M., *The autocritique of Enlightenment: Rousseau and the philosophes*, Cambridge, Mass. 1994

Isambart, G., *La Vie à Paris pendant une année de la Révolution*, Paris 1896

Israel, J. I., *Radical Enlightenment: philosophy and the making of modernity, 1650–1750*, Oxford 2001

Jacob, M. C., *The radical Enlightenment: pantheists, freemasons, and republicans*, London 1981

Jainchill, A., 'The constitution of the year III and the persistence of classical republicanism', *FHS* xxvi (2003), 399–435

Janssens, J., *Camille Desmoulins: le premier républicain de France*, Paris 1973

Jarrett, D., *The begetters of revolution: England's involvement with France, 1759–1789*, London 1973

Jaume, L., *Le Discours Jacobin et la démocratie*, Paris 1989

Jones, P. M., 'The "agrarian law": schemes for land redistribution during the French Revolution', *P&P* cxxxiii (1991), 93–133

Kaiser, T. E., 'Money, despotism, and public opinion in early eighteenth-century France: John Law and the debate on royal credit', *JMH* lxiii (1991), 1–28

Kaplan, S. L., *The bakers of Paris and the bread question, 1700–1775*, Durham, NC 1996

Karsten, P., *Patriot-heroes in England and America*, Wisconsin 1978

Kates, G., *The Cercle Social, the Girondins and the French Revolution*, Princeton 1985

—————— *Monsieur d'Eon is a woman: a tale of political intrigue and sexual masquerade*, New York 1995

—————— 'The transgendered world of the chevalier/chevalière d'Eon', *JMH* lxvii (1995), 558–94

—————— (ed.), *The French Revolution: recent debates and new controversies*, London–New York 1998

Kelsey, S., *Inventing a republic: the political culture of the English commonwealth, 1649–1653*, Manchester 1997

Kennedy, M. L., *The Jacobin clubs in the French Revolution: the early years*, Princeton 1982

—— *The Jacobin clubs in the French Revolution: the middle years*, Princeton 1988

—— *The Jacobin clubs in the French Revolution, 1793–1795*, New York–Oxford 2000

Keohane, N. O., *Philosophy and the state in France: the Renaissance to the Enlightenment*, Princeton 1980

Kramnick, I., *Bolingbroke and his circle: the politics of nostalgia in the age of Walpole*, Ithaca 1968, repr. 1992

—— *Republicanism and bourgeois radicalism: political ideology in late eighteenth-century England and America*, Ithaca 1990

Lacorne, D., *L'Invention de la république: le modèle américain*, Paris 1991

Las Vergnas, R., *Chevalier Rutlidge: 'gentilhomme anglais', 1742–1793*, Paris 1932

Leigh, R. A., 'Jean-Jacques Rousseau and the myth of antiquity in the eighteenth century', in R. R. Bolgar (ed.), *Classical influences on western thought, AD 1650–1870*, Cambridge 1979, 155–68

Lewis-Beck, M. S., A. Hildreth and A. B. Spitzer, 'Was there a Girondist faction in the national convention, 1792–1793?', *FHS* xv (1987–8), 519–36, 537–48 (commentaries by M. J. Sydenham, A. Patrick and G. Kates)

Lilla, M. (ed.), *New French thought: political philosophy*, Princeton 1994

Linton, M., 'Robespierre's political principles', in Haydon and Doyle, *Robespierre*, 37–53

—— *The politics of virtue in Enlightenment France*, Basingstoke 2001

Livesey, J., 'Agrarian ideology and commercial republicanism in the French Revolution', *P&P*, clvii (1997), 94–121

—— *Making democracy in the French Revolution*, Cambridge, Mass. 2001

Lockitt, C. H., *The relations of English and French society (1763–1793)*, London 1920

Lucas, C. (ed.), *The French Revolution and the creation of modern political culture*, II: *The political culture of the French Revolution*, Oxford 1988

Lutaud, O., *Les Deux Révolutions d'Angleterre: documents politiques, sociaux, religieux*, Paris 1978

—— 'Des Révolutions d'Angleterre à la Revolution française: l'exemple de la liberté de la presse ou comment Milton "ouvrit" les états-généraux', *Colloque international sur la Révolution française*, Clermont Ferrand 1986

—— 'Emprunts de la Révolution française à la première révolution anglaise', *Revue d'histoire moderne et contemporaine* xxxvii (1990), 589–607

McDonald, J., *Rousseau and the French Revolution, 1762–1791*, London 1965

Manin, B., *The principles of representative government*, Cambridge 1997

Marshall, P. D., 'Thomas Hollis (1720–74): the bibliophile as libertarian', *Bulletin of the John Rylands University Library of Manchester* lxvi (1984), 246–63

Mathiez, A., *La Théophilanthropie et le culte décadaire (1796–1802): essai sur l'histoire religieuse de la Révolution*, Paris 1904

—— *Le Club des Cordeliers pendant la crise de Varennes et le massacre du Champ de Mars: documents en grande partie inédits*, Paris 1910

—— 'Pourquoi parut le "Vieux Cordelier"?', in Desmoulins, *Le Vieux Cordelier* (ed. Calvet), 33–40,

Mazel, G., 'Louise de Kéralio et Pierre François Robert: précurseurs de l'idée républicain', *Bulletin de la Société de l'histoire de Paris et de l'Ile-de-France* (1990), 163–237

Miller, P. N., *Defining the common good: empire, religion and philosophy in eighteenth-century Britain*, Cambridge 1994

Monnier, R., 'Paris au printemps 1791: les sociétés fraternelles et le problème de la souveraineté', *AHRF* (1992), i. 1–16

——— *L'Espace public démocratique: essai sur l'opinion à Paris, de la Révolution au Directoire*, Paris 1994

——— 'Cordeliers, sans-culottes et Jacobins', *AHRF* (1995), ii. 249–60

——— 'L'Invention de la république et la dynamique culturelle démocratique', *History of European Ideas* xx (1995), 243–52

——— ' "Démocratie representative" ou "république démocratique": de la querelle des mots (république) à la querelle des anciens et des modernes', *AHRF* (2001), iii. 1–21

——— 'Républicanisme et révolution française', *FHS* xxvi (2003), 87–118

Mornet, D., *Les Origines intellectuelles de la Révolution française, 1715–1787*, 5th edn, Paris 1954

Mossé, C., *L'Antiquité dans la Révolution française*, Paris 1989

Murphy, A. E., *John Law: economic theorist and policy maker*, Oxford 1997

Nicolet, C., *L'Idée républicaine en France (1789–1924): essai d'histoire critique*, Paris 1982

Norbrook, D., *Writing the English republic: poetry, rhetoric and politics, 1627–1660*, Cambridge 1999

Pachet, P., 'La Restitution du texte de Camille Desmoulins: une exigence politique', in Desmoulins, *Le Vieux Cordelier* (ed. Pachet), 13–31

Pagden, A. (ed.), *The languages of political theory in early modern Europe*, Cambridge 1987

Palmer, R. R., *The year of the Terror: twelve who ruled France, 1793–1794*, 3rd edn, Oxford 1989

Parker, H. T., *The cult of antiquity and the French revolutionaries: a study in the development of the revolutionary spirit*, Chicago 1939

Pasquino, P., 'The constitutional republicanism of Emmanuel Sieyès', in Fontana, *Invention of the modern republic*, 107–17

Peyronnet, P., 'Le Babillard' and 'Calypso', in Sgard, *Dictionnaire des journaux*, i. 137, 195

——— 'J. J. Rutlidge', *Revue d'histoire du théâtre*, iv (1992), 330–59

——— 'Rutlidge', in Sgard, *Dictionnaire des journalistes*, ii. 891–3

——— 'Introduction' to Rutledge, *Les Comédiens ou le foyer* (ed. Peyronnet), 9–24

Pocock, J. G. A., 'James Harrington and the good old cause: a study of the ideological context of his writings', *JBS* x (1970), 30–47

——— *The Machiavellian moment: Florentine political thought and the Atlantic republican tradition*, Princeton 1975

——— 'The Machiavellian moment revisited: a study in history and ideology', *JMH* liii (1981), 49–71

Raab, F., *The English face of Machiavelli: a changing interpretation, 1500–1700*, London 1964

Rahe, P. A., *Republics ancient and modern: classical republicanism and the American Revolution*, Chapel Hill 1992

Raskolnikoff, M., *Des Anciens et des modernes*, Paris 1990

——— *Histoire romaine et critique historique dans l'Europe des lumières*, Rome 1992

Raynaud, P., 'Destin de l'idéologie républicaine', *Esprit* xii (1973), 17–29

Reesink, H. J., *L'Angleterre dans les périodiques français de Hollande, 1684–1709*, Paris 1931

Remer, G., 'James Harrington's new deliberative rhetoric: reflection of an anti-classical republicanism', *History of Political Thought* xvi (1995), 532–57

Robbins, C. A., 'Algernon Sidney's *Discourses concerning government*: textbook of revolution', *WMQ* (1947), 267–95

——— 'The strenuous Whig: "Thomas Hollis of Lincoln's Inn" ', *WMQ* (1950), 406–53

——— *The eighteenth-century commonwealthman: studies in the transmission, development and circumstance of English liberal thought from the restoration of Charles II until the war with the thirteen colonies*, Cambridge, Mass. 1959

——— 'Library of liberty – assembled for Harvard College by Thomas Hollis of Lincoln's Inn', in Taft, *Absolute liberty*, 219n.

Rodgers, D. T., 'Republicanism: the career of a concept', *Journal of American History* lxxix (1992), 11–38

Rose, R. B. *The Enragés: socialists of the French Revolution?*, Melbourne 1965

——— 'How to make a revolution: the Paris districts in 1789', *Bulletin of the John Rylands University Library of Manchester* lix (1977), 426–57

——— 'The "red scare" of the 1790s: the French Revolution and the "agrarian law" ', *P&P* ciii (1984), 113–30

Rosenblatt, H., *Rousseau and Geneva: from the First discourse to the Social contract, 1749–1762*, Cambridge 1997

Rubini, D., 'Politics and the battle for the banks, 1688–1697', *EHR* lxxxv (1970), 693–714

Russell Smith, H., *Harrington and his Oceana*, Cambridge 1914

Salmon, J. H. M., 'Liberty by degrees: Raynal and Diderot on the British constitution', *History of Political Thought* xx (1999), 87–106

Schama, S., *Citizens: a chronicle of the French Revolution*, Harmondsworth 1989

Scott, J., *Algernon Sidney and the English republic, 1623–1677*, Cambridge 1988

——— *Algernon Sidney and the restoration crisis, 1677–1683*, Cambridge 1991

——— 'The rapture of motion: James Harrington's republicanism', in N. Philipson and Q. Skinner (eds), *Political discourse in early modern Britain*, Cambridge 1993, 139–63

——— 'Classical republicanism in seventeenth-century England and the Netherlands', in Van Gelderen and Skinner, *Republicanism*, i. 61–81

Shackleton, R., 'Montesquieu, Bolingbroke, and the separation of powers', *French Studies* iii (1949), 25–38

——— 'Montesquieu and Machiavelli: a reappraisal', *Comparative Literature Studies* i (1964), 1–13

Shalhope, R. E., 'Towards a republican synthesis: the emergence of an understanding of republicanism in American historiography', *WMQ* (1972), 49–77

——— 'Republicanism and early American historiography', *WMQ* (1982), 334–56

Shklar, J. N., 'Ideology hunting: the case of James Harrington', *American Political Science Review* (1959), 662–91

——— *Men and citizens: a study of Rousseau's social theory*, Cambridge 1969

———— 'Montesquieu and the new republicanism', in G. Bock, Q. Skinner and M. Viroli (eds), *Machiavelli and republicanism*, Cambridge 1990, 265–79

Skinner, Q., 'The idea of negative liberty: philosophical and historical perspectives', in R. Rorty, J. B. Schneewind and Q. Skinner (eds), *Philosophy in history*, Cambridge 1984, 193–221

———— 'The paradoxes of political liberty', in S. M. McMurrin (ed.), *The Tanner lectures on human values*, vii, Cambridge 1986, 225–50

———— *Liberty before liberalism*, Cambridge 1998

Slavin, M., *The Hébertists to the guillotine: anatomy of a 'conspiracy' in revolutionary France*, Baton Rouge–London 1994

Sonenscher, M., *Work and wages: natural law, politics and the eighteenth-century French trades*, Cambridge 1989

———— 'Artisans, *sans-culottes* and the French Revolution', in A. Forrest and P. Jones (eds), *Reshaping France: town, country and region during the French Revolution*, Manchester 1991, 105–18

———— 'The nation's debt and the birth of the modern republic: the French fiscal deficit and the politics of the French Revolution of 1789', *History of Political Thought* xviii (1997), 64–103, 267–325

———— 'Enlightenment and Revolution', *JMH* lxx (1998), 371–83

———— 'Republicanism, state finances and the emergence of commercial society in eighteenth-century France – or from royal to ancient republicanism and back', in Van Gelderen and Skinner, *Republicanism*, ii. 275–91

Steinberg J., *Why Switzerland?*, Cambridge 1976

Swenson, J., *On Jean-Jacques Rousseau considered as one of the first authors of the Revolution*, Stanford 2000

Sydenham, M. J., *The Girondins*, London 1961

Taft, B. (ed.), *Absolute liberty: a selection from the articles and papers of Caroline Robbins*, Connecticut 1982

Thomson, A., 'La Référence à l'Angleterre dans le débat autour de la république', in Vovelle, *Révolution et république*, 133–44

Tønnesson, K., 'La Démocratie directe sous la Révolution française: le cas des districts et des sections de Paris', in Lucas, *The French Revolution*, ii. 295–306

Trevor, D., 'Some sources of the constitutional theory of the abbé Sieyès: Harrington and Spinoza', *Politica* (1935), 325–42

Van Gelderen, M., *The political thought of the Dutch revolt, 1555–1590*, Cambridge 1992

———— and Q. Skinner (eds), *Republicanism: a shared European heritage*, I: *Republicanism and constitutionalism in early modern Europe*; II: *The values of republicanism in early modern Europe*, Cambridge 2002

Van Kley, D. (ed.), *The French idea of freedom: the old regime and the declaration of rights of 1789*, Stanford 1994

Venturi, F., *Utopia and reform in the Enlightenment*, Cambridge 1971

Viard, J. (ed.), *L'Esprit républicain: colloque d'Orléans, 4 & 5 septembre 1970*, Paris 1972

Vidal-Naquet, P., *Politics ancient and modern*, trans. J. Lloyd, Cambridge 1995

Viroli, M., 'The concept of *ordre* and the language of classical republicanism in Jean-Jacques Rousseau', in Pagden, *Languages of political theory*, 159–78

———— *Jean-Jacques Rousseau and the 'well-ordered society'*, Cambridge 1988

Vovelle, M. (ed.), *Révolution et république: l'exception française*, Paris 1994

Walzer, M. (ed.), *Regicide and revolution: speeches at the trial of Louis XVI*, Cambridge 1974

Weber, C., *Terror and its discontents: suspect words in revolutionary France*, Minneapolis–London 2003

Whaley, L., *Radicals: politics and republicanism in the French Revolution*, Stroud 2000

Whatmore, R., 'Commerce, constitutions, and the manners of a nation: Etienne Clavière's revolutionary political economy, 1788–93', *History of European Ideas* xxii (1996), 351–68

—————— 'The political economy of Jean Baptiste Say's republicanism', *History of Political Thought* xix (1998), 439–56

—————— *Republicanism and the French Revolution: an intellectual history of Jean-Baptiste Say's political economy*, Oxford 2000

Whitfield, E. A., *Gabriel Bonnot de Mably*, New York 1969

Winch, D., *Riches and poverty: an intellectual history of political economy in Britain, 1750–1834*, Cambridge 1996

Wokler, R., 'Rousseau and his critics on the fanciful liberties we have lost', in Wokler, *Rousseau and liberty*, 189–212

—————— 'Situating Rousseau in his world and ours', *Social Science Information* xxxiv (1995), 515–37

—————— (ed.), *Rousseau and liberty*, Manchester 1995

Wolfe, D. M., 'Milton and Mirabeau', *Publications of the Modern Languages Association of America* xlix (1934), 1116–28

Wood, G. S., *The creation of the American republic, 1776–1787*, Chapel Hill 1969

Wootton, D., 'Ulysses bound? Venice and the idea of liberty from Howell to Hume', in Wootton, *Republicanism, liberty, and commercial society*, 341–67

—————— (ed.), *Republicanism, liberty, and commercial society, 1649–1776*, Stanford 1994

Worden, B., 'Classical republicanism and the Puritan revolution', in H. Lloyd-Jones, V. Pearl and B. Worden (eds), *History and imagination: essays in honour of H. R. Trevor-Roper*, London 1981, 182–200

—————— 'The commonwealth kidney of Algernon Sidney', *JBS* xxiv (1985), 1–40

—————— 'English republicanism', in J. Burns and M. Goldie (eds), *The Cambridge history of political thought, 1450–1750*, Cambridge 1991, 443–75

—————— 'James Harrington and *The Commonwealth of Oceana*, 1656', in Wootton, *Republicanism, liberty, and commercial society*, 82–110

—————— 'Marchamont Nedham and the beginnings of English republicanism, 1649–56', in Wootton, *Republicanism, liberty, and commercial society*, 45–81

—————— 'Harrington's *Oceana*: origins and aftermath, 1651–1660', in Wootton, *Republicanism, liberty, and commercial society*, 111–38

—————— 'Republicanism and the restoration, 1660–1683', in Wootton, *Republicanism, liberty, and commercial society*, 139–93

—————— 'Wit in a Roundhead: the dilemma of Marchamont Nedham', in S. Dwyer Amussen and M. A. Kishlansky (eds), *Political culture and cultural politics in early modern England*, Manchester 1995, 301–37

—————— *Roundhead reputations: the English civil wars and the passions of posterity*, London 2001

—————— 'Whig history and Puritan politics: the *Memoirs* of Edmund Ludlow revisited', *Historical Research* lxxv (2002), 209–37

Wright, J. K., 'National sovereignty and the general will', in Van Kley, *French idea of freedom*, 199–233

———— *A classical republican in eighteenth-century France: the political thought of Mably*, Stanford 1997

———— 'The idea of a republican constitution in old regime France', in Van Gelderen and Skinner, *Republicanism*, i. 289–306

Unpublished dissertations and articles

Hammersley, R., 'The influence of English republican ideas on the political thought of the Cordelier Club', DPhil. diss. Sussex 2002

Henry, N. O., 'Democratic monarchy: the political theory of the marquis d'Argenson', PhD diss. New Haven 1968

Ramaswamy, J., 'Reconstituting the "liberty of the ancients": public credit, popular sovereignty and the political theory of the Terror during the French Revolution, 1789–1794', PhD diss. Cambridge 1995

Robertson, G. M., 'The society of the Cordeliers and the French Revolution, 1790–1794', PhD diss. Wisconsin 1972

Whatmore, R., 'What was revolutionary about 1789?', unpublished paper

———— and J. Livesey, 'The democratic republicanism of the Girondins', unpublished paper

Index

188

Ramaswamy, Jaikur, 150
ratification of laws, 47–50, 78, 109, 127–9,
142, 160
Raynal, *abbé* Guillaume, 63
religion, 72–3, 110–14, 145–6
representative government:
Brissot/Brissotins and, 18, 23–4, 45,
54–5, 71, 142, 159–60; communal
assembly and, 18, 22–4, 25, 26;
Confédération des amis de la vérité and,
30; Cordeliers' rejection of, 45, 48, 55,
71, 125, 135, 142, 159–60; different
from ancient democracy, 125–6;
Mandar's rejection of, 71–2; Rousseau's
rejection of, 33, 45, 48, 159; Rutledge's
rejection of, 105–6
republicanism, American, 2–3, 164–5
republicanism, British/English: Cordeliers
and, 55, 160–3, 165, Desmoulins and,
150, 153–4, 155–6, 156–8, 161, 163,
influence on *Essai d'une déclaration des
droits*, 130, influence on *Idées sur
l'espèce de gouvernement populaire*,
123–9, influence on *Quelques Pensées
sur l'unité du législateur*, 131–3, Mandar
and, 62–75, 76, 79, 80–1, 83, 159, 163,
Rutledge and, 83, 88–92, 96–115,
134–5, 160; influence in America, 164,
165; influence in France, 10–14, 116,
161–3, 165; tradition of, 1, 2, 81–2
republicanism, classical/ancient, 6, 8–9,
41–3, 75, 81, 84, 160, 163
republicanism, democratic: Cordeliers and,
45–50, 54–5, 76, 81, 142, 157–8,
159–60, 161, 162–3, Desmoulins and,
38, 45, 46, 153, 158, Girardin and,
47–50, in *Essai d'une déclaration des
droits*, 130–1, in *Idées sur l'espèce de
gouvernement populaire*, 124–9, La
Vicomterie and, 39, 45–6, 47, Mandar
and, 71–2, 72–4, 76, 81, Robert and,
46, Rutledge and, 104–6, 114–15,
134–5
republicanism, Dutch, 3
republicanism, French: Brissotins and,
42–4, 47, 50, 52–3, 54, 54–5, 159–60;
Cordeliers and, 14, 41–2, 44–5, 45–50,
50–2, 53, 54–5, 135, 159–61, 162–3,
165, Desmoulins and, 38, 41, 44–5, 46,
47, 151–4, 155–6, Girardin and, 47–50,
in *Essai d'une déclaration des droits*,
129–31, in *Idées sur l'espèce de
gouvernement populaire*, 123–9, in
Quelques Pensées sur l'unité du

législateur, 131–3, La Vicomterie and,
39, 45, 47, Mandar and, 62–75, 76–82,
Robert and, 41–2, 45, 46, 50–1,
Rutledge and, 97–115; early examples
of, 36–7; historiography of, 1–2, 5–9,
11–12; Jacobins and, 34–6, 163;
Montesquieu and Rousseau and, 32–4
republicanism, modern, 8–9, 42–5, 54–5,
68–9, 104–6, 125–9, 135, 157–8,
159–60
republics: America, 43, 44, 55; ancient
41–3, 45, 68–9, 108, 125–9, 140;
Athenian, 42, 45, 69, 75, 108, 125,
155; English, 1; Dutch, 3; French, 1,
34, 39, 46, 50–5, 61, 116, 159;
Genevan, 43, 44, 55; Roman, 41–2, 68,
69, 75, 80, 140, 155; Spartan, 42, 108;
suitable only for small states, 33,
104–6; Venetian, 44, 89, 96, 108–11,
113, 124, 126, 160
Richelieu, Armand Jean Duplessis, duc de
(Cardinal Richelieu), 98–9
Riqueti, Honoré-Gabriel, comte de
Mirabeau, 12–13, 96, 117–18, 150 n.
60, 157; *Théorie de la royauté, d'après la
doctrine de Milton*, 157
Riqueti, Victor, marquis de Mirabeau, 63,
137
Robert, Pierre François Joseph, 36–7,
39–41, 43, 45, 46, 50–1, 53, 124, 159;
Avantages de la fuite de Louis XVI, 51;
and Cordeliers, 40; *Mercure national, ou
journal d'état et du citoyen*, 40;
Républicanisme adapté à la France, 36–7,
41, 45, 46, 51, 124
Robbins, Caroline, 154, 157
Robertson, George, 15, 29, 31 n. 75
Robespierre, Augustin, 150
Robespierre, Maximilien, 6, 15, 35, 37, 41,
118, 136–41, 144, 146–50, 151–2, 156,
158, 160
Roland, Jean-Marie, 35
Roland, Manon Philipon, 40
Rome, 2, 13, 41–2, 68–9, 75, 140, 155
Rose, R. B., 142
Rota Club, 90
rotation of office, 71–2, 90, 105–6, 115,
126–9, 160, 164
Rousseau, Jean-Baptiste, 19
Rousseau, Jean-Jacques: and civil religion,
110; and idea of revolutionary
measures, 137; and impossibility of
popular government in a large state,
33, 43, 105, 124, 159, 160; and